GREENER PASTURES

T0317135

GREENER PASTURES

Politics, Markets, and Community

among a Migrant Pastoral People

ARUN AGRAWAL

Duke University Press

Durham and London 1999

© 1998 Duke University Press

All rights reserved

Printed in the United States of America

on acid-free paper ∞

Typeset in Sabon by

Keystone Typesetting, Inc.

Library of Congress Cataloging-in-Publication

Data appear on the last printed

page of this book.

To Ma, Bua,
and Barima
My three
Rajasthani
mothers

Contents

TABLES AND FIGURES

This is a study of the *raika* shepherds, migrant pastoralists who travel with their sheep through the semiarid parts of western India. It seeks to understand one of the central questions in the lives of all migrant pastoralists: why do they migrate? Not all residents of the semiarid western Rajasthan migrate, after all. Not only do the raikas migrate but they migrate collectively. The second task this book sets itself is to explain why they migrate jointly rather than as individual households. Collective migration produces dilemmas related to free riding, the leadership of the collective, and control over capricious actions of leaders. As its third task, this book analyzes the institutions shepherds have crafted to solve the problems inherent in any human attempt to address joint tasks. In solving these three puzzles, the book pays attention to politics insistently. Politics is ubiquitous in the interactions of the shepherds with their neighbors and state officials, in their exchanges in markets and with farmers, and in their internal relations as a community.

Two personal incidents illuminate the concerns that inform this book.

At the end of my fieldwork, just before I returned to the United States to write my dissertation, the shepherds took me through a long session of questions. They wondered what I would do with all I had written, taped, and photographed. Could I write something an outsider would understand without knowing them personally? What kind of stories would the book tell? Would I write the book by myself? Would the book contain many photographs? This book answers the questions they asked. It does not contain any photographs. Instead it describes their mobile lifestyle by narrating stories about their lives and work, actions and thoughts, struggles and triumphs.

The second incident dates back farther, to the time when I had just decided to travel to the United States to become a graduate student. One evening I shared dinner with Vijay Mahajan, a close friend and mentor who like me had been working with grassroots development organizations in India. He did not yet know I planned to tack a new course. Over dinner, I disclosed with some misgivings that I was soon leaving for the United States. I still remember his troubled comment: "After such knowledge, what forgiveness?" At the time, I did not realize he was quoting Eliot. I was also incapable of reflecting on the irony of his choice: he was using Eliot—a westerner—to question my decision to go to the West for further studies. And I was too ill read to know I could have quoted Eliot back to him: "[T]hink now, History has many cunning passages." This book is a continuing engagement with the worry he expressed about my decision: upon leaving India, I might forego the interests I had in development, political economy, and the impact of markets and states on marginal peoples.

The book is organized into three parts following the introduction and a discussion of the ways in which mobility, identity, and loss are recurrent themes in the lives of the shepherds. Each part is devoted to one of the central conceptual formations in the social sciences, each devoted to answering one of the three questions the book raises. Part I relates to politics and the state. It addresses the question of why the shepherds migrate. It does so by focusing on the relations of the shepherds with their landholder neighbors and how struggles between these two groups have led to the sociopolitical squeeze on the access of the shepherds to the fodder resources they need for their sheep. It also analyzes the relations of the shepherds with the state by critiquing attempts to sedentarize the shepherds. It explains why the shepherds migrate by focusing on the ways in which power structures their relations with their neighbors and with state actors.

Part II investigates why the shepherds migrate collectively. It focuses on market exchanges and the nature of markets. To understand the imperatives that move the shepherds to travel together rather than as individuals, I suggest, it is important to underline the ways in which the migratory lives of the shepherds depend critically on market exchanges. In examining market exchanges, part II also points to the social and political forces that influence price, shape value, and determine profit.

Part II focuses on how the shepherds solve problems of collective action that arise in joint migrations. The analysis hinges on the complex relationship between community and institutions. Joint migration depends on the delegation of powers to leaders, the division of responsibilities, and mechanisms shepherds have devised to control their leadership. Community and hierarchy emerge as mutually dependant.

The conclusion of the book uses insights from writings on resistance to articulate the question of agency. Briefly, it suggests that the attempt to divorce resistance from intentions of agents undermines the project of trying to cast marginal peoples as historical figures. Deploying discussions about the lives of the raikas, the conclusion suggests that the raikas are indeed conscious agents of their own lives.

The three-part organization of the book facilitates a double explanatory strategy. It allows me to relate stories about the lives of the raikas that focus on three central questions: why do they migrate, why do they migrate collectively rather than as individual households, and how do they address problems of collective action as they migrate, problems that are pervasive in all joint action? Telling the story of the raikas by organizing the book in three parts also allows engagements with the politically, practically, and theoretically critical concepts of power, exchange, and community. Migration is related to the political marginalization of the raikas, collective migration hinges on market exchanges, and solving problems stemming from joint migration requires institutions based in community.

I have taken on many debts in the writing of this book. The possibility of thanking those who helped allows me finally to view with pleasure the debts I have incurred. My friends felt free to give time and intellectual companionship. I felt free to ask them. I have filched, often without knowing (or telling), many ideas and thoughts from casual acquaintances and readings. This is perhaps an appropriate point at which to acknowledge these kinds of debts. But since the essence of theft is stealth I hope most of these unwary acts remain undetected! The patience and kindness of many acquaintances — during field research and the initial writing in India and after returning to the United States — have been invaluable to the development of the book's arguments. I would like to be half as patient when needed.

Work on the book began without my knowing it. My first debt, then, is to those who led me to understand what I was doing. The shepherds whose lonely camp I encountered in a pastoral common in Rajasthan generated in me the necessary curiosity about their livelihood. I thank Ranaramji and his family for their gracious hospitality and their willingness to talk to a stranger who dropped in unexpectedly. Dr. B. R. Joshi from Jodhpur introduced me to Ranaramji. Without his encouragement, I doubt that I would have gone beyond a provocative conversation. Subsequent interactions with raika shepherds, especially Dallaramji, Bhopalaramji, and others in different mobile camps only confirmed the initial impression that I had chanced upon a treasure. They were unfailingly courteous (if sometimes openly puzzled by all the questions I asked), vastly knowledgeable, and enormously humoring. Without their willingness to talk with me, the foundations of this book could not have been laid.

I wrote about my interactions with the shepherds first in the form of a report to satisfy the requirements of funded research. A small grant from the Drylands Program of the International Institute for Environment and Development, London, in 1989–90 had made the major proportion of the fieldwork possible. Camilla Toulmin and Margaret McKean's encouragement to push ahead with the writing on the shepherds helped me complete the initial report on time. Robert Bates at Duke University, as my dissertation adviser and intellectual challenger, helped me to realize that what I had written had a different potential as well. It was in numerous conversations with him that the idea of a book crystallized. Peter Lange's sardonic humor and penetrating criticism at an early stage forced me to confront the dubiousness of some of the arguments I was hoping to advance. His friendship and support at a later stage helped me complete this book. Although I dare not admit it in print, George Tsebelis continues to inspire (and provoke), even if from a distance. Jeff Romm at the University of California at Berkeley, in his own thoughtful fashion, made me rethink the plan of a book on shepherds and the grazing commons.

Initially, the research on the shepherds was to form one part of a manuscript on multiple types of community-managed resources. But the particularities of a moving social group and the general relevance of such a mobile lifestyle for received notions about politics, exchange, and community forced a different treatment. How do the interactions of shepherds with settled neighbors and state actors force a reexamination of political analyses that hinge upon settled existence? How does a mobile group create markets and perform in existing ones? And how can community be constructed by "placeless" social groups? For encouraging me to place upon each of these questions the necessary weight, I thank Sabine Engel and Louise Newman.

The intellectual debts for this enterprise are so numerous and stem from so many different contexts that memory will ill serve me on this score. I would like to blame my graduate training for not turning me into a better recollector, but that, at best, would be an act of laziness. Let me, then, begin by acknowledging the inspiring influence of Professor Anil Gupta at the Indian Institute of Management in Ahmedabad for introducing me to the pleasures and disappointments of an academic career. Without his support, drive, and explicit push, I would probably have become a cog in the machine that is the Indian bureaucracy. I will never know if being an academic has been the better alternative.

Robert Bates's scholarship sets standards that one always (only?) dreams of emulating. The clarity of his writing is a lesson to all who believe complex ideas need convoluted constructions. I thank him for forcing me to question myself and reevaluate my arguments constantly — a way of thinking that will extend far beyond this book. It is impossible to acknowledge the specific aspects of Elinor Ostrom's direct and indirect influence on the ideas in this book. My amorphous notions about common property began to crystallize in close interactions with her in Indiana. She continues to inspire. James Scott has shaped the arguments and prose in the following pages in ways he does not know but might nonetheless recognize (and disavow). I remain indebted to him now and look forward to incurring more such debts in the years to come.

A number of friends — for how else can one refer to those who voluntarily or under duress read first drafts of arguments — have been kind enough to subject themselves to the various versions through which the work evolved. Many individuals have read one or more chapters of the manuscript and incisively commented on the merits of the arguments. For reading the entire manuscript, I thank Rebecca Karl, Louise Newman, and five anonymous reviewers. I received valuable and significant comments on various chapters from (deep breath!) John Aldrich, Paul Alexander, Jennifer Alexander, Venkatesh Bala, Rita Brara, Jeff Campbell, Ben Crow, Glen Cutting, Gudrun Dahl, Ann Farnsworth, Terry Filicko, Kathryn Firmin, Kirsten Fischer, Clark Gibson, Michael Goldman, Sanjeeu Goyal, Paulette Higgins, Hsain Ilahaine, Alice Ingerson, D. L. Johnson, B. R. Joshi, Martina Jones, Courtney Jung, Stuart Kasdin, Purnendu Kavoori, Hee Min Kim, Herbert Kitschelt, Fabrice Lehoucq, Mary Moore, Ilse Kohler-Rollefson, Sangeeta Luthra, Mary Beth Mills, Donald Moore, Sutti Ortiz, Pauline Peters, Harold Pollack, Amy Poteete, Aseem Prakash, Kent Redford, Frances Rosenbluth, Steven Sanderson, Marianne Schmink, Michelle Sipe, K. Sivaramakrishnan, Carol Smith, Michelle Taylor, Leslie Thiele, George Tsebelis, Leonard Wantchekon, Allison Wylie, anonymous referees at the journals *Human Ecology* and the *Journal of Theoretical Politics*, and officials at the Sheep and Wool Development Board in Jodhpur. I must also acknowledge the influence of Amitava Kumar, Carol Stack, and Anna Tsing in my choice of form for chapter 1 of this work. Kimberly Pfeifer knows the many ways in which she has provoked and helped the discussions in the following chapters. She also knows how grateful and appreciative I am.

I began working out the specific arguments for the book while a Ciriacy-Wantrup fellow at the University of California, Berkeley, and as I taught at the University of Florida. But the bulk of the book was completed at Yale University during my tenure as a postdoctoral fellow with the Program in Agrarian Studies. Revisions continued while I held a fellowship at the Workshop in Political Theory and Policy Analysis at Indiana University, Bloomington. Friendships made during the tenure of these fellowships have made the writing of this book not only pleasurable but also exciting. I am especially thankful for the opportunity to get to know and learn from Christine

Glaser, Vinay Gidwani, Jesse Ribot, and Nancy Peluso. Kay Mansfield's persistent (nettlesome?) questioning in New Haven made certain I would write every day, even if only a little. I think she knows how much she has done and continues to do to make New Haven a livable place.

Perhaps it is my good fortune that I suffer from a bad memory. A better one would have required the acknowledgment of the profound debt I owe to a much larger number of individuals, conversations, and challenges that have remained unmentioned. The pleasure and the relief of forgetting is, finally, what allows me the luxurious presumption of putting my name on all the arguments in this book.

Research and writing often hinge on goodwill and the concrete signs of support in the shape of funding. I would like to thank the International Institute for Environment and Development and the Population Council for supporting the fieldwork on which this book is based. Small grants from the Division of Sponsored Research and the Tropical Conservation and Development Program at the University of Florida allowed me to collect and analyze additional data. The writing effort was supported by a number of universities in multiple ways: a James B. Duke fellowship from Duke University, a salary from the University of Florida, the Ciriacy-Wantrup fellowship from UC Berkeley, a fellowship from the Program in Agrarian Studies at Yale University, and a fellowship from the Workshop in Political Theory and Policy Analysis at Indiana University at Bloomington. Lest I appear totally inefficient, I must say that I did do some things apart from this book during these different fellowship tenures!

Three of the chapters in this book have appeared in earlier versions in the following journals: chapter 4 in *Human Organization*, chapters 6 and 7 in *Human Ecology*, and chapters 6 and 7 in *Journal of Theoretical Politics*. I wish to thank the Society for Applied Anthropology, and Sage Publications Ltd. for permission to use parts of the work they published first. I also wish to acknowledge the professional care of Janet Opdyke in copyediting the manuscript. Her promptness and thoroughness are a model. Pamela McElwee crafted the index in record time and with the exemplary speed and intelligence that anyone who has worked with her has become accustomed to seeing.

The communities of scholarship of which I was fortunate enough to become a part at each of these stellar research institutions not only contributed to my intellectual growth but created the sociality without which a writing project will always be far more painful than this one has been. Nothing accounts for friendships, nor can one ever repay them. I would like to thank Courtney Jung, Donald Moore, Suzana Sawyer, and Ajay Skaria just for being my friends and for the pleasures of conversation. To Shivi, I owe the debt of the knowledge that collaborative ventures can enthrall. For contributing to my sanity through their willingness to listen and to talk, I send hugs to Patty Dalecki, Susan Emery, Paula Kellogg, Mary Moore, Hazel Pridgen, Marty Swilley, and Debbie Wallen. I thank Paula for all her help in the preparation of this manuscript.

Sabine's companionship and love have gone into many pages of this book. They have at times facilitated the arguments and at times interrupted their completion. How can I not be grateful for both?

GREENER PASTURES

Rajasthan and Gujarat showing the location of Jodhpur

Introduction:

Politics, Markets, and Community

among a Migrant People

That is the introduction. Writing one allows a writer to try to set the terms of what he will write about. Accounts, excuses, apologies designed to reframe what follows after them . . . — Erving Goffman, 1974

The limitations of any field of study are most strikingly revealed in its shared definitions of what counts as relevant. — James Scott, 1985

Theory is very important. Life is more important. — Ranajit Guha, 1997

"Arrey Sa'! (Hey Mister!), what is there to research about us? We are nothing! Just spend our lives running after sheep and goats. Neither home, nor an address. Sleeping under the open sky, in winter, summer, and rains. Depend all the time on the whims and fancies of government officers. Year after year we measure the length of roads by our feet, carrying cooking utensils on camels and mules. Can't even rest in one place for a week. Why waste time, then, yours and ours? There is nothing to find out about us. If you spend your time with brahmins and rajputs (*babhan-thakeran*), it will be better used. You will even get better refreshments (*sa-pani*) from them." These are the words with which Bhopalaramji greeted me one morning, two months into my research on the raika shepherds in western Rajasthan in India.

The day had begun like many others I had spent in Patawal, a village close to the district headquarters in Jodhpur. It was October and still hot. I no longer had the appreciation I had found for clear, sunny days in my two years in the United States. The patina of uncertainty that had surrounded even routine actions when I first arrived in Patawal had given way to a ritual feel to everyday activities. Such a transformation of daily life must be familiar to many who belong to the academic tribe of "field-workers": the original excitement of beginning research giving way gradually to the realization that fieldwork involves many repetitive, even boring tasks; and the painstaking enumeration of observations in the hope that poring over them later would reveal missing patterns. Today I had talked to villagers and made notes on conversations, then talked to more villagers and made additional notes. The process seemed unending.

I had met members of most of the 212 households in Patawal. Although I was interviewing and talking with all the villagers, the 50 or so households of the raika shepherds were the ones in which I was the most interested. The raikas are migrant agro-pastoralists, sometimes classified as peasants. I was soon to travel with them along their migration routes. Their lives and livelihoods, their transhumance and the communities they create while migrating, and their interactions and conflicts with farmers and government officials seemed experiences rich with meaning, bursting with analytical possibilities. I was hooked.

Initially I had been the target of insistent stares, the object of many a gaze: a stranger in my own land. But after two months of fieldwork most of the shepherds and the other villagers had become accustomed to my presence and curious questions, even if not entirely to the idea of being the subjects of research. Bhopalaramji, Hadkaramji's cousin, had arrived the previous evening from Patla, the neighboring village. His reservations, the doubts he expressed about the reasons for my research and my choice of the shepherds as allies and subjects, came as a small surprise. Probing to the heart of my desire to understand the lives of the shepherds, his questions undermined it by asserting that I was wasting my time. His declaration that the shepherds could not tell me much seems especially incongruous in light of current preoccupations of analysts with marginal communities, local knowledges, and indigenous peoples.

Had I been paying greater attention, however, I would have recognized generosity in the impassive amusement that seemed to motivate the words. Such deprecating aggression was belied by the friendly, quizzical expression on the lined face of the man who was putting down his own community. As if I were being tested; were I to take Bhopalaramji's advice literally, I might not be worth *his* time. The raikas may seem one of the most marginal groups in one of the most marginal physical environments in India. But did I have the right to make that judgment, even if I made it only indirectly by agreeing with what he said?

The ostensible meaning of Bhopalaramji's words was also belied by the consistent efforts of the different raikas I met to make time for and talk with me. If one of them so much as hinted that he had something else to do, others would scold him. "When next do you think an Umrikan (American) will come to write about us?" My affiliation with an American university and my "normal" brown skin, coupled with my ability to speak Marwari, had bestowed upon me a curiously ambiguous status: simultaneously American and Rajasthani. It was an identity with which I had begun to feel comfortable. The shepherds clearly felt it was appropriate.

In the eagerness with which the shepherds often told me their stories, their words would come out in a rush that my attempts to record could not match. Then they would stop, wait, make sure I had got what they were saying. The river of words would resume. When I taped their stories, an experience they liked so much that they wanted me to send back several cassette recorders, they would listen to their words being played back again and again. Why, I now wonder, would they have taken such care to ensure my attention if they thought I should have gone to talk to "brahmins and rajputs" or had little that was worth telling. Perhaps they were simply fascinated by technology. A different interpretation is also possible: the raikas did not believe they were peripheral or unimportant. Instead they thought their experiences required as much attention as I could give. Their marginality was a state of my mind.

The marginality of a people means something very different to those who live it than to those who write about it. For those who write, marginality — understood as the lack of access to institutionalized power — traditionally ensured that a group would receive scant analytical attention. Migrant pastoralists are a case in point. Few political scientists have written about them. This form of livelihood, many believe, is doomed to oblivion, scarcely worth attention, belonging properly to the rubbish heap of History. For many others, writing about marginal peoples is license to embellish and embroider, to suitably exaggerate wretched conditions. Anthropological writings about pastoralists, it sometimes seems, inhabit a niche of their own, separated from more "mainstream" writings on development, peasants, markets, states, or communities. But for those who live it life is no less central or important for all their recognition that they may be marginal to power. This refusal to accept marginal status even as they live it, this clenched fist in the face of History, as I like to imagine it, is one of the things that makes working with the raikas so satisfying.

In recent years, the value of marginality as a source of unique insights about power has begun to suffuse much social-scientific research.[1] As de Certeau has observed, somewhat sardonically: "Marginality is becoming universal" (1984: xvii). Constructed around the lives of the raikas, this book argues that the very marginality of the shepherds can contribute substantially to our understanding of the nature of everyday politics, exchange relations, and the formation and dissolution of communities. Politics, markets, and community: these central social-scientific concepts form the context in which I examine the mobile lives of the raikas. If political scientists, economists, or scholars working on community have only rarely examined migrant peoples who depend on animals for their livelihood, a study of such peoples can help explore the boundaries of our understanding of politics, markets, and community as we deepen our analyses of their lives. Such a study may also provide unsuspected insights into the nature of these intertwined concepts. By situating the raikas in more general conversations about the formations of everyday politics, markets, and communities, this book seeks to reach out to those who might consider the lives of migrant pastoralists, if they consider their lives at all, to be unconnected with these formations.

Raika agro-pastoralists are one of several, but perhaps numerically the largest, migrant groups in India. Exact census figures are hard to come by since the Indian state no longer collects demographic data by caste, but various estimates place their population at around half a million people.[2] The number may well be higher since migrant populations, because of their mobility, are often underestimated.

The raikas are also distinguished from other pastoral and agro-pastoral groups in India such as the *gujars*, *ahirs*, *jats*, *gaddis*, or Sindhi Muslims because of their historically strong identification with the camel. In the past, the raikas managed the camel herds of royal houses in Rajasthan and Gujarat. Even today, they can tell any number of stories detailing their prowess in handling the "ship of the desert."[3] Today raikas largely have adopted sheepherding. But as a group they are still renowned camel breeders and herders in Rajasthan and Gujarat, where most of them live. Popular destinations for European tourists during the winter, these states are the source from which streams of shepherds flow with their sheep every winter in search of greener pastures.

Within Rajasthan, raikas dwell primarily in the drier western districts of Jaisalmer, Barmer, Bikaner, Jodhpur, Jalore, Pali, and Nagaur. The verb, *to dwell* possesses quite a different meaning in the context of a migrant group than it does for a settled community. The meanings become further complicated because of the various patterns of mobility that different groups of the raikas create. Depending on their access to water and fodder, the amount of cultivable land they possess, the size of their flocks, and the composition of their households, raikas may migrate for anywhere between three to twelve months a year. In Patawal, the village where I began my research, the largest owners possessed flocks of three to five hundred sheep and migrated during about eight months of the year. They traveled long distances into the neighboring states of Haryana, Uttar Pradesh, and Madhya Pradesh, and often had the most interesting, if occasionally harrowing, stories to tell about their travels. The smaller herders could usually scout browse for their flocks within one hundred miles of their villages and seldom migrated for more than three months during the winter. The smallest flock owners, with less than fifty sheep, did not migrate at all in the time I spent in the village. That, of course, could change drastically were local browse to become unavailable.

That pastoralists migrate in search of fresh sources of water and fodder is a commonsensical inference and a widely accepted fact in the literature on pastoralism. Mobility is the most evident feature of the lives of migrant pastoralists. It seems critical if humans and their animals are to survive in regions with low rainfall and high variability in precipitation. This is true of most arid lands around the world. Pastoralists in sub-Saharan Africa, West Asia, western India, and the high altitude regions of the Andes, Alps, and the Himalaya all resort to mobility to address risks stemming from environmental fluctuations. The precise patterns of mobility vary tremendously, but mobility itself seems as natural as the occurrence of seasons. It should not be surprising, then, that a significant set of writings on mobile pastoralists concerns itself with the nature, causes, and consequences of mobility. Where pastoralists in harsh environments are concerned, mobility has become a naturalized fact.

This book begins with a puzzle that suggests that the normalization of mobility in the face of "natural" risks may be misleading. In Patawal, a village that is typical of many others in western Rajasthan, some of the shepherds migrated, others did not. While raikas often took recourse to mobility, few other villagers did. If environmental risks are a natural phenomenon, mobility is equally clearly a socially shaped and produced response. My attempts to untangle the reasons for the differing degrees of mobility in Patawal led my analysis directly to the networks of social obligations in the village, to structures of power and dependence that helped guide interactions, and to claims and counterclaims signifying an intensely politicized existence. Mobility, far from being a simple, natural, and easily justified strategy to address fluctuations in biomass production, emerged as layered and tremendously complex in its origins and execution.

The year I arrived in Patawal, Hadkaramji began his migration in mid-October. Except for two brief visits, he was gone nearly eight months. He took with him all his animals: 155 sheep, three camels, and a horse. A sixteen-year-old son and a fourteen-year-old nephew—on the side of his wife's family—went with him. The nephew would serve as an apprentice. Hadkaramji's parents, wife (Ranki), an eight-year-old son (Udhoji), and a younger, unmarried brother (Mohtaji) remained behind. The group of three travelers joined hands, perhaps I should say feet, with another relative who had 210 sheep. The resulting flock of 365 sheep was part of a migrating camp that had fourteen other flocks. Altogether the camp comprised nearly 6,000 sheep, forty-two camels, and four horses from six different villages around Jodhpur. Not all of the five raika families that left Patawal in 1989–90 joined the same camp. They migrated with three different camps. These diverse loyalties and affiliations reflect social and economic networks that play a critical role in the formation of transient mobile communities of shepherds — a role that is at least as important as that of spatial contiguity in the creation of more familiar settled communities.

In the time I was in Patawal, I became close to Hadkaramji's father, Harji, and brother, Khangji. Hadkaramji himself I met twice. The first time he returned from his travels barely five weeks after leaving the village. Their camp had walked 120 miles. But it had moved in a zigzag fashion to get to the best and most easily available sources of fodder: these seldom lie in a straight line. So he had to return only 40 miles to see his family. He left within two days to rejoin the camp. His wife and the eight-year-old son went with him. Hadkaramji's camp was going to Haryana, more than 500 miles away. The wife, Ranki, and the son, Udhoji, would travel with the camp for five months and then return to the village by bus — before the return migration began in early April.

The reason for the next visit was more practical. The migration this year had been difficult: a number of sheep had died. Hadkaramji returned for the second time in March, bringing his wife and son with him. He asked his father and brother to arrange for the family to sharecrop nearly one hectare of land (five *bighas*) belonging to one of the larger landowners in the village. Few raikas possess much land for cultivation, and several rent or sharecrop, especially when migration does not provide the expected economic return. The need to sharecrop from the *patels* (an upper-caste group in the village), who owned the most land in the village, was particularly galling to Hadkaramji. He explained.

> Three years ago, the number of shepherds migrating from Patawal was half that leaving today. Ever since the patels fenced the village common (*oran*), we have been in trouble. Earlier, sheep and cattle grazed on the village common when the fields were planted during the rains. Now there are more people and less land. If there is a fence around the common pasture, what can the sheep eat? We have hardly any land, unlike the patels and the rajputs. Those guys also know government officials. And they have the elected village council (*panchayat*) in the

palms of their hands. If they had been more willing to live as a village, they wouldn't have tried to sew the pasture shut. And what have they achieved with the fenced pasture? So much government money spent on planting acacia (*Prosopis juliflora*), and most of the plants now dead. All this for what? So that we can leave the village? So that they can live in peace? But unjust income (*haraam ki kamai*) can never earn peace.

If justice is the first virtue of social institutions (Rawls 1971), Hadkaramji was telling me that the social institutions in Patawal had failed the raikas.

The clarity of thinking this Gramscian organic intellectual displayed was impressive. Here was an astute political analysis combined with a moral indictment. The anger resulting from the blow to his livelihood was the source of both. I had learned the details of what had happened during the time I spent in Patawal (see chapter 2). To reduce the political influence of the raikas in the village, the landowners had fenced the grazing common and forced the larger of the shepherds to migrate from the village more often. The concern I felt was nothing compared with the deep burn that Hadkaramji and many other raikas in Patawal still experienced. To have to rent or share-crop land from those whose initiative had pushed them out of the village was not a palatable morsel. Nor is the story in Patawal an isolated account. Village common lands are being converted into private holdings, or being fenced, sometimes in the name of the environment, all over the western districts of Rajasthan. The resulting squeeze on fodder availability and access to what little fodder is available is as much socially created as it is environmentally generated. It has pushed migration to higher levels (Kavoori 1996; Robbins 1998).

If the networks of the everyday social and political-economic relations that determine access to pasture are slanted perilously against the shepherds, formal institutions of power — in the shape of government officials, the projects they design, and the rules they enforce — pose a heavy burden as well. The state inflicts its fragmented rationality upon the shepherds in diverse forms — some direct, others not so immediate. The heterogeneous policies followed by different arms of the government have effects that, even when unknown to their designers, may be quite disastrous. "When wheat is milled into flour, the weavils are also ground to death," is a saying I often heard among the raikas. Another was, "When the python turns in its sleep, many twigs break." The raikas have many ways of depicting oppressive relationships.

Not all actions of different government agencies, however, can be dismissed as the restless uncoiling of a python in its sleep, hard as even that may be to bear. Some are far more calculated. While in Patawal, I learned of a project to help the shepherds that the state government had promoted in cooperation with the World Bank. The Pasture and Sheep Development Program, as it was optimistically named by some unknown (to me) committee, was organized under the Drought Prone Area Program (DPAP) of Jodhpur District. Launched in 1974, it covered nearly fifty villages by the mid-1980s. It then ground to a halt because fresh funds ceased to lubricate its functioning.

The underlying logic of the project to develop pastures and sheep raising was straightforward. Shepherds, as they migrate, are seen to have an adverse impact on vegetation. Preventing them from moving would therefore benefit pastures, sheep, and the environment. This understanding of the relationship between pastoralism and the environment led to a program of action.[4] The scheme implemented a simple set of guidelines: select plots of one hundred hectares each in different villages. Fence them. Construct storage tanks to harvest rain water. Enroll shepherds into the scheme as members of a cooperative. Their sheep could count as their shares in the cooperative. Keep the sheep confined within the fenced plots. Cross them with improved varieties of rams. Development would then come to the pastures and sheep. The shepherds themselves were lost somewhere in translating the objectives of development into practice.[5]

Many of the pasture plots (eighteen out of forty-nine) were located in the driest part of Jodhpur District, near Phalodi in the north.[6] When I reached Jod Village, near Phalodi, one bright afternoon in early December — with the onset of winter, I had regained some of my appreciation for sunny, clear skies — few villagers were around. Jod is a dispersed settlement. The huts of its residents lie in agricultural fields, scattered in the uneven dune-covered desert landscape like so many black dots on a crumpled sheet of yellow paper.

Over the next few days, I came to meet many of the villagers. Some had been members of the cooperative society of shepherds that had been created in Jod. For most of them, it was hard to recollect what the project had done for them. One of them, Devji, who remembered where the "fenced" plot had been located, took me there. I saw no sheep in it nor any other features that could help me discern the plot from the surrounding area. "Yes, there had been barbed wire and fence posts (*taarbandi*)," Devji confirmed. "They were valuable. Someone stole and sold them." His expression was noncommittal as he imparted that bit of knowledge. I kept my face equally expressionless. Neither of us was interested in further discussing who might have stolen or sold the barbed wire and the fence posts. But the point had been made. If you take an unwilling horse to water, be ready for it to kick you.

Devji also guided me to the raised holding tank that had been built to save the sheep from thirst in the summer. It was dry. He drew my attention to the drain that was supposed to fill the tank during the rains. Clogged with sand, it seemed not to have seen the passage of water for years. We walked back to his home in silence.

As I shuttled between Phalodi, and other villages where the scheme had been implemented, and the Jodhpur office of the Drought Prone Area Program, I learned that the results had not been similarly bleak in all the forty-nine plots. The infusion of more than 10 million rupees spent on the program between 1973 and 1983 (about 600,000 dollars at the prevailing exchange rate) had left, at times, a deeper trace. In some villages, rusty strands of barbed wire could still be seen. In others, remnants of a shepherd's shed, the water tank, and its cemented catchment area were in remarkably good shape. And in a number of places shepherds remembered the activities undertaken through the program quite easily. But in scarcely any of the places I visited were the cooperative societies functional. At that, I felt, the shepherds could count themselves lucky. The program had at least not rendered them destitute in contrast to sedentarization projects in other parts of the world, which have often converted their beneficiaries into paupers. Nonetheless, the lack of insight into pastoralist livelihoods that marked the conception and implementation of the project was striking.

All government projects to develop inscribe what Foucault, referring to the communication of knowledge more generally, has called a "double repression" (1977: 219). First, they authorize an exclusionary process. In applying specific criteria of eligibility for programs, they separate populations into different groups and create or reinforce social divisions. Second, they impose standardizing models of behavior on those selected. Only through conformity to specified codes are benefits from a program assured.

At the same time, Devji's cryptic references to the value of barbed wire and fence posts was a reminder that the shepherds found their own uses for the development brought to them (see chaper 3). Recent scholarship has begun to use poststructuralist insights to critique the massive global apparatus that has institutionalized development into a universally desired goal (Escobar 1995; Ferguson 1994). Other works, also using political reworkings of poststructuralism, remind us that it is critically important as well to consider the practices and struggles through which the subjects of development redefine, renegotiate, and redeploy the original intentions and programs of those who will institute development (Gupta 1998; Moore 1997; Pigg 1992). The interactions of the raikas with their landed village neighbors and state officials show how the interests of those one would normally consider marginalized can operate within the crevices that the splintered nature of power always affords. They indicate also that being located on the receiving end in asymmetrical structural relations does not necessarily determine political outcomes against one.

Beginning in March, I spent several stretches of time with the shepherds as they migrated. I realized how mobility is critical to survival. To arrive at this recognition is not to buy into the "mobility is a natural response to risk" rhetoric. It is, rather, to begin prospecting the multiple layers of a complex social phenomenon.

Sandford, in a simple thought experiment, has demonstrated that mobility can allow a more efficient use of pastoral resources (1983: 33–36). The argument hinges on fluctuations in biomass production within a given area over time. Consider two different ecological zones in a region over three consecutive years. Assume that there are fluctuations in net annual biomass production within the two zones. If confined to a zone, the number of animals that zone can support over three years will be determined by the worst year in that zone. The region will sustain the sum of the number of animals supported in the worst year of biomass production in each zone. But, if animals can move across the two zones, then in a bad year in one of the zones some of its animals can move to the other zone. The larger the number of different ecological zones in a region, and the more the differences among them, the greater are the benefits of opportunistic movement across zones.[7] As studies of pastoral systems in Kenya, Ethiopia, and Zimbabwe have begun to question received wisdom in rangeland management, it has become clear that in regions with highly erratic rainfall pastoralists can derive the greatest benefits of mobility by moving their animals "sequentially across a series of environments each of which reaches peak carrying capacity in a different time period" (Behnke and Scoones 1993: 14). To some extent, this is what the raikas also attempt.

The demonstration that economic gain is possible through migration is insufficient as an explanation of movement, however. Especially in South Asia, where the thickly peopled landscape is at once agrarian and environmental,[8] movement with animals is not just a physical task. Mobility is the simultaneous execution of a set of social understandings through which the raikas build bridges with many different actors and construct transient but deeply experienced communities among themselves. Movement creates a variety of possibilities. They can be realized only in constant social negotiations.

For one thing, mobility enhances production levels. Greater production of sheep and wool, in turn, requires that the raikas find markets for exchange as they travel. Wool must be sheared, and those who shear the wool must be paid, usually in cash. Because the raikas do not eat meat, sheep must be sold and grains bought in exchange. The myth of subsistence-oriented production that often colors views about peasants is especially inappropriate for the raikas. The need to shear sheep and pay shearers, sell sheep and wool, and buy daily necessities and small comforts—in short, to engage the cash economy in all the ways necessary to the survival of any specialized producer—means that the raikas cannot rely on mobility as their only response to environmental risks and fodder deficits. They must also enter and nurture different forms of exchange relationships. The success of the migrant economy depends critically on participation in markets.

Movement with valuable sheep can also lead to encounters that threaten security. Traveling in the countryside, where minor government officials are as often predators on the weak as they are protectors of the strong, means that the shepherds must protect themselves against external depredations. A single shepherd migrating through unfamiliar territory with his animals would be easy prey to a variety of hunters: thieves, bandits, local bullies, and unscrupulous villagers. So it is not surprising that the raikas migrate as collectives (see chapter 4). Only as a group can shepherds undertake the level of protection effort required to keep their sheep and other valuables safe.

The literature on mobile and transhumant pastoralists, however, often takes the act of mobility itself to be a natural phenomenon. That is to say, even when scholars recognize the social causes that lead some groups to migrate when others remain stationary, the performance of mobility is analyzed primarily in terms of its physical characteristics. How far do pastoralists travel? What is the frequency of their movements? In which seasons do they travel? What patterns can be discerned in their migrations? To which destinations do pastoralists go and why? These questions occupy considerable space. The social characteristics of the enactment of mobility, on the other hand, seldom receive significant attention. Collective mobility, in comparison with individual movement, necessitates a radically different social organization. But it is common to find descriptions of mobile groups that make it difficult even to infer whether migration is collective or whether individual families travel on their own.

The failure to examine why some pastoralists migrate as collectives and others move as a single household may be explained in part by the limited influence of the literature on collective action and institutions on the work of scholars of pastoralism. But the lack of attention also reveals deep-seated, silent assumptions about the naturalization of mobility. These assumptions require unpacking, not acceptance. Indeed, once the issue of collective versus individual mobility is addressed, a series of questions social scientists ask in many different contexts becomes inescapable. When humans solve problems as a collective, the organization of that collective response requires social actors to construct institutions. The failure to create institutions often leads to a concomitant failure to solve problems.

I use the term *institutions* in the Durkheimian sense, the sense in which it has been deployed in the recent scholarship on institutional change (Bates 1989; North 1990; Ostrom 1990).[9] They represent provisional equilibria in human interactions constantly under negotiation. The informal institutions raikas construct while migrating are critical in facilitating interactions within the camp and with other social actors. In the absence of institutions, the raikas would migrate much less.

Movement through a landscape dense with humans also depends upon the ability to find one's way in a thicket of dynamic property rights regimes in land. Enforceable property rights increase security of tenure. Greater security of tenure, of which privatization is one of the prime examples, is often believed to be a step toward more efficient utilization of resources. But creation of enforceable property rights inevitably also increases transaction costs. This is especially true where established property rights are yielding to others.

Over much of the area through which the shepherds migrate, farmers used to raise one wet season crop. Usually this would be a low-value crop such as millet. Productivity of land was low. Few of the farmers felt that their land produced an output high enough to justify the expense of fencing. In consequence, shepherds migrated during the postharvest months through land that was unfenced and in which rights to graze were open to all. The manure sheep deposited was payment enough for the grasses or the fallow they browsed. Even today, there are numerous instances of farmers inviting shepherds to camp in their fields. Sheep manure is considered far better than inorganic fertilizers or cattle dung.

But the situation is changing relentlessly. In the last three decades, irrigation has become far more common. The efforts of the Indian state to promote agricultural production have extended canal and tubewell irrigation to many more parts of northern Rajasthan, Haryana, western Uttar Pradesh, and Gujarat. To belabor the obvious, irrigation encourages higher capital investments in agriculture, raises the productivity of land, and makes production less volatile. It also leads to agricultural intensification because land can be cropped a second, or even a third, time in a year. With irrigation, therefore, farmers intensify efforts to enclose land.[10] Their wariness of shepherds increases. If shepherds feel that irrigation and fencing are their enemies, farmers, reciprocally, believe sheep to be the enemies of their crops.

The changing production dynamics in agriculture redefine the relations between the shepherds and the farmers. That is not to say that their relations become uniformly more hostile. Kheenvji, who led one of the migrating camps in which I spent time, summed it up succinctly, if indirectly: "Where there are utensils, there will be noise. Some may even break. But without that noise, you cannot cook, cannot eat."

Browse for the sheep sometimes becomes scarcer as farmers enclose their fields. But intensified agricultural production can also increase the availability of biomass because new crops may be introduced and because crop residue may be present in the fields more than once a year. By timing their movements more precisely, shepherds can take advantage of the new production niches. The changed situation necessitates, however, that shepherds and farmers renegotiate established understandings about the use of available biomass. It also means that the shepherds have less social and physical space in which to maneuver and less time within which to do so. The limited room to negotiate is reflected in the low prices they receive from farmers for the products they sell.

Recent anthropological discussions on markets and value, especially in the wake of Appadurai's influential intervention in the debate, have appropriately pointed to the ineradicably social and political nature of all economic transactions, even when such transactions are seemingly voluntary and take place among equals. These analyses have highlighted the role of politics in new and unexpected ways. But in trying to focus on a particular stage in the life of a commodity as the most prominent in determining value, many theorists unnecessarily constrain their analyses. Appadurai's assertion that it is "exchange that is the source of value" (1986: 57) or Miller's claim that "consumption has become the vanguard of history" (1995: 1) move us beyond hoary disputes about whether capital or labor is the source of value. But they still elide issues that could receive attention if analysis were kept more open-ended.

An examination of the grain-manure exchanges between the farmers and the shepherds, and an elaboration of the factors that contribute to price formation, create room to discuss the nature of markets, value, and barter versus cash exchanges (see chapter 5). The discussion highlights the intensive bargaining that goes into each exchange. Frequent revisions of initial offers, alterations in tone of voice, changing facial expressions, impatient body movements, and explosive gestures form essential elements in the negotiations. But statistical analysis of more than eighty exchanges reveals that shepherds receive a relatively low price during migration for the manure their sheep deposit in farmers' fields. Their returns are just about half of what they can get in their home villages.

Kheenvji, whose words, to recall Geertz, reminded me more than once that I was not studying the raikas, only studying with them, had this to say: "Our sheep can't eat their fill in one place because we don't have enough land at home. We are strangers (*pardesi*) here, as well, in these lands (*des*) through which we travel. We don't belong, so everybody mistreats us. Why else do you think that for the manure of the same sheep penned in a field we get such a low price here and a higher price at home?" He thought for a moment and continued: "I call it home, but I don't really have a home. Didn't I have to leave it last year? Wouldn't my sheep have died of hunger if I didn't leave it? Didn't I have to miss the birth of my first son?" Kheenvji's "voracious taste for the concrete," as Fanon would have put it (1963: 95), hints at some of the ways in which property and power, production and place, are tightly linked. To disentangle the interwoven factors determining the value of goods sold during migration, we must pay more insistent attention to the political economy in which the shepherds are located, to the variable social relations of the shepherds with the farmers, and to the ways property mediates the consumption of forage by sheep.

The prices negotiated during migration often apply to all the members of the collective. Thus, the leader of the camp haggles with traders and farmers over the price of the wool and sheep manure that is sold, but all members of the camp abide by the negotiated price. Similarly, medicines and a significant amount of grain that is consumed in the camp are bought at prices negotiated on behalf of the collective. The community that exists in the shepherd migrant camps is substantially responsible for the trust shepherds display when they accept the collectively applicable prices. But the community found in migrant camps is founded upon grounds that would be troublesome to much of the recent literature on community, both from those on the left and those on the right, and from those who consider their positions to be beyond left or right (Etzioni 1993).

Much of this literature, drawing its cues from works written around the turn of the century, focuses on structural characteristics and conceptualizes communities as being egalitarian collectives with stable memberships (Agrawal 1997a). The members are supposed to be resolutely connected to specific places and to interact regularly and frequently over the long run. Migrating camps of shepherds, in comparison, are connected not to place but to the processes of decision making, prospects of economic gain, hierarchy, and mobility. Their membership fluctuates; they are transient. They are, nonetheless, communities.

Members of the migrating camp delegate the power to make decisions on their behalf to the camp leader (*nambardar*). Successful migration depends heavily, then, on the ability of camp leaders to make the right decisions. Joint market exchanges, collective migrations, and communal defense are underpinned by a particular organization of decision making within the camp that is highly informal but still tremendously effective. The camp leader, because he is particularly knowledgeable about numerous aspects of the migration experience, makes the majority of decisions for the entire migrating camp. In the thirty camps I studied, the nambardars made more than two-thirds of all decisions (see chapter 6).

Such delegation of decision-making powers to specialists is widespread in all organizational contexts. Among the raikas, it reinforces hierarchical relationships between the shepherd and the nambardar. However, one must exercise care in using *hierarchy* to describe the interactions between the shepherds and their leaders. The shepherds are under no compulsion to heed what their leader says. If they find decisions especially onerous, they have the option of leaving the camp in midmigration. But the nambardar's social status and authority to make decisions are correlated with a multitude of attributes related to knowledge, age, social connections, ownership of sheep, qualities of leadership, and kin networks. The combined weight of these factors lends a nambardar an authority that is difficult to ignore without significant cause and often not even then.[11]

The authority a nambardar exercises operates through no visible instruments and may often not even be perceived or described as power. As Arendt suggests, "authority precludes the use of external means of coercion; . . . [it] is also incompatible with persuasion" (1993: 93). A prime example of what Foucault has called "capillary power," the exercise of authority during migration is constitutive of the social relations and interactions in the camp. Among its effects are inspiration and loyalty to the group. Collective migration would be impossible in the absence of hierarchy and the cooperation it frequently inspires.

Inequalities in leader-led relations create the contingent potential for significant gain and significant abuse. If camp leaders exercise authority in the service of the collective good, shepherds stand to harvest critical and significant economies in everyday tasks. They can save money in their purchases, they can land the best deals when selling their sheep, they can graze their sheep knowing that the strength of the collective is at their backs, and they are spared the trouble of making a raft of routine decisions that could consume inordinate amounts of time. But asymmetric allocation of decision-making powers also means that unscrupulous camp leaders can exploit camp members and wreck the prospects for a financially successful migration.

All collective action in the real world is, of course, troubled by the specter of deceitful conduct, especially when authority and resources are delegated to specialists. But over time shepherds have created informal monitoring mechanisms that deter most potentially dishonest behavior. Shepsle and Bonchek point out that monitoring goes hand in hand with delegation (1997: 309–10). But monitoring is not enough. Without the prospect of sanctions when fraudulent actions are discovered, the information recovered through monitoring is likely to be worthless in nudging inappropriate actions in a more reasonable direction. And here shepherds face a problem. How credibly to threaten someone who is manifestly in a position of greater authority? This is the issue chapter 8 addresses. The answer depends on identifying the ways in which the camp leader depends on the shepherds for his future reputation. It is these reciprocal relations of gains and losses between the camp leader and the shepherds, this dependence upon each other, that hold the key to the delegation of decision making and the collective organization of everyday tasks in the raika migrant camps. Understanding them provides the answers to questions about why collective action is feasible in the raika migrant camps and how shepherds limit the possibilities of abuse.

Not only is collective decision making the key to a financially successful migration, but it also forms the cornerstone of the transient communities shepherds craft as they traverse thousands of miles every year. Their communities are transient in the obvious sense signifying mobility. They are also transient in that they come into being each year for six to nine months during the migration and then dissolve, or, more accurately, are then suspended, until the next year. Similarly, they are communities not just in the physical senses of the term — regular and frequent interactions during migration, interdependence and mutual vulnerability, or similar material endowments of members. Rather, they are also communities in a deeper sense, in that members feel bound to their migrating camps by shared experiences, common goals, and common identities.

Contemporary appeals to community take place in the shadow of the apprehension that old forms of solidarity are disappearing or have disappeared and in the hope that in specific, localized communities may be found the resources to create new forms of political engagements. Shepherd communities form an example that cautions against identifying community too strongly with a locality, against equating the erosion of community with increased mobility, and against too strenuously separating deeply felt solidarities from the presumably more shallow desire for economic gain. Their communities come into being without affiliations to particular local spaces, even as the shepherds move constantly, and together with the needs, desires, and specific processes oriented toward economic gain. They underline the fact that when we consider particular social processes or phenomena antithetical to the possibility of community our theoretical lenses may require reorientation, even replacement. Paraphrasing Althusser, one might say, theories exist only in the concrete contents they enable us to think ([1969] 1996: 217).

As the shepherds relate with their settled neighbors, state officials, merchants, and farmers along their migration paths, and among themselves, they bring to their interactions particular understandings of themselves that are generated in diverse fields of social negotiations. Mobility, by bringing the shepherds into many new contexts, perhaps affords them numerous opportunities to create fresh understandings of who they are and to act based upon these understandings. Their understandings, colored always by their marginality, may also be understood as identities, habitus, or "orientations to action." Identities, thus, always mediate the engagements between structures and actions, opportunities and choices (but see Elster 1989: 13–16). The complex and variable relationships between contexts, identities, and actions, each helping to constitute the others, underpin all possibilities of social change for the shepherds.

"What can you say about us, sa'. We are here one day, gone the next. That is our way of life. We go where there is better browse, more friendly farmers, less trouble. Our possessions are so few, it is easy for us to move. We live our own lives. 'The python doesn't serve anyone; birds don't work for feed / Our ancestors told us no one provides but He!' " Kheenvji's couplet has lost much in translation, including the rhythmic tempo of the lines he uses to describe his livelihood. But the words in this conversation are similar to those in a different conversation with Bhopalaramji early in my fieldwork. The tone and the meaning are subtly different this time. Within a mobilized marginality, Kheenvji suggests that there is reason to hope for a better life. Under the cover of an ostensible fatalism that relies on divine agency, Kheenvji also asserts the importance of what he believes to be the shepherds' right to lead their lives in a particular fashion. His words are a reminder that hegemony, power, and marginality are never complete, are always under revisionary contestation.

1 · Mobility, Identity, Loss:

Recurrent Themes in the Lives

of a Marginal People

[T]his research activity, which one can thus call genealogical, has nothing to do with an opposition between the abstract unity of theory and the concrete multiplicity of facts. . . . What it really does is to entertain the claims to attention of local, discontinuous, disqualified, illegitimate knowledges against the claims of a unitary body of theory which would filter, hierarchise and order them in the name of some true knowledge . . . — Michel Foucault, 1976

I am a methodological opportunist who believes in doing or using whatever works. If game theory works, I use it. If what is called for is a historical accounting, I do that. If deconstruction is needed, I will even try deconstruction. So I have no principles. — Adam Przeworski, 1995

In so far as the science of man exists, it finds its materials in the "trivial," the everyday. — Henri Lefebvre, 1947

The mobility of the shepherds is irreducibly, if variably, constitutive of their identities. Forged in the crucibles of their everyday actions and the opportunities they encounter, identities are also central links between actions and opportunities. A consideration of the dynamic relations between mobility and identity reveals the ways in which the shepherds engage developments adverse to their interests. It also suggests a healthy caution against contemporary assertions that the way of life of the raikas is eroding and that it will soon disappear. There is some irony to such assertions. After all, many theorists view increased mobility as a defining symptom of modernizing societies. Migrant pastoralists, however, are taken to be nothing but remnants of outdated social formations that have no place in our modernity. To point to the mobility that is the hallmark of the lives of many shepherds is not to suggest that they are already living the postmodern condition. It is rather to focus on those forces of change that not only shape the lives of pastoralists but underlie larger societal trends — and concern other analysts.

Mobility, identity, and loss are recurrent motifs in the lives of the raikas. These themes are implicit in the discussions in the three parts of the book, which concern politics, markets, and community among shepherds. In this chapter, I consider them explicitly.

Each section in the chapter is dedicated to one of these themes and is written in two distinct voices. The first, enactment, uses the words of the raikas drawn from conversations and documents. With as little textual intervention as possible, it enacts, as it were, a circumscribed performance in their voice. To use the words of the raikas is not to make a claim about authenticity or unmediated representations. Rather, it is to elaborate on the selected theme in words that evidence the immediacy and relevance of that theme to the lives of the raikas. The second voice, refraction, connects the motifs of mobility, identity, and loss with the observations of other scholars on these same motifs. Together the texts in these two voices provide evidence about the multiple ways in which it is possible to explore the same theme.

My use of two voices can be viewed as an attempt to unravel the double code through which accounts of other peoples inevitably express themselves.[1] Most texts, and this applies to studies in comparative politics, seek to achieve coherence by integrating different voices and sources, by polishing the seams that mark their differences. This applies to information that is collected during fieldwork, in conversations with colleagues, or through research in a library or archive. My use of dissimilar registers attempts to produce a different kind of coherence by making two distinct voices speak to each other. Recovered from particular kinds of silences, each voice tells its own story but also reflects on the other voice (see Barthes 1977: 146–50). The two segments of each of the following sections thus form a diptych that speaks in different tongues about the same subject.[2]

MOBILITY

"Three weeks ago, when we camped near the Kaneda train station, Ghewarji fell asleep on guard duty in the night. The poor man had just returned from his home and is still recovering from all the work his wife made him do." The listeners gave snorts of meaningful laughter, to which Ghewarji protested. "Don't deny it, you did fall asleep." Thus began a conversation with Dallaramji, the leader of one of the migrant camps whom I interviewed.

"In the morning Modaramji found seven sheep missing from his flock. You ask how he knew exactly seven were missing out of more than three hundred? Well, Moda knows all his sheep by name." At this point I smiled. The thought that Modaramji knew each of his three hundred sheep by name seemed unlikely. "Don't smile. Each sheep has a name, and when Moda calls

they come running. And the same is true for all shepherds who are their mothers' sons." Dallaramji demonstrated the truth of his assertion by beginning to whistle and call his own sheep by name. And several of them did come running (as far as it is possible for sheep to run), looking reproachfully at their owner at being interrupted in their browsing.

"Two of the seven were newborn lambs. One was Moda's prize ram, just bought for eleven hundred rupees.[3] *We could clearly see the footprints of the bastards who took off with the sheep.*

"We traced the footprints of the thieves two miles to the homes of the sansis *[one of the lower castes in Rajasthan] near the village. All of us went. There must have been at least thirty in our group. You should have heard the noise we made. A huge crowd gathered. Those sister fornicators had already eaten one of the lambs. First they denied everything. Then they gave back four of the animals and said they only had stolen four. But once we started threatening them with the police their story changed quickly. I played a trick on them and asked Moda and Ranaramji to leave as if they were going to the police station. The sansis could not take that and gave back the other two sheep and two hundred rupees for the sheep they ate. I'll bet that has been their costliest meal.*

"We were lucky. Sometimes the sheep are stolen at the point of a gun. You can trace all the footprints you want! We were also lucky that it was the sansis who stole the sheep. If it had been a thakur *[an upper caste], even God might not have been able to get it out of his stomach. God helps us in many ways. You are smiling, but think about it. We wander around the whole year. Without divine help, things would never turn out right."*

I interrupted the flow of Dallaramji's words. "Why do you leave your village? Isn't there enough grass on the common? Would you leave if the common was big enough for your sheep?"

"That is the problem. We don't have enough grass on the common. And there are too many enclosures (taarbandi). *Sa' (Mister), we curse having to leave the village and home and family. And all for a few sheep!"*

In the above description, the raikas emerge as more or less victorious in their conflict with a settled group. But this is not the only kind of story about mobility I learned. Another incident powerfully brings home the dangers of mobility. It is extracted from a letter written by a legislator in Madhya Pradesh.[4]

"You can imagine what happens when hundreds of thousands of sheep invade your standing crops for miles. Village after village begins to weep.... For a whole fortnight these nomads terrorized the place. They even did criminal things like snatching money from people and rotis from mothers

*and sisters going to the fields. . . . Last year I had about five hundred thou-
sand sheep removed from my area. This year, at the time when sheep were
being massacred in Dahinala, policemen, village councils, and forest officials
in my area were trying to rid farmers' fields of about one hundred thousand
sheep. During the time of the Janata government [the political party then in
office], Shiv Charan Mathur [Rajasthan's chief minister under an earlier
Congress Party government] himself was the chairman of the local Sheep
Removal Committee. Half a dozen shepherds were killed by the local farmers that year, and the Shekhawat government filed a police report of serious
offense against Mathur."*

Mobility confounds settled relationships. It raises uncomfortable questions
about teleological theories of history,[5] undermines attempts by states to ter-
ritorialize and control their populations, and confounds accepted understandings of the relationships between property rights and efficiency, place
and community. The raikas' variable relationships with their village neighbors, interactions with state officials, use of resources, negotiations in markets, and organization of their migrating camps are each linked closely to
their mobile existence, demonstrating its complexity. In each of these cases,
the positive or negative alignment of mobility with politics and power is
critical in influencing what happens to migrants.

Simply understood, and it was thus understood for a long time in the
context of migrant pastoralism, mobility is a strategy raika shepherds deploy
to accommodate the spatial and temporal structure, intensity, and unpredictability of environmental variations.[6] Even understood in this simple fashion,
mobility can unsettle established interpretations of the relationship between
different forms of property rights and the efficient use of resources. For
example, those who study resource use and management commonly accept
that some form of property assigning exclusive rights to users[7] is critical to
efficient use of resources.[8] Indeed, Garrett Hardin's mistaken analysis of the
tragedy of the commons hinges on the assumption that open access to resources will necessarily lead to their decline and degradation (1968).[9] Theorists of various persuasions have asserted that exclusive ownership, through
either common, private, or state ownership, is necessary to effect more efficient management of resources.

In the case of the raikas, however, it is upon open access to fallow fields
that additions to animal wealth and increases in income are predicated.[10]
The migration cycles of the raikas (see figure 1.1) begin at the end of the
monsoons and vary between three months and the entire year.[11] The survival
of the migrating sheep depends most importantly upon the forage that may

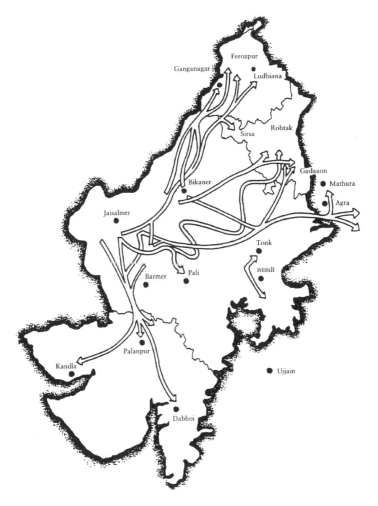

Figure 1.1   Migration patterns

be available along the migration routes on fallow private fields (Agrawal 1992). Over much of the region traveled by the raikas, cultivated fields are harvested by late October and then lie fallow, open to all animals. In this sense, the private fallow seasonally provides *open access* for grazing.

Without the availability of seasonal forage on this open-access fallow, raika migrations would be far more difficult, even impossible, for many. Mobility and open access to grazing on the fallow make it possible for the raikas to herd the number of sheep they do. If rights to forage were strictly specified, the incomes of the raikas would be much lower and their livelihoods at far greater risk. Nor is the case of the raikas an exception. Smith, speaking of the Richtersveld, argues: "In environments characterized by infrequent and highly localized rains, free access to land, as practiced by herders in the Richtersveld, may well be the best way to optimumly use the sparse resources" (1991: 109).[12]

Open-access fallow, where forage is browsed for a day or two before the raikas move on to a new pasture, is not only critical to the raikas' migration; it is also instrumental in permitting a higher level of return for the larger society of which the raikas are a part. If sheep did not graze the postharvest fallow it would scarcely be used. The fields would also be less fertile in the absence of the manure sheep deposit on them. At the same time, formal arrangements to manage low-productivity pastures would necessitate contractual arrangements whose transaction costs (of enforcement) are likely to far exceed possible profits. The lesson is general. Where raises in productivity are very low in relation to the transaction costs necessary to effect exclusive rights to resources, open-access regimes are likely to be more efficient than those that confer exclusive property rights.

In social theory, the concept of mobility has other meanings, positive as well as negative. Increasing mobility disrupts the regularity and predictability of the social interactions that undergird community. It is the solvent that unglues communal relationships. As Giddens and a number of other scholars writing about modernity have suggested, mobility is the shifting state in which humans find themselves with the advent of modernity, the force that potentially shatters tradition. If individuals are mobile and constantly meet new people (as do the raikas), customary rules and understandings about ethnicity and community are likely to be disrupted. But the mobile lives of the shepherds pose a question about such understandings of mobility. The raikas create vibrant communities while migrating. They demonstrate that there is no necessary antagonism between travel and the existence of community, between mobility and the emergence of solidarity.[13]

Other understandings of mobility identify it with freedom and the capacity to accomplish tasks. Those who are mobile are marked as agents. Braidotti, speaking of migrancy and nomadicity in the context of female subjects, suggests: "Mobility is one of the aspects of freedom . . . a superb achievement" (1994: 256). This equation of freedom and power with mobility corresponds well with popular and official understandings of who is capable of moving. Rural populations are less mobile, as are tribal and indigenous groups. Those who study them can move, and so can government officials. The ability to move is a mark of freedom, incarceration a stripping away of power. State officials recognize the dangers mobility can pose to authority by rupturing territorial integrity; they attempt to sedentarize no-mads. Scholars find in mobility the possibility of diversity and efficient use of spatially heterogeneous resources; they argue against sedentarization.[14] Tsing, in discussing mobility among the Meratus, suggests that it "expands social spaces and shapes political communities . . . [and] opens transcultural conversations that bring extra-local concerns into local negotiations of lead-ership, gender, and community" (1993: 150). The Meratus she talks about attempt to be mobile in an effort to mimic and gain power.

These views of mobility have much to recommend them, including their intuitive appeal. For example, by resorting to mobility the raikas sometimes create tension and concern among the settled populations through whose villages they move. They escape from dominated positions within relations of power (see chapters 2 and 3). They can increase their incomes (see chapters 4 and 5). Yet, in the easy identification of mobility with power, one is apt to ignore another possible interpretation of movement, one that the raikas' example should bring home with particular force. The raikas come from villages where the larger part of the population, especially the more powerful village actors, does not resort to mobility to support livestock. The control landowners exercise over resources, especially land but also the power to purchase feed from markets, obviates the need to migrate. To consolidate their position within the village, they exclude raikas from village commons and force them into greater mobility (see chapter 2). In such situations, when mobility becomes a reflection of the structured deprivation of power, it be-comes inscribed by marginality. It binds migrant populations to their exis-tence, leading scholars to view nomadism as a mode of livelihood more traditional than any settled existence. Mobility has no necessarily negative or positive relation to power, only contingent ones. Existing theoretical lenses are apt to occlude this contingency of possible relationships between power and mobility. The ability to move, it can be easily imagined, is a precious gift of power. But it can also be a valued refuge from those in power.

IDENTITY

"We are Shiva's ghosts.[15] He looks after us. Without His blessing how could we survive months and months, even years, away from home? You can see that we go where our sheep and camels go, where there is grass. We have no choice. Yet no one can stop us!

"From where do we come, you ask. Well, Parvatiji, Lord Shiva's wife, was playing idly with clay one day because He had gone off, as usual, to spend His time with His ghost and demon friends and followers. As She molded it in different shapes, She created a strange-looking animal with five legs and

was entranced by it. When Shivji returned, She asked Him to bring this animal to life. He was reluctant — the animal was awkwardly shaped, and once brought to life would find it difficult to move. But Parvatiji insisted, and in the face of women's insistence what man can stand by his words?

"Shivji gave way, and after breathing life into the animal, He said, 'Uttha,' which means 'get up.' This is the secret behind the camel's name." (In Hindi, the camel's name is phonetically almost the same: Oontha.)

"Becase the fifth leg of the camel prevented it from moving, Shivji cut it and put the leg on the camel's back, which gives the camel its characteristic hump. The remnant of the fifth leg is the boss on the belly of the camel.

"After its fifth leg was removed, the camel began running about and proved difficult to control. To take care of the camel, then, Shivji created a man from the dirt of His skin. This man, Pinda, was supposed to subsist on the milk of the camel. He fell in love with a heavenly beauty, Rai. From their union, permitted by Shivji, all the raikas have sprung. The twelve daughters of the couple were married to rajput grooms, and the son was married to a rajput woman. The present day subcastes of the raikas come from these thirteen original couples. Because it was Shivji's will that we subsist on the milk of the camel, we still never sell camel's milk."

I am still uncertain about the different interpretations of this myth of origins. Most raikas, including children, can recite it with minor variations to explain their fascination with the camel, the meanings they ascribe to camel's milk, and their unwillingness to sell it. They also use it to indicate a relatively high position for themselves in the caste hierarchy. But their attempt to reconcile divine creation with the dirt of the divine body is characteristic of other contradictions and fractures in their lives.

The discussions of the origins of the raikas by Kohler-Rollefsson (1992), Srivastava (1991, 1997), and earlier by Westphal-Hellbusch (1975) provide some historical depth in answer to the question: "Who are the raikas?"[16] Through the sources mentioned in these writings, it is possible to trace the raikas back to Baluchistan and Persia from which places they migrated to settle finally in their present-day locations in Rajasthan and Gujarat.

Given the arid environment of these states, the expertise of the raikas in breeding and tending camels made them invaluable to the ruling houses. The maharajas of Jaisalmer, Bikaner, Jodhpur, and Jaipur all maintained camel corps for desert warfare. The raikas usually looked after these camels. They also served as messengers for some of these same ruling houses. Today they trace kinship to rajputs, often calling themselves "younger brothers of the rajputs" (Srivastava 1997: 13).

Socially, the raikas are divided into thirty-four exogamous subcastes, several of which are further subdivided into lineages.[17] Caste councils, called *nyaats*, exercise a significant influence on the social life of the raikas and wield substantial authority in settling disputes related to marriage contracts, land, and conduct that is considered unsuitable for caste members. There are significant spatial differences in the power exercised by caste councils in different parts of Rajasthan and Gujarat.

Raikas differentiate among themselves on the basis of where a particular individual is from: Marwar and Godwara in Rajasthan or Kutch and Patan in Gujarat (Randhawa 1996; Srivastava 1997). In recent years, some raikas have attempted to mobilize greater organizational strength for their communities by establishing raika associations in different parts of Rajasthan. Most often these associations are led by educated raikas. They are different, thus, from the more "traditional" institutions of the caste councils or those that facilitate decision making in the migrating camps. The newly created raika associations can be seen as part of an effort to construct what Srivastava (1997) calls a "social-identity movement" among the raikas.

In contrast to this political project of creating a single body that will include all raikas, the caste councils attempt to establish social boundary markers that can be quite restrictive. Some councils have attempted even to prescribe the appropriate dress, food, and marriage rules for members (Srivastava 1997: 29). Clearly, the identity "raika" is a negotiated outcome, not simply an ascriptive category.

Nor can the views of the raikas about themselves be reduced to a single dimension. In response to questions about whether they are a caste or a group united by a single occupation, I often heard the story of origins that begins this section.[18] At other times, I heard assertions that they were a caste, an occupational group, or both. Such structural identifications as caste, poor, or pastoralist often point toward an identity that others confer upon a group rather than being a dynamic or subjectively felt identity.[19] Although there is no direct correspondence between such sociological classifications and felt identities, sometimes classifications are also critical in producing the effects that they are only supposed to signify. The multiple, variable answers that the raikas gave in response to my questions about their identities mesh well with recent writings on the subject.

Calling for a move beyond static notions, beyond what Appiah and Gates call the "regnant cliché-ridden discourse of identity," recent scholarship on identity advises us to eschew essentialist conceptions (1995: 1). It demands greater attention to locality and history as significant factors for understanding how identities are constituted. It also suggests the importance of paying attention to the ways in which members of groups see themselves in relation to others. It may be useful, in this connection, to remember Benjamin, who conceptualizes history as an open field rather than a linear progression or a necessary development (1978). Identities as well must be seen as the consequences of processes and interactions that do not have determinate ends. They are neither the necessary consequence of particular structural relations nor the automatic effect of a social location.

Attempts to think about who the raikas are, or how they came to be what they are, must also engage the ways in which they constitute, mobilize, and rework existing beliefs about themselves. Memories of their history, conversations, songs, stories of origin, and communally performed tasks during migration serve to congeal the concrete effects of repeated interactions with groups along their migration routes and in the villages where they camp. What seems critical to their views of themselves, thus, are their relationships with place/movement, work, and caste and the variable ways in which these constructs are mobilized to give new meanings to the term *raika*.

Place, whether conceptualized traditionally as landscape or more recently as a complex amalgam of language, environment, and history, figures in the raikas' views of themselves more as an ellipsis, or a displacement, than as an identifiable and fixable location. For the migrating raikas, there is, perhaps, no place called home if one defines place as a stable point in space. Instead, home emerges as a socially defined and communally imagined site. Instead of being the intersection of lines on a map, it is a configuration of social forces. Such perceptions of home are also found among other migrant or marginalized populations.[20] This nullity, or the lack of a geographically fixed point called home, can also be framed positively by abstracting and reconceptualizing it as mobility. The process of substituting place by means of socialized movement is indicated in specific phrases the raikas use to talk about their lives: "[W]e go where our sheep and camels go, where there is grass. We have no choice but no one can stop us!"

In the absence of stable connections with a particular place, the raikas identify themselves with the camps into which they are collectively organized during their migrations; these are usually named after the camp leader. Achieving an identification with the camp, especially because it is produced annually within a relatively short period, requires an immense investment in work and sociality through conversations around evening fires, songs, and communal buying, selling, guarding, and cooking. Even young raikas can tell stories of divine origins, myths of valorous deeds performed by ancestral figures, or accounts of conflicts between raikas and farmers. Such storytelling is a critical task in community building. Together with the more material aspects of camp life, such as the allocation of decision making and the performance of collective tasks such as camel grazing and cooking, it breathes life into the migrating camps of the shepherds. At the same time, the identities shepherds create during their migrations become more explicable in light of the political-economic forces and fissures in village communities that push them together as migrating groups (see chapter 2).

The two other axes that the raikas use most readily when speaking of their identity — caste and work — are often framed negatively as well. They usually talk about their caste status by contrasting it with that of upper caste individuals, and of their lives and occupations as something that is naturally different from a life of settled farming and landowning. To point to these different ways in which my interlocutors among the raikas see themselves in relational terms is to insist upon something many feminist scholars have long recognized: any collectivity (in their case women, in this book raikas) is "historically, discursively constructed, and always relatively to other categories which themselves change" (Crosby 1991: 155; see also Riley 1988: 1–2). No ontological or epistemological foundation is made available for an identity because of a particular social-structural location such as "poor and marginal" or a seemingly concrete point of reference such as "caste." Identities are constructed on the basis of different experiences in multiple fields of social engagements (de Lauretis 1986).

How identities are constructed and which identities will become relevant in particular interactions can only emerge through specific contests among different groups over resources, power, and status. Although the conflicts themselves also shape identities, we should note that individuals do not begin social interactions as empty slates onto which their interests during conflicts etch a new identity. As different participants within a conflictual (or cooperative) process interact, they must, even if shortsightedly and tenuously, assess who they are, where they are located in relation to others, and what actions will best serve them. This process of renegotiating who they are, and an emergent understanding of how they are peripheralized, is decisive in the struggles of the raikas with other groups: over control of resources, negotiations over prices of commodities, and attempts to secure benefits from government officials.

Loss

The following is a translation of a letter the raikas sent to the chief minister of Rajasthan in 1990 as a protest against the worsening fodder situation. Bhopalaramji, who shared the letter with me, is active in lobbying state legislators on behalf of the shepherds.

In the service of:
Shri Bhairon Singh Shekhawat, Chief Minister
Rajasthan Government
Jaipur, India.
Re: Application from the Animal Herders' Association

Respected Sir:
Gochar[21] *(common grazing lands) should remain untouched. This year the price of wool has fallen to Rs 1,200 per hundred kilos.[22] Other prices are rising, and that harms the shepherds extremely. To graze animals, we need grazing lands, but unauthorized controls on such lands increase each year. It results in the destruction of commons grazing and other commons such as ponds (naadi), and the catchment areas of the ponds (agor). District magistrates and deputy district magistrates are permitting these trends. They should be stopped. If not stopped, all commons will vanish and our problems will become excessively severe. It is the duty of the state government to protect ponds, their catchments, and grazing commons. It is also the duty of the village councils (pan-chayat). The Rajasthan Tenants Act specifies these rules, but they are broken. In 1971, the Wool Marketing Federation was organized to reduce the exploitation of the shepherds by middlemen. But the federation is not buying wool, and exploitation has not stopped. Keeping in mind these facts, please ensure appropriate action and implementation.*
Respectfully,
Bhopalaram Dewasi, Chairman
Animal Herders' Association

Jodhpur (Member, Bharatiya Janata Party)

A number of writings, from Salzman's documentation of the declining pastures in Rajasthan and Gujarat (1986, 1987) to other recent works on pastoralism in India (CSE 1985; Prasad 1994), indicate that migrant pastoralism does not possess a bright future. The inference to be drawn from these analyses is that, dependent as they are on pastures and mobility, the orbit of raika lives must progressively diminish as pastures disappear, as more lands come under irrigation and become privatized, and as governments attempt to sedentarize nomadic populations. Crooke ([1896] 1975) expressed similar sentiments more than a hundred years ago when he suggested that the *banjaara* (another migrant group in India) were disappearing and used this "fact" to justify an account in which migrant groups are viewed as anomalies in a modernizing society. The banjaaras still exist today, and their continued existence attests to the resilience of migrant groups (Randhawa 1996: 220).

Writings about pastoralists have moved through phases that are easily distinguished. Earlier writings on nomadic pastoralists, under the influence of structural functionalism, emphasized the stability and boundedness of pastoral groups (Evans-Pritchard 1940) and often "attempted to reconstruct 'traditional' social organization" (see Dyson-Hudson and Dyson-Hudson 1980: 16). More recent works stress the links of mobile pastoralists with other groups and social formations and focus on the ways in which their societies are undergoing change (Ensminger 1992; Fratkin 1991; Khazanov [1984] 1994; Rigby 1992; Schlee 1989).

Analogous changes also mark views about the relationship of pastoralists with their environment. Beliefs that pastoralists are irrational or inefficient users of grazing lands or are forced by circumstances to degrade their environments (Hardin 1968; Herskovits 1926; Lamprey 1983; Picardi and Siefert 1976; Pratt and Gwynne 1977) have yielded to interpretations that view pastoralists as shrewd managers of livestock who can use resources with a sensitive recognition of the capacities of their environments (Anderson and Grove 1987; Behnke et al. 1993; Bonte and Galaty 1991; Homewood and Rodgers 1991; Sandford 1983). As misperceptions about whether pastoralists can effectively use their environments have been modified by new research, scholars have begun to focus more on how state policies constrain the actions of pastoralists and vitiate the viability of pastoralist livelihoods.

Migrant pastoralism is an inconvenient fact for facile teleological accounts of historical change that see human development as a progression through stages: from hunting and gathering to pastoralism, agriculture, and industrialization (Khazanov [1984] 1994). In the evolutionist scheme, the demise of pastoralists is inevitable. Empirical accounts that highlight the challenges confronted by pastoral groups fit well with the perception that such societies are doomed to disappear in any case. With the loss of faith in a teleological history, however, studies that examine whether and to what extent pastoralists are really vulnerable have also emerged.[23] These later studies emphasize instead the abilities of pastoralists to devise innovative strategies in uncertain physical and social environments (Behnke 1994; Hogg 1992; Homewood and Rodgers 1984).

To draw these points together, the literature on pastoralists, including that on the raikas, sees them in one of two ways. Either their lifestyles are seen to be under threat because they are irrational creatures, unable to address environmental constraints, modernization, and market forces, or they are highly innovative but threatened owing to shortsighted policies followed by unsympathetic or myopic government bureaucracies. Recent studies of pastoralists attempt, in this sense, a dual redemption. First, they seek to redeem their subjects by pointing to how pastoralism is economically and culturally viable and how the actions of the pastoralists are not going to lead to the loss or disappearance of pastoralist lifestyles.[24] Second, by producing an account of the lives of the pastoralists, they prevent at least the loss of knowledge about these lives. Even were pastoralists under threat, writing about them preserves knowledge about them. It is in this sense that Clifford refers to all cultural descriptions as "allegories of salvage" (1986: 115).

Narratives that suggest pastoralist lifestyles are disappearing, or that pastoralists are a group under threat, coincide in striking fashion with an enormous literature that views indigenous peoples as losing their identities, customs, languages, knowledges, and cultural specificity.[25] The very pervasiveness of these arguments might indicate the persistent desire of authors to see themselves as saviors of the people about whom they are writing.

Accounts of loss and recovery may, on the other hand, be connected less to grand allegorical images than to specific processes of change and transformation. It is to this specificity that any account of other peoples must attend, even as it recognizes the possible complicity of specific descriptions with larger allegorical visions. Ethnographic accounts run the risk of marginalizing their subjects and conceding center stage to theory when they do not insistently attend to history over allegory, local truths rather than sweeping generalizations, and particular subjects in preference to macrolevel political-economic forces. Stories cannot prevent meanings from being read into them, especially new meanings that emerge in relation to the changing contexts within which they are read. It is neither necessary nor desirable to prevent new and unintended meanings from emerging in the texts that are written. But what would constitute a "real" loss would be allegorical readings of texts that ignore the specificity and historicity of the experiences that the subjects of these texts undergo.

Allegories of loss and recovery always raise suspicions about exactly what it is that is disappearing and why it needs saving. Do changing lifestyles signify that something "culturally pure" is being lost, being destroyed? Or do they denote new relationships in response to social change? Power, who exercises it, and how it is instrumental in transforming specific relationships are crucial to answering such questions. Without denying the marginality of groups that are located in politically or spatially peripheral positions, it is worth pointing out that precisely at the margins might the influence of centralized authority be the least and the influence of markets and modernization trends the weakest. In such instances, focusing only on how marginal groups change in ways beyond their control is to present a lopsided picture at best. Such an imbalance is precisely what I attempt to guard against in the stories this book recounts. In various chapters, I describe and analyze the ways in which the raikas contest attempts to marginalize them, the organizations they create to influence politicians, their negotiations in market settings, and their decision-making arrangements during migration. Throughout, the objective is to make it clear that their lives may be stories of acceptance, accommodation, and compromise, but they are as much stories of renegotiation, resistance, and adaptation to forces over which they seemingly have little control. Broad generalizations, posed either as grand allegories within which the meanings of specific events can be fitted or as macrolevel and structural changes that particular stories exemplify, provide willfully one-sided accounts of what happens in the lives of particular peoples.[26]

Rather than reading the chapters that follow as stages in a sequence that unfolds to reveal ever more significant and central elements about the raikas, they are better taken as local insights into different aspects of their lives. The ensuing chapters are divided into three parts — on politics and power, markets and exchange, and community and hierarchy. It is not the intention of the book to attempt the impossible task of presenting a "holistic account" of raika society or even to pretend that there is a raika society. The representations of writers are always incomplete, focusing, like the human eye, on what strikes them as significant. The book elaborates, as well, important influences on particular areas of raika lives and actions. Although each part of the book primarily investigates a particular set of relations, it does so with the recognition that power, exchange, and community are closely connected. Exchange, power, and community, after all, are crucial parts of all social lives and of our imagination about what counts as relevant.

I · SUBALTERN POLITICS,

DEVELOPMENT,

AND THE STATE

In fall 1989, I arrived in Patawal Village in Jodhpur District in Rajasthan to investigate how villagers use the grazing common. Many questions motivated me. What was the nature of the institutions guiding the access of villagers to fodder and fuelwood? How had these institutions come into being? What role had the village community played in maintaining local resources and creating the institutional rules to manage them? How could institutional arrangements be improved to manage common property better? The implicit questions, of course, were whether external actors could help create better village-level institutions and whether the relationship between the state and the local community was necessarily antithetical.

In addition to an inventory of institutions and their origins, rules and their effects, I came away from my research with lessons in the use of power, the influence relative power positions play in political struggles over resources, and the relationship of local political struggles with state initiatives on development. In contrast to my initial expectations and perceptions, I came to realize that the local community and its interests could be seen neither as antithetical nor as complementary to those of state actors. The concepts of the community and the state themselves came into question as their internal fractures and multiple constituents came into view.

The relations between actors within the community and the state turned out to be highly nuanced, greatly dependent upon context. In retrospect, it is clear that these relations always contain the seeds of new and surprising political alliances within the community, which in turn can reflect upon local actors in unanticipated ways. Further, the villagers — landowners, lower caste members, and the shepherds — turned out to be far more preoccupied with the politics of the allocation of resources than with creating efficient rules for managing pastures. The elections in Patawal for the village council seats were emblematic of the ways in which villagers used external political changes for their own ends.

The shepherds' political struggle with the landowners in Patawal Village captures significant aspects of their other struggles as they seek a livelihood. The struggles are usually unavoidable and the stakes asymmetrical — costs of losing the contest remain high, gains from a victory minimal. Often winning the political bargain simply implies the continuation of the status quo. The shepherds' entanglement with the landowners over the disposition of forage from the grazing common of the village embroiled them in a conflict in which the best possible outcome was merely continued access to the common pasture. Competing in the village council elections brought them face-to-face with the possibility of losing access to the common, as it was enclosed in the name of environmental conservation and the protection of trees.

In a long conversation, Hadkaramji, one of the shepherds in Patawal (see introduction) said: "When the question first came up about the elections to the council, we didn't know what to do. We couldn't win a majority in the council. But if they [the landowners] put an enclosure around the common land, we would have even less grass for the sheep. All around the country, we have less land for grazing our sheep. In our village, we have the same story. On one side, the snake and on the other the alligator. If we stood for elections, the upper castes would become upset. If we didn't, enclosure was almost certain. And even if we won a seat, politics in the village would change only a little. We would gain only limited power, we knew."

He continued, "We also knew that the upper-caste villagers have never been very happy with us. The sheep sometimes get into fields. Some are jealous of us because they think we are rich. We have always been looked down upon. When they talk, it is out of the sides of their mouths. Even their children think we are unclean. So, when the time came, we decided we needed to act. Even if nothing major changed, at least we would have shown that a cornered dog can turn to bite. Getting a seat in the village council when those in power are opposed is something of which we can be proud."

A seat on the council, however, required that the raikas put up a candidate in the village elections. Contesting the elections was a challenge to existing power relations in the village. Winning a seat was proof that the challenge had teeth, that the future hold of the upper caste, landowning families on the council was insecure. The landowners in Patawal reacted by forcing the raikas to migrate more often and for longer durations. They accomplished their designs by using state regulations to enclose the common in the name of increasing its vegetation cover. The enclosure has reduced the fodder available to the raikas' sheep, especially during the critical monsoon months between June and September when most fields are planted all over Rajasthan.

As Hadkaramji summed it up:

It is true that we have to live together with the other families in the village. But one also has to show that one's hands are strong. If you always say "Yes, yes," your tomorrows will be lost as sure as sheep eat grass. Thinking about it now, it is obvious we didn't play the election game well. But I also am not sure what else we could have done. There will, however, be other chances. There are always other chances. You just have to know how to make use of them. Next time we'll need to get the help of more villagers. Do you know the story of the sticks in a bundle? When the bundle breaks, you can break each stick one by one. But when they are together, try breaking the bundle! If we get together with others in the village — bhils, sargaras, meghwals [lower caste families], whoever is willing to see from the same eye — the election results will be hard to swallow for the upper castes.

Hadkaramji's observations about the village elections — the contest that forms the centerpiece of the analysis in chapter 2 — indicates some of the ways he thought about power. The attempt to use power always seeks to change existing social relations. A wily user of power is aware always of the possibility of defeat and ready to seize another chance. His words also hinted at the ways in which some raikas might have changed as a result of their struggle against the enclosure of the village common. Hadkaramji's words indicated little deference in his attitude toward the dominant upper caste individuals in the village, marking instead an impatience, a desire to shift the status quo.

Local politics, the experiences of the raikas suggest, is ineradicably enmeshed with macrolevel political changes. Government regulations about improving vegetation cover on the local grazing common precipitated the latent and simmering differences between the shepherds and the landowners. Higher levels of migration prompted by enclosures in different parts of Rajasthan may in turn provoke new state regulations. State initiatives to change social conditions often emerge in response to perceived local necessities and the larger impacts of these local conditions. The directional arrow of influence in the relationships between local and macropolitical developments can point both ways.

The Pasture and Sheep Development Program in Jodhpur District, undertaken under the Drought Prone Area Program in the 1970s, is the subject of chapter 3. It nicely illustrates how local adjustments to state policies can change relations of power and the terrain on which new power relations are played out.

"They started by asking us for land so that they could fence it into pasture plots. Then they told us they would make us into cooperatives. We thought, 'Let them make cooperatives. Maybe we will get some money out of it.' But we also wondered, 'Why do they want us to stay in one place to be part of this cooperative? Is it possible to find all the grass one needs for the sheep in just one place?'" Devji in Jod Village, whom I met in late 1989, five years after the Pasture and Sheep Development Program had breathed its last in his village, was clearly not very impressed with its accomplishments.

He was especially unhappy with the way members were chosen for the cooperative societies. "There was big trouble about who could become a member of the society and who couldn't. This is the problem with government schemes. They give to those who already have a lot. What could the poorer shepherds do apart from breaking the fence when no one was looking? It was already rusting and weak. And its presence didn't make any difference to the way we graze our flocks. Many of us just put our sheep with the ones inside the plot. Who was going to separate our sheep from those that were already within the pasture plot?"

In the same breath, Devji talked about two different aspects of the programs. First, he listed the reason why poorer shepherds in the village did not like the program for pasture development: although it was supposed to help the poor shepherds, it enlisted the richer villagers as members. Second, Devji told me how the villagers undermined the unequal effects the program could have created. They broke fences, not just metaphorically but also in reality, to graze their sheep in pastures the program had enclosed. Not only did they break fences, but they literally sold the barbed wire and the fence posts, effectively erasing the traces of the development brought to them.

Devji also had a more general critique of the program. "There are four kinds of famines," he told me.

> The first is *akal* — the normal kind. Crops fail. It comes every two years. Then there is *trin-kal*. Crops fail, pastures fail. There is no fodder. It comes every five years. You have to leave your home and go away with all your valuables. Even worse is *jal-kal*, which occurs every ten years. There is no water. Without help from outsiders, from relatives who live in other areas, from the government, you can't survive. But the worst is *maha-kal*, which comes every twenty-five years. Nothing helps. Plants, animals, human beings all die, and no one can prevent it. Why do you think it has the name of death itself? You just have to let maha-kal take its course. It means that God is really angry with the world. What the project people didn't understand is something every son of a mother in Rajasthan knows. In normal times, pasture plots are fine. But whenever there is a trin-kal, jal-kal, or maha-kal all the sheep will die if they are

jailed behind a fence. Grasses will come back with the rain but not the sheep.

Although the shepherd cooperatives that the government attempted to form under the auspices of the Sheep and Pasture Development Program did not work for any length of time, they were useful in another way. They became part of attempts by shepherds to construct a politically oriented federation to lobby at the level of the state legislature. The shepherds used their mobility as a strength. They used it as a basis upon which to petition state politicians. More importantly, the institutional forms that help them organize collective migrations helped in the creation of the larger political federation. The raikas, thus, contest their marginality by using the democratic electoral process. They participate in this process and attempt to wrest concessions from politicians in exchange for promises of votes. Through such contests, they evoke the possibilities of a better future for their children.

Chapters 2 and 3 explore the multiple facets of power and the ways in which it shapes the relationships of the shepherds with residents in the localities shepherds inhabit and with state actors. In so doing, I attempt to navigate through some recent writings on power. An impressive literature on the subject, substantially influenced by Gramsci and Foucault, has moved us toward more textured and insightful understandings. Reflected in writings on ethnicity and identity, on the state, about development, from feminist perspectives, on peasant communities, and on much else, these new insights provide a constant, if complicated, backdrop to my analyses of the unequal relationships into which the raikas enter. But the deployment of such concepts as hegemony, discourse, power/knowledge, and performativity in current writings does not displace earlier Weberian or Marxist optics on power. It cannot be otherwise given the different spectacles and manifestations of power with which these theorists concern themselves.

2 · I Don't Need It but You Can't

Have It: Institutions, Politics, and

the Village Grazing Common

These elections were the first time we tried to fight the upper caste villagers. Next time we will do better. We will build a thicker bundle of sticks, which will be harder to break. We will talk with the sargaras and the bhils so that they will vote with us. They will understand that they are cutting off their own hands by making us leave the village. We will talk with the raikas in other villages of the council. — Raika villager in Patawal, 1990

We have to live together with the other families in the village. We cannot afford to create differences with those who own everything. We have to think about our tomorrows. — Raika villager in Patawal, 1989

The grazing common in the village has declined completely. The animals have eaten all the grass, villagers have burned all the trees. . . . When the government is working so hard to improve our country's forests, isn't it also our duty to contribute even if it means making some sacrifices? — Village headman, Patawal, 1989

Raika pastoralists migrate annually, but most of them spend the four monsoon months from June to September tending their agricultural fields. In this period, their sheep and camels must subsist on the village common since few raikas possess sufficient land to afford private pastures. Without access to the browse on the common, the raikas would be forced to migrate more often. This chapter examines ongoing conflicts over the grazing commons in Patawal, elaborates on their social context, and analyzes the politics around the institutional arrangements to manage the local commons. In the process, it initiates a conversation with neoinstitutionalist scholars[1] whose insights have advanced our understanding of the importance of politics in the creation of new institutions. The case I describe adds to existing analyses of the creation of institutions by examining the conditions under which social actors may initiate strategies that *reduce* their total benefits under new institutional arrangements.

The administrative and geographical setting of Patawal Village is Jodhpur District in semiarid western Rajasthan. Although the raikas in Patawal are engaged in agricultural rather than pastoral production, their overall reliance on sheep rearing and migration increases their marginality to village social and political life. As migrating shepherds, the raikas are able to take advantage of spatially scattered grazing resources and improve their annual incomes. But their absence from the village for a large part of the year contributes to their inability to play an effective role in village politics. The politics that forces the raikas out of the village and into migration more often and for longer time periods provides a window on the complex negotiations that create the raikas as migrant pastoralists.

There are three social actors in the local struggles I describe: (1) the raikas; (2) the larger landowners in the village, who belong mostly to the upper castes; and (3) the agricultural laborers, who are mostly of lower caste. The raikas and the larger landowners are the main protagonists. At stake are the amounts the state expends on village-level development programs and the forage available from the grazing common. The terrain on which the actors struggle for advantage is the tilted landscape of social and political relations among the different castes and the changing policies of the Indian state regarding the use of land and land-based rural resources, especially the grazing commons.

The immediate occasion for the political contests in Patawal was the distribution of fodder from the *oran,* the village grazing common.[2] But long-term issues — existing tensions among different village factions, assessments of the threats shepherds might pose in the future, and changes in laws protecting common lands — also played a significant role in influencing the process of the struggle. Being a part of the struggle, in turn, changed the way the raikas think of themselves and their relations with other villagers.

I first introduce the village and the major factions into which its population is divided — the landholders and animal owners.[3] Political activity in Patawal is and has been influenced greatly by state policies. The politics of the distributional struggles in the village suffuses interactions among villagers and is crucial in altering institutions that affect grazing. The processes of institutional change in Patawal can be viewed as attempts by political actors to consolidate and enhance their existing power and their share of the economic pie, an investment in the future.[4] Institutions are thus always under negotiation rather than being settled equations.

The Village and Its Factions

Patawal is located near the district administrative headquarters,[5] the city of Jodhpur. Situated in the drier, flatter part of the district, the landscape of

Table 2.1   Population and Caste Distribution in Patawal

Caste	Number of Families	Proportion of Village Population
Raika	57	27
Meghwal	38	18
Patel	27	13
Bhil	24	11
Charan	14	7
Sargara	12	6
Brahmin	4	2
Rajput	3	1
Others	33	16
Total	212	100

Source: Household survey by the author, 1989–90.

Patawal is disturbed only by the *naadi,* a tank dug in the village common to conserve rainwater for the dry season. Water from the tank and an old well are crucial to the villagers, especially after the monsoons. Low and irregular rainfall make agriculture a risky business. According to the villagers, only every five years is there sufficient rainfall for a good crop. Most, therefore, have acquired some animals to diversify their assets.

The oran occupies 225 hectares, approximately a quarter of the cultivated area.[6] It is an administrative as well as an ecological unit. Orans with trees on them have existed in western Rajasthan for longer than people can recall, and their current status is protected by law (Brara 1987). The surface of the oran is distinguishable from cultivated fields because it has not been plowed for centuries. The oran also has a higher density of trees and shrubs. For many villagers and their animals, the oran and its vegetation represent important benefits. Its small trees provide villagers fuelwood and fodder; its grasses supply fodder for cattle and sheep.

The village contains 212 upper and lower caste families (see table 2.1). Between 1981 and 1988, the number of households increased by almost 25 percent, as was revealed in conversations with villagers and the patwari of the village. The two most numerous castes, raikas and meghwals (both of which are scheduled castes),[7] make up nearly half of the village population. Together the different lower caste groups comprise a majority—74 percent of the village households. Brahmins, rajputs, and charans, the upper castes, form just 10 percent of the population. These relative proportions of the different castes are representative of other villages in Rajasthan—lower castes form a majority, upper castes a minority. The patels in Patawal are primarily an agricultural caste and count themselves among the upper castes. Numerically they are the largest of the higher castes. During the last thirty years, they have been economically successful and have assumed a significant position in local politics. The factional struggles that I recount and analyze occurred between the patels, rajputs, charans, and brahmins on the one hand, and the raikas on the other.

The raikas are chiefly animal owners. This, apart from their lower caste, distinguishes them from the patels, charans, rajputs, and brahmins. Many upper caste villagers see the raikas as dirty and unclean, like the sheep they own. A small child once confided in me, "the raikas are unclean because they eat from the same utensils as their sheep." Some villagers believe the raikas eat the meat of their sheep. The raikas vehemently deny such allegations, but clearly their social presence and networks within the village are weak.

As tables 2.2 and 2.3 show, there is a large difference between the animal- and landowning patterns of the raikas and the higher caste groups.[8] Consider table 2.2, which reveals clear divisions between raikas and other castes in the species of animals owned. The raikas own most of the sheep and camels in the village (about 90 percent). They form only 27 percent of the population. Cattle ownership is more evenly spread. The four higher castes (charans, brahmins, patels, and rajputs), who together own about 50 percent of the cattle in the village, form 23 percent of the population.

The landholding pattern is highly skewed in favor of the higher castes (see

Table 2.2 Livestock Owned by Different Castes in Patawal

Caste	Cattle	Sheep/Goats	Camels
Raika	22 (0.4)	2,870 (50)	66 (1.2)
Meghwal	24 (0.6)	55 (1.5)	NA
Patel	49 (1.8)	18 (0.7)	NA
Bhil	8 (0.3)	152 (6.3)	4 (0.2)
Charan	42 (3.0)	97 (7.0)	1
Sargara	5 (0.4)	21 (1.8)	0
Brahmin	9 (2.3)	0	0
Rajput	8 (2.7)	0	0
Others	33 (1.2)	22 (0.7)	0

Note: Figures in parentheses indicate the per family holding by animal species.

Sources: Household survey by the author, 1989–90; patwari records, 1987.

Table 2.3 Land Distribution According to Caste Groups in Patawal

Caste	Area Owned (in hectares)	Number of Households	Per Family Holding (in hectares)
Raika	120	57	2.1
Meghwal	170	38	4.5
Patel	264	27	9.8
Bhil	40	24	1.7
Charan	155	14	11.1
Sargara	23	12	1.9
Brahmin	34	4	8.5
Rajput	10	3	3.3
Others	167	33	5.0
Outsiders	73	12	6.1
Total	1,056	212	5.0

Sources: Household survey by the author, 1989–90; patwari records, 1987.

table 2.3). The charans and the patels have the highest landholding figures in the village: 10.2 hectares per family.[9] The rest of the village households own 3.3 hectares of land on the average. The raikas possess just 2.1 hectares of land per household. Of the various castes in the village, the sargaras, bhils, and meghwals occupy the lowest position in the caste hierarchy. After more than fifty years of Indian independence, their economic circumstances remain congruent with their lower social status. They hold a little more land on the average than the raikas do. On the other hand, they possess very few animals. The rest of the villagers treat them as untouchables, and their houses are on the outskirts of the village. Some of them have encroached upon the village common to find space on which to build their huts.

Caste inequalities in land and animal holdings are further accentuated by the fact that just a few families within each caste hold most of the land and animals of that caste. For example, just 20 percent of the raika families own more than 50 percent of the camels and sheep in the village. Similarly, less than 10 percent of the upper caste households own more than 50 percent of the land and cattle held by the upper caste families.[10] Differences of caste, differences in land and animal ownership, and prolonged absences from the village render the raikas unequal participants in local political and economic life. None of the villagers are rich or powerful in any meaningful sense, but the raikas are marginal even to the affairs of the village.

Inequalities between the upper caste families and the raikas in terms of their land and animal holdings have an important effect in polarizing the interests of the two groups, especially when it comes to harvesting benefits from the commons. To understand how the unequal division of land and animals affects the interests of village caste groups in relation to the village common it is necessary to examine the economic activities of the villagers.

Most families in the village rely on agriculture. Almost all households possess and cultivate some land. Millet, fodder crops, legumes, and some oilseeds are the major crops grown in Patawal. They are cultivated during the summer monsoon. The first plowing occurs at the end of June or the beginning of July depending on the onset of the monsoons. To take advantage of every bit of available moisture after the first showers have fallen, farmers use tractors instead of bullock-drawn plows because tractors accomplish the task much faster. Once crops are sown, they mature quickly and are harvested in October and November. For the rest of the year, all the fields in Patawal lie fallow.

None of the fields is enclosed. Cultivated fields are private property, but they become common property for the purposes of grazing during the fallow period. There are thus two types of commons in Patawal: the oran, which is never cultivated, and the postmonsoon fallow. Animals graze on the oran throughout the year. The fallow is available for seven to eight months. The treatment of fallow as common is not a phenomenon unique to Patawal. Most villages in the dry regions of northern India lack irrigation and have only one cropping season. It makes sense, therefore, to treat privately owned fallow as "common" in the postmonsoon period when no crops are standing in the fields.[11]

After the harvest, when the productivity of the fields is limited by the lack of water, the costs of policing the fields are far higher than the potential returns. Since exclusion cannot be enforced, the fields effectively become common (Agrawal 1992). But the trees on the fields remain under private ownership. Other villagers can graze their animals on the fields and collect fallen twigs and branches for firewood, but they cannot fell a tree for its wood. The movement of the cultivated fields between private and communal use with the change of seasons points to multiple local understandings of property and resource use.

The understandings of the settled villagers about the relationship between land and property are similar, in this sense, to those of the migrating shepherds. Institutional arrangements for the use of land-based fodder resources are in flux — undergoing changes that mesh with the seasonal movements of the shepherds (and other pastoralists). More efficient use of resources in Patawal, rather than being synonymous with particular forms of property, is predicated upon social processes concerning the use of land and the creation of dynamic institutional arrangements that can attend to the ebb and flow of temperatures and precipitation, people and animals. The seasonally shifting nature of property arrangements in relation to the fallow is critical to understanding the use of resources in many rural contexts.

Because of easy access after the harvest, fallow is an important source of fodder for both the upper and lower castes. The lower castes do not benefit more from the grazing on the fallow than the upper castes do (but see Jodha 1987, 1988). Almost all caste groups in the village maintain cattle. Further, the number of cattle owned by different caste groups roughly matches the proportion of land owned by that group, and inequalities in cattle ownership parallel landholding inequalities (see tables 2.2 and 2.3).[12] For example, the four upper caste groups own 54 percent of the cattle and 47 percent of the land. The lower castes own 19 percent of the cattle and 24 percent of the land. None of the castes, therefore, gains much over the others through cattle ownership. The grazing patterns for the cattle and other village animals demonstrate that open access to the fallow for grazing confers no extra benefits on any caste group in the village.

Villagers graze their animals on the open fallow from November to May. Most of these animals are cattle. Many of the raikas, who own almost all the sheep and camels in the village, leave with their animals on their annual migration. The few sheep that are left behind browse more on the oran than on the crop stubble in the fields. Cattle, on the other hand, seldom graze on the oran after the monsoons because the vegetation quickly deteriorates to an extent that makes it unsuitable for cattle. As the quality of the crop stubble in the fields declines with the approach of summer, more cattle are fed from private fodder stocks. Families without sufficient stocks usually purchase fodder from neighbors or neighboring villages.

Benefits from the grazing common are distributed unequally among the different castes in the village. With the onset of the monsoon, private fields are sown with crops and closed to grazing. The grasses on the oran rejuvenate. Some of the cattle begin to graze on them.[13] A few farmers may set aside a part of their land as private pasture, but only a minority have such surplus land. A large proportion of the households, therefore, must rely on the vegetation in the oran during the monsoon months to feed their cattle. Both the upper and lower castes rely on the oran, although the upper caste families can feed their animals from private fodder stocks and crop residues as well.

The raikas return from their migration around the beginning of the monsoons. At this time, the sheep population of the village increases enormously. A similar situation exists in other villages in western Rajasthan since the pastoralists in these villages return from their migrations at the same time. Almost all the returning sheep browse on the village common because there is no other forage. As one villager described it: "In the monsoon months, the oran is so filled with sheep that it resembles the back of a flea-ridden dog."

The raikas and the upper caste groups depend, then, on the oran and private fallow to very different degrees. The upper castes own cattle that graze on the oran for only a short period during the year. Most of the time, the cattle are fed from private sources or on the privately owned fallow fields that turn into open fallow after the harvest. The raikas are sheep owners. They are absent from the village for most of the year but return for approximately four months. In this period, the vegetation on the oran is crucial to the survival of their sheep and their households because they possess little land that can be spared for grazing.

Where benefits from the grazing common are concerned, unequal land and animal (sheep and camel) holdings between castes polarize caste interests. The raikas would like the oran to be as large as possible so that their sheep can browse during the monsoon. Any reduction in the size of the oran directly reduces the fodder available to their sheep and camels at a critical time. Other groups in the village, especially the richer landowners, are not seriously affected by reductions in the size of the oran. At the same time, inequalities of wealth and assets *within* a caste facilitate joint political action to improve benefits for the entire caste. We shall see that the events that led to institutional change were precipitated by the more powerful and influential actors among raikas and the landowners.

POLITICAL PROCESSES

Historically, Patawal was a part of the feudal state of Marwar. Erstwhile patterns of administration and land use continue to influence some present-day dynamics in the village. Local institutions, especially the informal Village Council (panchayat) and the caste councils, function on principles that date back three to four hundred years. To appreciate the workings of institutional arrangements today, it is necessary to investigate their roots. The history of institutions of resource use retained in the collective memory of the villagers inspires many of the current rules that influence the use of resources.[14]

One of the most intriguing historical rules followed by villagers, for instance, requires that individuals who break rules regarding the common must feed the birds. To punish individuals who cut wood or grasses on the oran, the informal panchayats require them to stand in the village square and offer seeds or grains to the birds. The rule has historical roots, but many panchayats still apply it despite the fact that in the current context it makes sense only as an act of altruism. Three circumstances give the rule an economic rationale historically. First, birds often deposit undigested seeds in their droppings—thus, birds are efficient seeders. Second, the orans date back to the feudal period when even petty lords controlled large areas and many orans lay within their domains. Third, the lords would want to protect and enhance vegetation all over their fiefs. The rule for feeding birds, it can be inferred, was created by feudal lords to improve vegetation on the orans. Today, when orans are small, villagers do not necessarily gain the benefit of such indirect seeding of the oran. The rule persists nonetheless.

Take another example. The oran in Patawal, as in other villages, is also the catchment area for the water tank located in it. For a few weeks before the monsoons, all villagers are prohibited from grazing animals on the oran so that droppings do not contaminate the drinking water that collects in the tank. Recently, piped water has arrived in the village, benefiting richer villagers disproportionately because they receive its benefits directly in their homes. They are far less careful today in following the prohibition against grazing animals on the oran. Poorer villagers, more dependent on the water tank in the oran because few of them get the benefit of the piped water supply, are unable to sanction the more influential rule breakers.

To analyze how grazing resources are utilized in the village today, we need to consider two factors: (1) Patawal was once part of the centrally controlled *khalsa*[15] lands in the feudal state of Marwar, and (2) local community institutions played an important role in enforcing social and economic decisions at the grassroots level.

Prior to Indian independence, the princely state of Marwar was administered feudally with the king at the top and a congeries of nobles called *jagirdars*—fief holders—below him (Upadhayaya 1973: 256). The nobles ruled as minikings, administering their fiefdoms without much hindrance by the center (Sharma 1977; Sharma 1972: 216–18). They appointed their own officers to collect revenues, police the villages, and dispense justice in their lands. The crown, throughout the nineteenth and early twentieth centuries, sporadically attempted to limit the local influence of jagirdars. It favored local administrative bodies and village communities in their disputes with the petty feudal lords.[16]

On khalsa lands, however, the crown's decrees held sway, unmediated by the authority of local lords. A large number of local institutions, of which the most important were the informal panchayats and the caste panchayats, influenced social behavior, settled disputes, and guided the actions of villagers regarding resource use. Informal panchayats were judicial and administrative bodies that, on occasion, also settled intravillage disputes (Sharma 1972: 207–8). These panchayats still persist. Although they have lost their significance in many cases, the Patawal panchayat continues to influence social life. It comprises one representative from each of the major castes in the village and two each from among the patels and the charans. Although the members of the panchayat are drawn from different castes, charans, patels, and brahmins form a majority in it. Meetings of this panchayat are arranged by consultation among villagers. It settles most minor disputes; presides over significant events such as marriages and funerals; and, more recently, since the benefits of development have been introduced into the village, oversees the piped water supply, the school building, and the distribution of prizes in the school. The informal panchayat also manages the local common resources, something that has historical roots but in Patawal has been buttressed by the activities of its formal Village Council.

In most villages in Jodhpur state, some land was reserved for communal grazing during the feudal period (Patwa 1989: 112–14). All such land was controlled by the panchayats. They also possessed and managed other common resources. Some of these resources were naturally given (pastures, forests), some were provided by the feudal lords (orans, nadis), and still others, such as drinking water wells, were constructed by the panchayat itself.

Jodha details many of the rules that regulated access to community grazing lands (1990: 13–19). According to him, the scattering of watering points evenly in the grazing commons, deliberate rotation of grazing, periodic restriction on some types of animals, use of watchmen to prevent villagers from breaking rules, auction of rights to dung collection, top-feed lopping, and restrictions on the cutting of wood are some of the more prominent ways in which villagers protected and conserved the commons. Often the panchayats also levied user fees. The revenues gathered through user fees and taxes went to a village fund and were used for public purposes.

A number of rules regulated access to and the use of orans. Orans are also usually dedicated to a local deity who once protected the villagers and their animals from evil spirits. Villagers can often recount stories about how people illegally removing wood from the oran could not leave its boundaries because of the deity exercising its power. Today, with the decline and the disappearance of the formal feudal state, many of the rules have lost their force. This is the substance of a number of recent studies (Anantram 1988; Brara 1987; Jodha 1985). They argue that after India's independence in 1947 existing rules became ineffective especially rapidly. Jodha (1985: 255) studies two villages in western Rajasthan and concludes that out of nineteen rules that villagers used for managing commons in the past only two survive today.

Anantram also contends that local panchayats have become less effective in implementing rules for conserving common resources.

This chapter, however, suggests that, at least for Patawal, the "erosion" of community institutions has not proceeded apace. In the last fifteen years, the formal Village Council has attempted to resurrect and create new rules for utilizing the commons. In its efforts, it has enlisted the help of the existing informal panchayat, entrusting it with responsibility for protecting the oran and collecting fines from those who break rules of access. The partnership between the informal panchayat and the formal Village Council indicates the ways in which the traditional is less a dead and reified past, more a living history. The combined exertions of the panchayat and the council to protect the oran have been crowned with some success but at the cost of disadvantaging the raikas.

The Village Council[17] constitutes one of the most obvious forms of state involvement in local political processes. Mandated and funded by the Indian state since the late 1960s, the Village Council may be seen as one of the formal ways in which the state is present in the village. It is a thirteen-member elected body that carries out developmental tasks locally in four villages, including Patawal. Through more than 500 near unanimous resolutions in the past twelve years, its members have voted to construct local schools, lobbied the government to provide drinking water to the villagers, and undertaken relief work during droughts.

The head of the council is called the *sarpanch*. Its twelve other members, called ward *panches*, are chiefly upper caste individuals (patel, rajput, brahmin, and charan). The ward panches are so called because each of them represents a ward, the electoral units into which the four villages are divided. Patawal has four wards, and the sarpanch is the elected representative from one of them. The remaining three villages have seven wards. The wards in each village, including in Patawal, are divided spatially. The raikas have a clear majority in one of them. Together with other lower caste groups, they form a majority in all the wards.

Apart from the sarpanch, ten members of the formal Village Council are elected, and two are nominated by those who are elected. The nominated members must come from disadvantaged or lower caste groups. All the elected ward panches were from upper castes before the election of a raika in 1982. The raika ward panch was elected from Patawal during the struggle between the landowners and the raikas. The two nominated ward panches are a lower caste woman and a meghwal.

The fact that most of the elected members of the Village Council are from the upper castes, even when the lower castes are a majority in all the wards, speaks to the hegemonic sway of the upper castes in the villages. I use the term *hegemony* in its Gramscian formulation, as a "moving equilibrium" maintained by the provisional alliance of particular social classes to win and shape consent from a dominated majority. It is not universal, nor a given, nor total social control. It has to be won, sustained, and reproduced so that the dominated groups are contained within an ideological space that appears "natural," even permanent (Gramsci 1971; Hall 1977; Hall and Jefferson 1976; Hebdige 1979). Precisely because it has to be won and exercised, there are no determinate outcomes when hegemonic alliances are challenged.

The mutual compromises that the upper castes have crafted to ensure cooperation include an understanding that on relief and construction works financed by the state government the upper caste villagers will be the primary employees. The amounts involved are not trivial—exceeding Rs 15,000 in six of the last ten years.[18] For the eighty or so upper caste families in the village, this represents fifteen to twenty days of employment in the summer— when agricultural work is nonexistent. The idea that the state provides new forms for accumulation is literally true in Patawal.

Only 14 of the 512 resolutions of the panchayat concern the oran. Six aimed at converting part of the common into land for settlement. Two petitioned the government to remove encroachments. Three detailed sanctions for individuals who illegally harvested wood. The remaining 3 aimed at improving grass and tree cover. The final 6 resolutions (3 + 3) occupied center stage in the political struggle that led to changes in the institutional arrangements guiding use of fodder and fuelwood from the oran.

CHANGES IN INSTITUTIONAL ARRANGEMENTS

The vegetation cover on the oran in Patawal is superior to that on the orans in most neighboring villages. There are more trees, and they are less severely lopped. When asked the reason, villagers stated that trees are sacred objects, especially the *khejri* (*Prosopis cineraria*). They should therefore be preserved, not cut. But the villagers also admitted that prior to the action taken by the Village Council and the informal panchayat the vegetation was declining. Clearly, to translate people's feelings of respect toward trees into protective behavior reinforcement is necessary. Reinforcement can occur in several forms: new protective rules, economic incentives, punitive sanctions, or strengthened norms. The Village Council undertook to protect vegetation by creating new, enforceable rules.

Beginning in 1979, the council initiated resolutions that restricted the access of different villagers to the common. Although the new rules restricted the access of different caste groups equally, they most adversely affected the group that depended on the common to a disproportionately greater extent. These were the raikas. They own most of the sheep in the village, and sheep browse chiefly on the oran. Restrictions on access to the oran, therefore, affect the raikas more than they affect other groups. The political process whereby the Village Council accomplished its objective of restricting access to the common is interesting and instructive. Its description resonates with existing writings about how hegemony is exercised and the relationship between local and macrolevel politics.

The higher, landowning castes combined with the meghwals and encouraged them to vote against the raikas in the local council elections. They then used their dominance in the elected council to reduce the grazing area of the oran and effectively reduce the benefits to the raikas. Reduction of the size of the oran forced some of the raikas, especially those who have large numbers of sheep, to migrate for longer periods of time and become even more marginal to village politics.

In 1979, the council passed a resolution that banned villagers from cutting green wood from tree species such as *ber* (*Zizyphus nummularia* and *Zizyphus mauritania*) and khejri. This incident was not unique. Several similar resolutions had been debated earlier. There was, however, one difference this time. Coupled with the passage of the resolution to prevent villagers from cutting wood, council members debated whether part of the oran should be fenced to prevent animals from entering it. The debates in the panchayat assumed new meaning in 1979 because of developments that took place in the civil and revenue courts of the state and because around this time the state government began to consider a new forest bill.[19]

The Rajasthan Tenancy Act (1955) and the Allotment of Land for Agricultural Purposes Rules (1970) specify that certain village lands cannot be converted into agricultural land. Pasture lands (orans), lands covered by water (nadis), lands reserved for village forests, and lands earmarked for purposes of public utility fall under the provisions of these two statutes. These statutes safeguarded the interests of animal owners in Rajasthan by ensuring that grazing lands for their sheep would not be privatized as agricultural land.

A series of court decisions between 1961 and 1977 further strengthened the principle that certain categories of land in the western dry districts of Rajasthan could not be used for agricultural purposes. In the case of *Nanu Ram v. State of Rajasthan* (1961), the Board of Revenue decided that "grazing lands which were recorded as such . . . were to be frozen as *charagah*[20] lands. In *Ram Singh v. Parmoli* (1971), the courts reversed the decision that grazing lands could not be converted into agricultural lands. But this reversal of the earlier decision did not apply to grazing lands in the western semi-arid districts of Rajasthan. Shepherds in districts such as Jodhpur, Barmer, Bikaner, Jaisalmer, and other western districts, therefore, were still safe. In *Durga Prasad v. Pannalal* (1977), it was reiterated yet again that all lands in the villages that were unassessable for revenue were exempt from conversion to agricultural land. The oran in Patawal, recorded as community grazing land in land settlements prior to Indian independence, was exempt from conversion to private cultivated land. The interests of the raikas were protected.

In the late 1970s, however, villagers heard rumors about a new forestry bill that the government was considering. This bill contained a provision through which common lands in a village could be enclosed to improve vegetation cover. Once a formal Village Council passed a resolution to enclose a part or the whole of its oran, government Forest Departments or other agencies could fence the oran and help the Village Council plant trees and/or grasses. In addition to fencing and planting the oran, the Forest Department could provide the council with funds to hire a guard.

The raikas in Patawal were (and are) vehemently against enclosure of the oran. In the elections for ward panches for the formal council in 1982, they put up two candidates. They believed that once their candidates were elected they could attempt to persuade the rest of the members of the council to desist from enclosing the oran. They could also meet with higher district authorities, and as members of the Village Council their word would carry greater weight.

Although the rumors about the possible enclosure of the oran served to precipitate the decision by raika elders to put up two candidates in the panchayat elections, a second factor was possibly involved. The Village Council was and remains the conduit for much government largesse in the form of funds that the state disburses as development expenditures. The council uses these funds primarily for construction purposes undertaken in the summer months — the building of roads, schools, and embankments and the digging of nadis. It secures the labor for these projects by hiring individuals from the upper castes. The raikas hoped that by winning two seats on the council they might get a share in the employment opportunities created each year. As conversations with various lower caste group members, but especially with the raikas, indicated, they had long resented the near monopoly exercised by the upper caste members on state-funded temporary work during the summer. Yet there was little they could do about it except complain, usually among themselves.

The raikas had reason to entertain some hopes of success in the elections.

Numerically they are by far the largest caste group in Patawal. Elections are conducted on a "first past the post" basis, so in each ward the candidate who secures the highest number of votes is declared the victor. The raikas and lower castes have a clear majority in all the wards of the council. With a clear majority in one ward, the raikas also hoped to get the support of other lower caste groups in the other ward. If the interest of the raikas in preventing the enclosure of the oran would be served directly were their candidates to be elected, there would also be a chance that members of other lower castes could gain a share in summer construction jobs.

The hopes of the raikas proved illusory. These elections were the first in the village in which a lower caste group had threatened the unchallenged domination of the council by the upper castes. The candidacy of the raikas immediately united the patels, charans, and rajputs against the raikas. The threat to their monopoly on government-funded jobs was sufficient to forge a front that ultimately succeeded in avoiding the danger. The upper caste, landowning faction in the village, once united, acted predictably. It tried each of the four strategies prescribed by Chanakya[21] — *saama* (cajoling or persuasion), *daama* (bribes), *danda* (threats), and *bheda* (dividing the enemy) — to negotiate with the raikas to prevent them from putting up a candidate. None worked.

Failing to move the raikas, the upper caste faction used a carrot and stick policy with the other major lower caste group — the meghwals. If the meghwals voted for the raika candidates, the upper caste group made it clear that they would never again receive employment on the farms of the patels and brahmins. When the election returns came in, only one of the two raika candidates had been elected. While the exact voting pattern remains unknown, it was obvious that many of the meghwals had voted against the raikas, knowing that if the upper caste candidates lost they would know the meghwals had voted against them. Even in the ward where the raika households had a clear majority, the margin of victory was not overwhelming. The small margin reflected dissension among the raikas. Many felt sufficiently threatened by the dominant position of the upper castes to vote against their own candidate. The poorer raikas, who owned few sheep and could find browse around the village even if the oran were enclosed, were especially reluctant to confront the upper caste groups.

Although the senior and more established raikas partially got their way, their unprecedented attempt to join the Village Council polarized the landowning castes against them. Over the course of the next five years, the council passed five resolutions that effectively restricted the access of villagers to the oran and enclosed 30 percent of the area. The raika representative in the council predictably voted against all five resolutions. Apart from providing a voice of dissent, his vote had little effect.

The newly elected set of council members passed a resolution in 1982 that formally prohibited villagers from cutting trees on the oran without first obtaining the council's permission. Between 1982 and 1987, the council passed three resolutions that enclosed seventy hectares of the oran. Trees have been planted on the enclosed land with the help of the Forest Department and the Center for Arid Zone Research Institute (CAZRI) in Jodhpur. The area is enclosed by barbed wire, and none of the village residents is allowed to graze sheep or cattle on this part of the oran. A villager from the upper caste groups has been hired to sleep in the enclosed portion and guard it against grazing. He did not, however, seem to think that his presence effectively prevented illegal fuelwood collection. "I can't be here all the time. And even when I am here, I can't prevent villagers from taking away fuelwood in the night," he said. He did manage to control most illegal grazing.

Early in 1987 the Village Council passed a comprehensive resolution that fixed precise and graduated fines for illegal grazing and cutting wood on the oran. Where wood could be recovered from the offenders, the council handled the matter directly. If the wood could not be recovered, the council could call in the police. In the same meeting, the council specified that money collected as fines would be used for collective welfare within the village. Further, the amount of the fines in specific cases could be reduced at the discretion of the council. To enforce the rules, it appointed a five-member committee consisting of one ward panch and four prominent villagers. Members of this committee were not paid, nor were they supposed to act as guards. But they could seek the assistance of the informal panchayat members in protecting the oran.

The relationship between the multivillage formal council and the informal panchayat is difficult to pinpoint. There are no legally defined areas of authority and influence for the informal panchayat in Patawal. Nor does it have a legal standing or formal powers of enforcement. Within the village, however, its word carries considerable weight. It plays an important role in enforcing rules and protecting the oran. Since it comprises the elder and respected village residents, it is difficult to defy their decisions unless villagers want to cut themselves off from village community life.

The informal panchayat meets regularly. Meetings can be called for several reasons. The panchayat reaffirms rules about grazing and about the cutting of trees in the oran and on private fields. It arbitrates disputes related to the interpretation and application of rules. It also selects one or two guards to protect trees (or confirms the existing guards in their positions). The guard is

Table 2.4   Grazing Days Lost as a Result of Fencing the Common

| Caste Group | Grazing days available on the common[a] | | |
	Before Fencing	After Fencing	Days Lost
Higher castes (patel, charan brahmin, rajput)	8,238 (171)[b]	4,675 (118)	2,562 (53)
Raikas	70,897 (1,243)	48,840 (856)	22,056 (387)
Lower castes (bhil, sargara, meghwal)	7,770 (105)	5,342 (72)	2,417 (32)

Note: It is assumed that: (1) during the monsoon months, the sheep graze on the oran; (2) during the monsoons, 70 percent of the fodder requirements for the cattle are met out of private stocks for all villagers; (3) after the monsoons and harvest, sheep graze on the oran 25 percent of the time; and (4) the fenced area of the common possesses, on the average, the same level of productivity as the unfenced area.

[a] One grazing day equals one livestock unit grazing for one day (five sheep/goats = one livestock unit).

[b] Figures in parentheses are grazing days for each household.

paid a salary by the village families collectively. While the formal multivillage council is officially responsible for auctioning dry trees from the oran, in practice it is the informal panchayat that oversees this task. It retains the revenue from the sale of dry trees and uses the money for public purposes.

Because the raikas and the landowning castes in the village differ substantially in the animals they possess, the rules restricting fodder use from the oran have adversely affected the raikas. Indeed, 30 percent of the oran was fenced precisely because the landowning groups dominating the formal Village Council knew that the new rules would affect the raikas unfavorably. The new institutional arrangement was created to show the raikas who was the boss in the village. The arrangement, as one raika put it, also kicked the shepherds where it hurt the most — in their stomachs.

When seventy hectares of the oran were fenced, the benefits to the landowning castes declined a little because during the monsoons some of their cattle graze on the oran (see table 2.4). The reduction of benefits to the raikas, however, is much greater. The loss of forage during the monsoon months has hit them especially hard. Today, six more raika families have been forced into migration as a result of the fenced oran. The landowners in

Patawal not only reduced the economic benefits to the shepherds, but they reduced the threat of future political challenges in the panchayat by forcing many of the raikas to stay out of the village for longer periods. The enclosure of the oran has made the raikas an even lesser threat in the electoral politics in the village.

The Village Council passed resolutions to enclose part of the oran in the name of environmental protection. By preventing animals from grazing in this part of the oran, planting new trees, and guarding the enclosed oran, the Village Council declared that the future availability of biomass and fodder will increase. As the sarpanch of the council put it: "Without action by the panchayat, villagers would have consumed the entire oran. Their own poverty would force them to do so." Such assertions mesh well with global environmental discourses and the popular national environmental discourse according to which the poor are compelled to destroy their own environment because they have no choice. To save their long-term future from the harmful consequences of their short-term actions, those with authority must constrain them.

Whether the future will match the expressed hopes of the council remains unclear, however. Fencing the common has obviously reduced present benefits to all groups in the village. The villagers, thus, are making the "sacrifices" for the environment to which the sarpanch of the council referred approvingly. But the upper castes are making far more limited sacrifices (see table 2.4), and estimates about increases in the future productivity of the enclosed oran can be only gloomy at best. The Forest Department planted most of the trees on the oran about three years before I began my fieldwork. Survival rates for the trees are as low as 10 percent. Survival rates of less than 5 percent after five years are common[22] in other plantation programs of the Forest Department. The enclosed portion is distinguishable from the rest of the oran only by the rusty fencing that surrounds it, not because it has more vegetation. It seems clear, then, that not only have present benefits to all groups declined in the village, proportionately more precipitously for the raikas, but none of the village factions can hope to reap greater benefits from the oran in the future. The assertion of the village sarpanch that current sacrifices are needed to improve the future vegetation cover of the oran rings hollow!

The enclosure of the oran, by depriving the shepherds of grazing resources during the bottleneck monsoon months, has forced them into longer and more frequent migrations. The institutional effects accompanying this trend — exclusion of common lands from pastoralism — matches, paradoxically, the effects of agricultural intensification in western Rajasthan. Agricultural intensification has the similar result of reducing the forage available to pastoralists and requires changes in institutional arrangements that define who will have access to common lands (see Robbins 1998).

The unfolding of the events in Patawal continues to be a puzzle, however. Why should the landowning castes have reacted to the raikas by forcing them to migrate out of the village more often, seeking to marginalize them from village politics altogether? Even if two shepherds had been elected to the council, the landlords would still have enjoyed a wide enough majority on the council to defeat any proposals that were against their interests.

Before the raikas mounted a challenge to the domination of the council by upper caste households, the social understandings in the village meant that the benefits from grazing the common went mostly to the raikas and the benefits from government-sponsored, small, rural infrastructure projects were cornered chiefly by the upper caste landowners. In this situation, the landowners were dominant in village politics and the shepherds, as a migrant group, were subordinate despite their numerical superiority. This social understanding was underpinned by a specific structure of expectations and beliefs on the part of both the landlords and shepherds. Although there was always a possibility that the domination of the landlords might be challenged, the shepherds saw no pressing reason to challenge it. Although the landlords could attempt to marginalize the shepherds even further, they did not see why they should take such an action.

The rumors about the new forestry bill and worries that the village common might be enclosed, coupled with the temptation of a share in the development expenditures of the Village Council, altered the existing structure of beliefs on the part of the raikas. Their resulting actions forced the landowners to reevaluate the nature of the threat the raikas posed. The raikas put up candidates for the council seats; the landlords, seeing this action as a direct attempt to undermine their monopoly over government-financed labor on development infrastructure, revised their beliefs about the probability that the raikas would undermine their control. In response, they created new institutional rules to ensure that the raikas would be rendered marginal to village politics. The problem was not that in this particular election the raikas had won a seat. Rather, their winning a seat in this election signified the very realizable possibility that with their superior numbers the lower castes could become a majority in future elections. The upper castes, including the patels, comprise only about 25 percent of the village population. Faced with two bad future outcomes, they chose the option that seemed marginally better. Concerns about future stakes in village politics, thus, prove critical in explaining the sequence of events in Patawal. They are also critical in explaining why the dominant faction in the village was willing to reduce its absolute economic benefits in the short and the long run.

CONCLUSION

Political processes in Patawal possess substantial historical depth. They have helped shape, together with political developments outside the village, the emergence of new rules for using the village common. The actions of different village factions have led to outcomes that have further marginalized the shepherds from village politics. Their attempt to gain representation in the elected Village Council united the landowning castes in the village against them. The upper caste, landowning groups used their control over the Village Council to enclose the village common and force some shepherds to migrate longer and more frequently.

This description of the emergence of new institutions to manage grazing in the village thus challenges accounts that view institutions simply as mechanisms for efficiently allocating resources (Barzel 1989; North 1981; North and Thomas 1973). Most such accounts of institution formation rely on evolutionary mechanisms,[23] among them "marketlike forces" (Calvert 1995: 220), to drive institutional change toward efficient outcomes in the presence of transaction costs. These accounts are unsatisfactory, however, for at least two reasons. First, they do not connect the emergence of new institutions with choices made by agents. Second, they fail to address the tremendous array of evidence that reveals the importance of politics and shows how new institutions, rather than creating greater efficiency, can lead to Pareto inferior outcomes.[24] The logic of Pareto optimality that informs much institutionalist analysis does not hold very well in Patawal.[25]

To remedy these deficiencies, a growing number of analysts has highlighted the political nature of processes that lead to new institutions (Bates 1981; Knight 1992; Libecap 1989; North 1990). They have attempted especially to show that institutions are the outcomes of individual choices, even when these choices are made under the constraints of existing rules, and that they are attempts by social actors to consolidate asymmetric power relations and increase economic gains. In these accounts, actors choose institutional rules to increase their gains. Scholars such as Knight (1992) have pointed out that outcomes that improve overall benefits to society usually occur when no powerful group is ranged against them.

The discussion presented here not only adds to accounts that politicize institutional change; it also makes an extension. Existing analyses of institutional change seldom investigate situations in which social actors with the power to create new institutions rationally act so as to reduce the absolute amount of their discounted benefits. We see the landowners in Patawal adopting precisely this seemingly counterintuitive strategy. By enclosing the oran, they reduced the grazing benefits. Their other benefits (from the council's development expenditures) remained the same. They were willing to suffer a cut in their absolute benefits to protect their future shares.

Pareto inferior outcomes can fall into two broad classes: (1) where some members of a group subject to the changed institutions are better off as a result of the change, although the total benefits to the group decline; and (2) where no members of the group are better off and the total benefits are smaller. The second class of outcomes are ones few new institutionalist accounts have examined. Patawal is an example of these types of outcomes.

In Patawal, we observe the inescapably political nature of institutions in the crafting of new rules by those with the capacity to impose them on a collective. But we also see a dominant faction accept small economic losses in the short and the longer term to secure long-term control over existing resources. The upper caste villagers accept, indeed drive, politics around common resources to a Pareto inferior outcome. In analyzing the formation of new institutions, we also observe various village-level actors strategically using new political opportunities to renegotiate existing relations of domination and control. These renegotiations, we discover, can involve alliances between unlikely partners — the upper caste groups and the meghwals — that might exist for only as long as the current phase of the conflict lasts. These renegotiated understandings hinge on the desire for protection against the possibility of incurring large future losses.

3 Getting out from under the

Visible Foot: The Shepherds,

Development, and the State

Much of the disillusionment with the results of [development in] the past three decades originates with people who do not understand the importance of social wage, who have no idea what the conditions of the masses were like in 1950, or who have forgotten the extent to which LDC people live in semi-arid lands for which we have yet to make the technological breakthrough. — Arthur Lewis, 1984

The idea of development stands like a ruin in the intellectual landscape. Delusion and disappointment, failures and crimes have been the steady companions of development and they tell a common story: it did not work. — Wolfgang Sachs, 1993

Nearly all political questions and differences of opinion now turn upon the concept of the state. — Vladimir I. Lenin, [1917] 1924

The state is not the reality which stands behind the mask of political practice. It is itself the mask which prevents our seeing political practice as it is. — Philip Abrams, 1988

The legitimacy of the postcolonial state in the immediate aftermath of struggles for decolonization was founded upon the efforts of its leaders to gain independence. With the passage of time, however, leaders have sought and proclaimed a different justification for seeking power and office: rational plans to develop their countries and citizens. The success of the postcolonial state is measured not just by its capacity to maintain a semblance of order but by its willingness to initiate and its ability to accomplish "development." If "rationalization" is the primary characteristic of modernity in our times, the ensemble of practices and personnel that creates the "state" is perhaps the chief carrier of this rationalization.[1] This chapter engages one such attempt to rationalize and develop the shepherds in Jodhpur District: the Pasture and Sheep Development Program.

Specific programs directed at their lives are not the only way shepherds are influenced by state policies. Their livelihoods intersect with many other state undertakings as well. Government policies regarding irrigation, forests, agriculture, fodder, famine relief, and migration contribute to the political-economic context in which the raikas exist and shape the lines along which their lives flow.[2] Some of these policies are aimed specifically at the shepherds. Others affect them unintentionally even if directly. And the influence of still others unfolds almost as an afterthought.[3] The consequences in each case are determined jointly by the nature of the policies and the responses of the shepherds. The flow of influence between the raikas and the actors that comprise the state may be highly asymmetric; it is not entirely one way.

The raikas encounter the state and its attempts to develop in formal and informal, explicit and indirect ways. The shepherds evade, renegotiate, reshape, and are influenced by their encounters. The discussion shows that a consideration of mobility is necessary to productively think about raika-state interactions. Different perspectives on the state would see it as a set of organizational entities, an accretion of discrete institutional practices, or even the effect upon the lived performances[4] of the raikas. These views of the developmental state provide some insights into the articulation of state practices and raika livelihoods. Attending to mobility deepens the understanding of such articulations. I use the concept of territoriality in the latter part of this chapter to highlight how the mobile lives of the shepherds connect with attempts at control and development.

ARTICULATIONS WITH THE STATE IN EVERYDAY LIVELIHOODS

In the course of their everyday struggles for a livelihood, the raikas travel vast distances within the borders of the Indian nation-state. Their annual migration cycles span the better part of the year. Prior to India's independence, their migration routes took them across what is today the border separating India from Pakistan. After the British territorial possessions in the subcontinent were divided in 1947, the avenues for migration became more restricted. Since the raikas could no longer travel westward into present-day Pakistani Sind, Punjab, and Multan, they have been forced to create new routes and further develop existing ones in Haryana, western Uttar Pradesh, and Madhya Pradesh (Kavoori 1990). Today few raikas travel west, except for short journeys into the districts of Jaisalmer and Barmer.

Although the raikas seldom cross international borders, their migrations carry them across provincial boundaries every year. The migrating raika camps receive identification papers from government officials. These papers permit them at specific points to move across provincial borders into Haryana, Uttar Pradesh, Madhya Pradesh, and Gujarat. The papers also form a means whereby government officials can track the movements of the shepherds.

Their movements monitored and controlled at the borders, the raikas depend greatly upon the goodwill of the officials. The number of sheep and other animals that can enter a given district, forest range, or province are often set in advance. But whether the animals in a migrating camp fall within the set limits is less an objective numerical fact than a matter of judgment by a petty official. Such judgments are always susceptible to influence. Government officials let those subject to their decisions know that monetary influence is especially effective. Bribes, in consequence, are not only extracted but the shepherds are expected to pay them as a matter of course.

In recent years, as their access to fodder has diminished, some shepherds have been forced to migrate year-round. Especially during the monsoon months, when virtually the entire northern Indian landscape is under cultivation, these shepherds find fodder primarily in the forests of Rajasthan and Madhya Pradesh. The movement of the raikas into forested areas is directly regulated by state policy in the form of charges for grazing in state-owned forests. Grazing fees, grazing passes for specific locations, and the number of animals state governments allow to enter their forests have been the subject of extensive discussion and dispute. State governments, facing urgent demands from competing constituencies, are often unwilling to address the needs of the shepherds.

Competing demands are also evident in attempts by state governments to raise grazing fees so as to accommodate the concerns of forestry officials and environmentalists who perceive grazing to be disastrous to vegetation growth. In 1990, the Madhya Pradesh state government raised annual fees for animals entering its forests from Re 1.00 to Rs 10.00 per sheep or goat, Rs 10.00 to Rs 50.00 per camel, and Re 0.75 to Rs 2.00 per cow or buffalo. Whether such phenomenal increases in the fee schedule actually could have been enforced is uncertain.[5] But they did succeed in effecting the collection of larger bribes during the time they were in effect.

"Sa', we are tired of traveling, having to deal with government officers. Nowadays, you need papers and stamps for everything. At every checkpoint [when crossing state borders] there is someone asking questions. There are plenty of criminals around. Why not ask questions of them, why trouble us honest people? But the reason is straightforward. Can you tell me? It is because we are easy marks. Money flows more easily from our pockets. And once it is out, we are also out [of the hands of the government officers]." These words of Kheenvji, describing his interactions with government officials, on the one hand demonstrate the routinization of corruption in the daily lives of the poor. On the other hand, they evidence his shrewd understanding of and accommodation to the prevalent political-economic context.[6]

Bribes, whose giving and taking occurs under cover, expose two quite different faces of power. They show the power of state regulations to influence the action of those who are to be governed; they also reveal the stark limits upon state influence. That bribes are necessary to subvert policies set by state actors is an index to the powerful effects state regulations produce. State regulations on migration seek to limit it. They either must be followed or resources must be found to enable a different course of action. The intended effects of regulations can be overcome by recourse to another source of power — money in the form of a bribe. But the giving and taking of bribes is itself a powerful effect of regulation. Conversely, the fact that bribes render possible actions that are illegal and undesired by those state actors who create rules exposes the constraints on what state actors can accomplish by regulating. Bribes simultaneously mark the outer limits of plans and regulations and the nakedness of power.

The shepherds are an obvious and recurrent irritant to forest officials. Consequently, state policies expressly seek to regulate the movement of shepherds across state boundaries and into forested areas. The shepherds are almost invisible to irrigation managers. Irrigation policies influence the movements of the shepherds far more indirectly. Their effects, nonetheless, are highly significant. The increasing intensity of irrigation creates outcomes that are an excellent example of "unintended consequences."

The Indian state has pursued an active policy of extending irrigation in the postindependence years. Its attempts have been especially aggressive in the semiarid northern districts of Rajasthan, to which water is channeled from the Indus River system.[7] On irrigated lands, farmers can raise cropping intensity to 200 percent or more.[8] This is a result entirely in keeping with the intentions behind the extension of irrigation. But the extension of irrigated farmland in semiarid regions has at least three other results. First, it encourages enclosure as crop yields increase. Unirrigated lands all over north India are fallow after the harvest. They are available for grazing to animals from within and outside the village. But owners of irrigated tracts find it to their advantage to fence their fields. Enclosures reduce the grazing land available to raikas and other migrant pastoralists.

A second unanticipated impact is ecological. Because much of the length of new canals is unlined or only imperfectly lined, water seepage is common. Large areas along the canals have become waterlogged. In semiarid areas, even when irrigation facilitates higher crop yields initially, waterlogging or salt pans may follow within a few years because of the unsuitability of the soil for cultivation. In both cases, the areas through and into which the raikas can migrate become more limited.

But at the same time the extension of irrigation in northern Rajasthan, Haryana, and Uttar Pradesh has led to a third unanticipated effect: the formation of a new pastoral niche during the winter months. The story of migrant pastoralism in Rajasthan can be seen as a history of accommodation between agriculturists and pastoralists: movements of animals are highly dependent on the availability of crop residues in the fields of farmers along migration routes. In India, pastoralism has not developed independently of agriculture—either sectorally or spatially. As Kavoori puts it, historically pastoralism has reproduced itself within an overarching agrarian ecological order (1996: 76). The cultivation of a second crop with the help of irrigation has provided pastoralists an alternative grazing niche where earlier none was available. Within this niche, however, the shepherds have less room to negotiate with farmers (see chapters 4 and 5).

The State and the Raikas: A Sedentarization Program

In the sketch above, we see the raikas come face-to-face with state practices and personnel in different contexts, but the interactions can be characterized as unplanned rather than designed. The Pasture and Sheep Development Program, aided by funds from the World Bank and implemented under the Drought Prone Area Program of the Indian government, created a rather different dynamic in the relations between the shepherds and government officials. This encounter stemmed directly from attempts to impose a blueprint of "rational" development and conservation.[9] The story of the project in Jodhpur District illustrates three aspects of planned development: (1) state actors possess a significant capacity to intervene in the lives of the shepherds, (2) state actors seldom consider the range of political, social, economic, ecological, and physical factors at different levels that influence the performance of planned range management projects, and (3) those subjected to the rationalizing processes of planned development often find reasons not to cooperate with their subjection.[10]

The objectives of the program, summarized in its outreach documents, were as follows:

1. To convert land not used for agriculture into pasture plots
2. To maximize the utilization of rainwater for pasture development
3. To check soil erosion by means of tree plantation

4. To maintain soil fertility by rearing a limited number of animals

5. To check the migration of animals in famine years

6. To improve the quality of wool and mutton in the area through cooperation and to improve upon the financial status of the poorer sheep breeders.[11]

The Program Office attempted to meet these objectives by organizing
shepherds into cooperative societies. It also created fenced pasture plots of
one hundred hectares for each society. The members of a society contributed
share capital in the form of adult ewes, which could graze in the fenced plot.
The plots were carved out of existing common lands controlled by Village
Councils and could be used only by the animals of those shepherds who
qualified to become members. Project officials also sought to improve the
quality of fodder on the pasture plots by sowing grass in contoured furrows.
The carrying capacity of each plot was estimated initially at 4 animals per
hectare but was revised downward to 1.6 animals after irregular rains made
it clear that the earlier estimate was too optimistic. The government hoped
that after three to four years of instructing shepherds in how to use the
pastures management of the plots could be handed over to the cooperative
societies.

Project documents index the performance of the forty-nine cooperative
shepherd societies with statistical details on a variety of dimensions. We
learn that the membership of the societies increased from an average of
twenty-one members at the time of their formation to forty-five in 1983–84.
Nearly 75 percent of the societies also partially fulfilled the socially equitable
objective of gaining the membership of some lower caste individuals. The
pasture plots of the societies supported an average of 159 sheep each (7,800
sheep in all). The sheep earned their owners a total revenue of Rs 1.06
million over the life of the project. They cost them only Rs 0.51 million,
yielding a surplus of Rs 0.55 million. The average annual surplus for each
society was Rs 2,368. These are encouraging figures. Combined with the
assertions in the project documents that the vegetation cover improved in the
fenced pasture plots, the project seems to have been a resounding success.[12]

There is another side to the picture, however, which is revealed by considering some other facts officially mentioned in project documents but left out
of the analysis. This aspect of the performance of the program becomes
obvious in conversations with its "beneficiaries" — the shepherds. To incorporate these new facts into the analysis is not to make a claim about presenting a complete picture. Rather it is to focus on the occlusions from which
official development discourses often suffer. It brings to light the strategies
organizational actors use to further their existence and justify their activities.

Project documents state that by 1983–84 the government had spent close to Rs 10.5 million on the program, dwarfing the revenues and expenditures of the societies themselves.[13] Most of this money was spent on salaries of the government officials in charge of the project, vehicles and office space, infrastructure development in the pasture plots, official visits, and documentation. Less than 20 percent was spent on direct services to shepherds in the form of feed and medicines for sheep or attempts to organize the cooperative societies that would eventually manage the pasture plots. Even this fraction of the total government expenditure on the project outstrips the total income of all forty-nine shepherd societies.

None of the cooperative societies of the shepherds, despite the stated intention of the program, ever received any pasture plots to manage. The Program Office advanced the reason that recurring failure of the rains prevented the shepherd societies from getting out of the red without aid from the government. Devji in Jod Village had a different take on the matter. "They talked a lot about forming societies and handing over pasture plots. That is the way government officers always talk. Show pleasant dreams that never work. We knew better. They were *taking* common pastures. Why would they *give* it back? If we wanted the land, we would have to take it back ourselves." The simple logic Devji offered proved to be a far more realistic description of what happened than the convoluted rationality contained in project documents.

In Orwellian fashion, project documents offer apologies and reasons for not reaching anticipated levels of performance even while they brag about their achievements. Villagers, the documents complain, provided the more unproductive common pasture lands for development of the pasture plots. Village animals competed for grazing with sheep owned by the societies. The grasses sown in the pasture plots could not establish themselves owing to high grazing pressure from the sheep and the repeated failure of the rains. Nonmember villagers had broken the fences around the plots and begun to graze their animals inside. Because of funding uncertainties surrounding the continuation of the program, many shepherds were unwilling to join the societies established for their villages. The list goes on.

Some of these reasons appear to contradict each other. If the plots offered for pasture development were of poor quality and grasses had not been established, why did nonmember villagers break the fences and graze their animals there? Other reasons that might have been operative remain unmentioned or unimagined. The program called for contributions of nonagricultural common land from Village Councils that could be converted into pasture plots. But the common land that Village Councils provided to the program was already being used for grazing by many of the villagers. In fencing these lands, the program sought to overturn existing practices in villages and ran squarely into resistance from those livestock owners whose animals grazed the local common and who did not gain membership in the cooperative societies. There was no reason for such shepherds to constrain the grazing habits of their sheep. As Ranaramji, one of the shepherds, put it: "We got neither money nor sheep from the project. It just came, and it just went. We didn't even notice it." Ranaramji may have been exaggerating the extent of his indifference to the project but not the extent to which his life remained uninfluenced by it.

Ranaramji's words also subtly draw attention to the processes whereby membership in the cooperative societies might have been decided and the effects of such processes. The societies formed a fertile source of tension by creating groups of losers and winners, privileging mainly those who were already better off, those who had the resources to gain access to project officials, and those who could put themselves forward as the most suitable participants in the project. The frustration engendered by being made marginal to the distribution of government largesse prompted many nonmember villagers to ignore the demands of the program not to graze their sheep on the fenced pasture plots. Their sheep "encroached" on the forage available in the plots. Other villagers, incensed by the enclosure, stole and sold the barbed wire and fence posts that marked the boundaries of the plots.[14] The project did not just "come and go." The explicit actions of many villagers "made it go."

Foucault speaks of a double repression — exclusionary processes and standardizing impositions — in the context of the communication of knowledge (1977: 219), which can fruitfully be extended to analyses of development programs. The Sheep and Pasture Development Program included some and excluded others; it imposed certain standards of behavior on those it included and promised inclusion to excluded others who were willing to conform to the new standards. But it is important as well to recognize that the repression generated by development programs occurred only in conjunction with the active connivance of at least some of the people who were supposed to implement these programs. The criteria for exclusion such programs authorize are often sidestepped or evaded. The standards of conformity they inscribe can similarly be dodged.

By 1983–84, it was clear that some of the objectives of the program had been foundationally misconceived. Others had not been met. Fodder production on the pastures improved in some cases but only when very few sheep were introduced. Where sheep were forced to graze within the hundred-hectare plots, program managers desired another round of investment in grass sowing after four years. Few pasture plots were planted with trees. The objective of maintaining soil fertility by limiting the number of grazing animals was defeated as villagers broke fences and grazed their animals in the pasture plots. Program documents also concede that wool and mutton production from sheep kept on fenced pasture plots was worse in comparison with local breeds precisely in the periods when rainfall was poor.

The Pasture and Sheep Development Program seems simply wrongheaded in its attempt to sedentarize shepherds. Rainfall and fodder production in parts of semiarid Rajasthan are irregular and unpredictable. Local social tensions and ongoing privatization of the commons often lead to the exclusion of the shepherds from even available common grazing lands (see chapter 2). In the absence of changes in existing patterns of access and ownership of grazing commons, changes that would alter the highly asymmetrical existing relations of power in villages, migration is not just significant for the livelihood of shepherds, but it may be the best strategy to counter the fodder deficits and unpredictable variabilities they experience. The kind of development Pasture and Sheep Development Programs of the state embody — intentionally apolitical, simpleminded, accommodationist — is unlikely to change anything in the lives of pastoralists.

An impressive body of research now shows why migrations may be the most appropriate strategy for shepherds in the face of infrequent and irregular rainfall, prolonged and variable site-specific fodder deficits, and inequitable and shifting access to forage. The attempt to sedentarize migrant populations can scarcely be explained by the inherent merits or performance of sedentarization projects, especially because sedentarization or resettlement programs are deaf and blind to the social and political context in which migrations and grazing take place. Sedentarization programs must be located in the desires of state officials to control the movements and migrations of citizens. In this light, the recommendation of program officials in 1983–84, despite ten years of evidence that the program seemed not to be working, is at best tragically innocent: "[T]he main consideration right now should be to go ahead with the programme and to clarify where adjustments are needed" (Jodhpur Spearhead Team 1985: 11).

RAIKA ORGANIZATIONAL RESPONSES

In contributing to the formation of shepherd cooperative societies in some of the villages in Jodhpur District, although these societies do not manage pasture plots as they were supposed to, the Pasture and Sheep Development Program produced an "unintended consequence" that might have long-term

Table 3.1   Distribution of Sheep and Sheepherders' Societies
in Semiarid Districts of Rajasthan

District	Rainfall (mm)	Number of Sheep (000's)	Migrating Sheep (000's)	Number of Societies
Jaisalmer	160	484	275	16
Ganganagar	253	537	86	7
Bikaner	263	823	493	29
Barmer	277	482	267	20
Jodhpur	319	769	371	48
Churu	323	505	178	32
Nagaur	389	927	333	38
Jhunjhunu	404	212	68	7
Jalore	404	420	159	38
Pali	415	1,031	329	9
Ajmer	440	567	110	31
Sikar	455	293	38	13

Source: Pasture and Sheep Development Program, Jodhpur District.

repercussions *favoring* the interests of the shepherd. These societies have aided the efforts of the shepherds to effect a collective organization to lobby the Rajasthan state government. The most visible attempt of the shepherds to lobby the government about its policies exists in the form of a federation of shepherd societies. Drawing the bulk of its membership of 353 sheepherders' societies and nearly ten thousand households from the semiarid western districts of Rajasthan, the federation gives a useful weight to the conversations of the shepherds with state-level politicians and ministers (see table 3.1). One of the raikas told me, "Our government is democratic (*prajatantra*). But it still listens best to money and guns. If you don't have money and can't use guns, you must, at least, have numbers and make a lot of noise."

More than 80 percent of the member societies come from the twelve drier districts of Rajasthan. The chairman of the federation of the sheepherders' societies is Bhopalaramji, a raika shepherd who was earlier a full-time migrant. He communicates regularly and frequently with members of the state legislature and midlevel officials of the state bureaucracy to represent to them the concerns and complaints of the shepherds. During my fieldwork, I discovered that he was able to persuade members of the legislature to ask questions in the Legislative Assembly on behalf of the shepherds, meet with them to deliver grievances, and provide them with information about specific incidents in which shepherds had suffered in their interactions with state officials. The sympathies of Bhopalaramji, and of a large number of sheperds who are members of the federation, were clearly on the side of the Bharatiya Janata Party, which had won the elections and formed the government in Rajasthan shortly before I began my fieldwork. Earlier Congress Party governments had been less sympathetic to the needs of the shepherds. Since their federation represents the interests of a significant number of shepherds, and it supported the Bharatiya Janata Party even when the party was out of power, it is not surprising that its president is able to gain access to those in power, limited and fragmented as that access may be.

Overall, only a small proportion of the shepherds have been attracted to the societies. It is also unclear whether the federation constitutes the nucleus out of which a more permanent and vocal organization of shepherds might ultimately emerge. Further, the federation has had few concrete successes, measurable mostly in terms of successful lobbying to raise the number of sheep permitted to graze in a forest area or reduce grazing charges. But the existence of the federation and its lobbying efforts are remarkable in light of the dispersed and marginal nature of migrant life.

The presence of the federation attests to the recognition by the shepherds that in a democratic polity they must voice their demands as a collective that is seen to control a small but sometimes critical bloc of votes. In the western districts of Rajasthan, the shepherds form only a small minority of the population, but as a bloc they can swing election results in a close contest. They recognize the significance of this fact. According to Akharam, one of the shepherds with whom I talked at length: "Politicians in our democracy are no different from a king. They will do something only if they find it in their interests. And most of the time what they do will only be in *their* interests." The actions undertaken by the shepherds through the Federation of Sheepherders' Societies are a concrete result of their awareness of how a democracy works.[15]

The shepherds' attempts to lobby state officials represent the incipient beginnings of collective action on the part of a highly marginal group. Even if the group has not achieved significant successes, the more critical fact to be explained is its very existence. How can we account for the emergence of this organization among the shepherds? In light of the well-known problems in organizing rural populations, especially peasants,[16] the ability of the shepherds to act as a collective is quite surprising. After all, the shepherds are even more dispersed than most peasants in addition to being mobile.

Paradoxically, the most important fact accounting for collective organization among the shepherds may be their mobility. Shepherds migrate as collectives, and collective mobility is more profitable for them than individual-oriented movement (see part II). They use institutional mechanisms to reduce the costs of collective organization during their migrations (see part III). These institutional innovations, emerging in response to the mobile economy and social organization of the shepherds, also confer on them a unique potential to organize for political gains in a democratic context.

A typical migrant camp comprises between fifteen and twenty flocks and forty to sixty shepherds. Most of these shepherds own a higher than average sized flock.[17] Each camp is led by a nambardar. Members of the camp live together for the greater part of the year and have developed institutional arrangements that allow them to overcome collective action problems related to free riding, moral hazard, and adverse selection (see chapter 7). These institutional innovations also facilitate everyday cooperative interactions among camp members. Without interactions that possess this reliable character, the camp is unlikely to survive beyond one or two cycles of migration. The basic problem of organization at the microlevel is thus overcome for the shepherds by the everyday practices of their migratory lifestyle. The formation of shepherd societies through the Pasture and Sheep Development Program also sought to take advantage of this collective organization.

Given the existing organizational resources present among the shepherds, a political entrepreneur can profitably economize on the costs of creating a larger structure. Contacting the camp leaders, many of whom are politically savvy as a result of their experiences with minor state functionaries, and impressing upon them the benefits of a federated organization is a far simpler matter than trying to organize each shepherd household into a large enough collective. Bhopalaramji is well aware of this fact. He travels constantly among shepherd camps to renew his acquaintances with the camp leaders. He provides medicines for the sheep at cost, playing a role in safeguarding the health of the most cherished possessions of the shepherds. Most shepherds in the camps I visited knew him personally and respected his actions on their behalf. He appears as one of those paradoxical rarities: a trustworthy and trusted politician.[18] His efforts have helped form the shepherds into a significant-sized federation of cooperative societies.

STATE ACTORS AND THE ''DEVELOPMENT'' OF SHEPHERDS

In seeking a more nuanced understanding of state-raika interactions, we find two central facts the most relevant: the mobility of the shepherds and the formal democratic character of Indian politics. They are the structural backdrop against which the raikas interact with state officials. They simultaneously possess the potential to advantage and disadvantage the raikas. Mobility prevents the raikas from creating the glue of social relations with those in power in a given place, and it constitutes them persistently as a threat to the settled mode of livelihood. But it also places other kinds of resources at their disposal — most prominently the internal cohesion of their migratory camps and the possibility of escaping exploitation through movement (chapter 2). The democratic character of the Indian state implies that the shepherds can use their numerical strength to influence politicians even if their strength is limited by their small numbers overall.

To carry out its claims to improve the lives of the poorer and less developed groups in society, the Indian state has undertaken multiple programs of economic development and social change. These can be classified into three broad categories.[19] Household-oriented programs are aimed to improve incomes through asset and skill endowment and wage employment. The Integrated Rural Development Program (IRDP), Training of Rural Youth for Self-Employment (TRYSEM), Development of Women and Children in Rural Areas (DWCRA), National Rural Employment Program (NREP), and Rural Landless Employment Guarantee Program (RLEGP) fall in this category. A second group of programs attempts to ensure basic amenities such as drinking water or school lunches. An example is the Minimum Needs Program (MNP). Finally, a third category of development programs attempts to benefit specific areas, especially regions that are ecologically fragile and have hostile agro-climatic conditions. The Drought Prone Area Program (DPAP) and the Desert Development Program (DDP) are examples. The Pasture and Sheep Development Program falls into this category as well.

State actors create these programs with a certain vision of what development entails and the direction in which society should move. Existing critiques often focus on the design and implementation of these programs and more recently on the very notion of development.[20] This study adds its voice to existing critiques by focusing on a central assumption of most development programs — development is most effective within a settled mode of life. The underlying vision of social change in development programs has little place for a group of people who constantly and regularly move across boundaries, interacting with a range of social actors during their movements. The raikas may fit the image of a poor people for whom the developmental state caters along many dimensions, but their mobility simultaneously constitutes them as outsiders. Since they do not conform to the idealized mold of the "poor," they must be sedentarized so that they can be recast in the image of those who need development. Only then can the state implement rational programs to "improve" their condition. It is in this light that we must view the attempt by the World Bank and the Rajasthan state government to sedentarize pastoralists on hundred-hectare pasture plots.[21]

Clues to how mobility threatens the authority of the state can be gleaned from an examination of the notion of territoriality.[22] While earlier writings on the state took the territorial nature of the exercise of state power for granted,[23] recent formulations have focused more pointedly on territoriality as integral to the exercise of power by the state (Vandergeest and Peluso 1995). *Territoriality*, defined as the "attempt by an individual or group to affect, influence, or control people, phenomena, and relationships by delimiting and asserting control over a geographic area,"[24] emerges as an orientation meant to define physical space through a homogenizing metric and secure control over resources within it — even if the construction of this space takes place only in a social context.[25] Territoriality thus contrasts with tenure, or property, which refers to relationships among individuals or groups over resources contained within a given spatial grid.[26] Of course, territoriality may be seen as a characteristic of the way all power is exercised rather than being a characteristic only of the exercise of power by state actors.[27]

Territorial regulation by the state, according to Vandergeest and Peluso (1995: 388),[28] depends on the creation of abstract space that is linear, can be divided into discrete and comparable units, and can be located and fixed on a grid. Abstraction, and simultaneously the objective definition of space, depend on a combination of overwhelming force and the emergence of cartographic technologies. Those who are mapped, however rational the technologies of mapping, have little say about being mapped. Command over space is such a fundamental source of power over everyday life, as Lefebvre reminds us,[29] that mapping techniques and their representational products are themselves seen by some to be producers of power.[30] But it is not abstract space, ultimately, that states attempt to control. Control over maps and representations of space is aimed at facilitating the surveillance, recording, and control of what is contained within this abstract space. Although state power in the modern era may pretend to be faceless, rational, and technocratic, one can only regard as fictional the idea that territorial regulation can be dispassionately exercised over abstract spaces. The abstract representational space is filled with particular objects. Control of these varied objects requires equally varied and nuanced strategies.

The strategy of situating and fixing individuals, households, or communities within specific locations is extremely useful in the exercise of control. But the raikas, by the very mobility of their existence, stand against this strategy. Their mobility, while it is an uncertain refuge from the exploitative context of their social lives, also constitutes a "site" from which to resist blueprints of development that spatially fix them. Against the territorial imperative of state construction stands their migratory form of earning a livelihood. Whereas state actors attempt to create particular localities and spaces as contiguous but separated units, the raikas knit the same spaces together by the simple expedient of living their lives across multiple sites.

Mobile objects and populations necessitate, therefore, subtle variations and nuances in strategies of control. According to Thongchai, territorial strategies involve "a form of classification by area, a form of communication by boundary, and an attempt at enforcing" (1994: 16). The everyday lives of the shepherds as they migrate challenges each of the strategies of classification, communication, and enforcement of rules through spatial practice. The unpredictable movements of the shepherds make it impossible to classify and record objects according to their location or to enforce a fixed location for animals and dwellings. The attempts by the state to sedentarize the shepherds begin to make better sense in light of the territorial nature of the exercise of power. Sedentarization of mobile groups allows state officials to exercise power over them without the need to discriminate on the basis of the complexities introduced by mobility.

But sedentarization can be accomplished only at tremendous costs. When livehood depends upon mobility in bad times, only brute force can lash a fixed location to migrant groups. This is precisely what we see being attempted in the Pasture and Sheep Development Program. The project sought to create parcels of grazing lands for shepherds, but it did so by ignoring the tremendous variations in precipitation that could eliminate all fodder on the fenced plots. It also ignored established social practices around grazing. Shepherds who were members of the cooperative society were forced to move their animals during periods of uncertain fodder production. Other shepherds refused to accept the boundaries that the fences of the pasture plots marked. The state found it impossible to defend these boundaries against the attempts of the shepherds simply to survive. Nor could it deploy the necessary brute force needed to overcome the shepherds' requirements for a livelihood.

But sedentarization is not the only alternative available in the exercise of control over spaces filled with particular objects. If control by imposing a fixed spatial location is not a convenient option for the state, it can and does use other, more subtle and pervasive means to monitor and control the uncertainties introduced by mobility. Chief among these are the attempts to monitor movement by means of a system of passes issued to the leaders of each mobile camp, the presence of border guards at the boundaries of different provinces, and the quotas fixed to regulate the entry of a fixed number of animals into particular forest areas. Each of these strategies is founded on territorial control but at the same time each moves beyond the attempt to fix objects in an abstract space. These strategies constitute instead an adaptation to the necessity of movement on the part of the shepherds. Exercise of power by the state is thus less dependent than one might imagine on attempts to territorially fix its citizens, resources, or objects. It relies, rather, on control over information that is systematically and retrievably collected, analyzed, and stored.

Attempts by state actors to control mobility provide further clues about the nature of power and its relation to mobility. Mobility on its own does not pose a threat to the exercise of power. It is mobility that is unregulated, movement that takes place outside the strategies of control exercised by state actors, that threatens power. After all, most modern states have adapted to the movement of citizens within their borders. In many instances, periodic migrations are encouraged by state actors to meet the interests of agricultural production (as from northern Bihar and eastern Uttar Pradesh in eastern India to Punjab and Haryana in the west) or the need for industrial labor. The invention of travel documents also permits movement across state borders.

The ability of state actors to invent strategies that can address the shifting locus of the challenges to power that mobility poses demonstrates how power can be used to tame. It is not just resistance that is flexible, adaptable, or variable; so is the exercise of power in the defense of existing states of affairs. It is to this aspect of power that Foucault points in his illuminating exposition of biopower in *The History of Sexuality* (1978). Sovereignty resides in the capacity to regulate social processes. The regulation of these processes, especially when they are highly complex and unpredictable, as they are in the case of the raikas, depends upon two possibilities: (1) access to brute force to simplify complexity or (2) access to and control over relevant information about complexity so that it becomes explicable and therefore nonthreatening.

The mobile existence of the raikas is an inconvenient fact for unilinear visions of historically progressive change. It disrupts attempts by state actors to police and control territorial boundaries. Sedentarization and monitoring of mobility represent the two possible strategies that the state can employ to limit the unpredictability engendered by a mobile lifestyle. If the attempt to sedentarize failed because the shepherds simply rejected it, the more subtle strategies of control — information collection, regulation of movements, quotas for entry into foraging areas — are far more successful. They are successful because the pastoralists are willing to treat them as legitimate attempts at constraint and to engage them by seeking higher quotas for grazing or more freedom of movement. They are also successful because they do not depend for success on an excessive resort to force, as do attempts at sedentarization. It is not that such force would be beyond the capacity of the Indian state. Rather, given the character of the Indian polity and its formal democratic character, unreasonable force is an unviable political option.

The democratic institutional arrangement, which political power seekers must engage, is thus a signal factor in the shepherds' search for better political outcomes. Their small numbers overall constitute them as relatively minor actors in the political horse trading that takes place in Jaipur, the capital of Rajasthan. But their better social organization, their ability to travel long distances, and the internal leadership that they have created in the process of migrating permits them to overcome the disadvantages of being dispersed. It is to their ability to overcome the problem of distance and dispersion that one must trace their mobilization in a federated organizational structure and their lobbying of political and bureaucratic actors within the state.

In addition, the very strategies that state actors initiate to sedentarize shepherds contribute to the effectiveness of attempts by shepherds to organize and gain a share in power. The Rajasthan government, in issuing identity cards to the migratory shepherd camps, connects them to particular villages as it constitutes them as citizens of the Indian state. Fixed residence is, after all, an important part of the being a citizen. It is precisely because the Indian state is willing to recognize the raikas as citizens that they can leverage their membership in the Indian polity to gain political advantage in the electoral arena. Consider, in contrast, the more marginal status of the gypsies in European countries, where they are at best second-class citizens, unable to parlay their mobility into political capital.

CONCLUSION

The state exercises a significant impact on the lives of the shepherds through policies that treat them as nonexistent (as, for example, in the case of irrigation policies) or are carefully and intrusively designed to develop them (as in the case of attempts to improve sheep and pastures). But much of the existing literature on state-society interactions sheds only limited light on the ways in which the raikas interact with state actors. The questions with which this literature remains preoccupied — what is the state, is the state autonomous and to what extent? — prevent a consideration of issues that are more pressing, certainly for the raikas and possibly for most subordinate and marginal groups. These issues relate to the concrete forms and strategies through which power is exercised in the interactions between state actors and members of marginal groups.

The mobility of the shepherds throws into disarray traditional forms of territorial power states use to control their populations. Attempts to impose such control, for example, through policies of sedentarization, fail to consider the reasons why particular populations are mobile. Without the possibility of recourse to massive levels of coercive force, attempts to impose territorial control fail. But state actors can always use more subtle means of exercising power territorially. For these strategies, greater levels of information and monitoring over movement are critical. By collecting and using such information, state actors obviate the need to convert mobile lives into sedentarized ones. To contest these strategies of the normal forms of domination, the raikas have attempted to engage state actors in the arena of democratic electoral politics.

Attempts by the shepherds to engage power is never exercised unidirectionally, just as it is always exercised asymmetrically. The mobility of the shepherds proves to be a productive site of resistance — not simply because they move, but also, and perhaps more importantly, because of the organizational resources it generates for them. The internal cohesion of shepherd groups, forged in response to the exigencies of a mobile lifestyle, permits them to engage state actors energetically and recalcitrantly. If mobility undermines the more familiar strategies of territorial control, it also creates the possibility of subverting those that are more nuanced or subtle.

To understand the lives of the raika shepherds, one must understand mobility. After a few months in Patawal village, trying to get a better sense of the relations between the shepherds, landowners, and lower caste village residents, I came to realize that the shepherds' mobility was Janus-faced. It was the condition into which they had been forced because of limited access to fodder and because they were unequally situated in their interactions with the landowners in the village — in a sense, it was the last refuge of the weak. It was also, simultaneously, the alternative that offered the shepherds greater incomes and the option to build communities based on a foundation of sociality rather than spatial propinquity. Once shepherds opted to migrate, they could rear larger flocks of sheep and earn higher incomes. Because they migrated collectively, mobility is also implicated in the creation of new communities. It is essential, therefore, to understand the migratory experience of the shepherds both as a business enterprise and an attempt to construct community.

I had taken the decision to walk with the shepherds with only a hazy idea about how they used movement to earn a livelihood. Among my background assumptions was a misperception that shepherds were not particularly closely connected with markets. I was soon to realize that I must revise my initial assessment about the role of markets. As I traveled with the flocks, I became convinced that migration critically depends on market exchanges.

Shepherds migrate jointly. Migration becomes necessary because of all the social and physical constraints that the environment imposes on them — limiting the availability of forage and their access to it. But migration is also a risky enterprise. It brings the migrant into a host of potentially threatening situations, creates very real possibilities of loss of life and property, and requires active negotiations with outsiders. Individually oriented migration would be a disaster. Chapter 4 shows that, despite the problems of coordination, monitoring, and control that plague all joint efforts, the shepherds prefer to migrate in groups. Economies of scale and security benefits from being in a collective during hostile encounters make joint migration perhaps the only feasible option.

The shepherds do not just travel collectively; they also enter exchange processes collectively. Sale of wool, whatever the variations in quality, takes place at a uniform price for the entire shepherd camp. The shearing of sheep, sale of manure, purchase of grains, negotiation of bribes, and a host of other market-related activities affect the shepherds as a camp of flock owners. The economic fortunes of individual shepherds are substantially and unambiguously tied to the fate of the group of which they are a part.

Market exchanges, however, are fraught with the possibility of losses. Shepherds graphically portrayed how middlemen and the vagaries of price movements threaten their survival.

"First of all, there are the middlemen," Ranaramji began.

> Everything we buy or sell — medicines, feed, sheep, wool — goes through them. It is hard to get to a market where one can get a good price. We might be in Degana, and the market for selling the wool may be in Delhi. How do we carry the sheared wool with us everywhere? So, of course, we have to sell the wool to someone else. We seldom have much cash, but we always need money. And whoever needs, bends lower. The wool merchants are willing to give us an advance on the wool. That makes life simpler, but we know we lose money this way. . . . And do you know, the price of wool changes every year? Up and down, up and down. But, brother, mostly just down. There is nothing we can do about it. The government imports second-hand wool from foreign [places]. You know, it is the waste wool of those outsiders that we use. From their sweaters and woolen clothes they unknit the wool and export it to our country because we are a poor people. When there is so much oversupply in the market, the price of wool is completely below what it costs to produce. Take this year, for example. Wool is stuck at Rs 1200 a quintal (one hundred kilograms). And it is all because of foreign wool flooding the market. Forget profits, we are not even going to be able to buy feed for the sheep. We will be lucky if we survive at the end of this migration.

Extensive and frequent participation in the market for products (wool, manure, sheep), consumption goods (foodgrains, vegetables, pulses), and inputs (feed and grazing costs, labor, costs of shearing) implies that the shepherds must pay constant attention to changing prices. But the shepherds also recognize that their returns are at least partially determined by factors entirely beyond their control. Talking about the market for sheep, Ranaramji said: "These markets are very hard for us. We seldom get the best prices because we sell when we need the money. Sheep and goats are like ready cash because one can sell them anytime one wants. But never can one sell them at the right price. This is why we remain poor."

The anonymity of many of the factors that structure prices cannot be seen as an unmixed evil. Indeed, anonymous interactions among negotiating parties and the absence of systematic influences that structure outcomes in favor of specific parties can be seen as defining characteristics of "free" markets. Shepherds use the uncertainties in their exchanges with farmers and traders to bargain and influence the terms of exchange in their favor.

Uncertainties in exchange stem from limited knowledge about exchange partners and other fluctuations over which the shepherds do not have much control because they are constantly on the move. Mobility creates new contexts in which shepherds must bargain to sell their products or to buy daily necessities. Shepherd camps not blessed with an articulate leader or one who is attuned to the environment would find it impossible to survive. Mobility helps negotiate risks, but it is a harsh mistress. From the inattentive or the ignorant she exacts a high price. It is understandable, then, that in almost all interactions the shepherds impress with their tremendous curiosity about prices, rainfall, and the location of friendly farmers. Accurate information improves the chances of an economically profitable migration.

Hadkaramji, one of the shepherds I met in Patawal, vividly illustrated the advantages of an articulate camp leader when I asked how shepherds could ensure a good bargain. "You ask how we get a good price? Take even something as low as sheep dung. We can make money from it—black gold we call it. But if the camp leader doesn't know his job, this black gold just remains black sheep shit scattered in the fields. Why? Because not too many people know when to press a farmer and when to walk away. Knowing when to say no is critical. Everyone can talk. How to talk is the secret."

The shepherds bargain actively and vociferously to arrive at the terms of their exchanges with farmers, wool and sheep merchants, sheep shearers, and government officials. Chapter 5 focuses on manure sales to examine the factors that drive price formation. In documenting the details of how verbal contracts between shepherds and farmers are set, the chapter fulfills two other objectives as well. First, it shows the importance of bargaining when prices are set competitively among formally equal negotiators. The freedom implicit in the possibility to abandon negotiations and search for a different possible partner allows those who negotiate to use their bargaining skills to the utmost. Second, it shows how structural inequalities influence outcomes in bargains struck between actors who have asymmetric power even if formal equality. To the extent political factors always influence bargaining, including settings of formal equality, the idea of free markets must remain chimeric.

4 Profits on the Move:

The Economics of Migration

among the Raika Shepherds

For poor rural households in western Rajasthan, survival depends upon eking out an existence from multiple sources: agriculture, labor, and animal keeping. The small size of landholdings and low levels of productivity account for the low agricultural income of the average rural family. Uncertain and variable rainfall and a sociopolitical squeeze on common grazing lands account for the need to migrate with flocks.[1] Farming their small holdings between three and five months around the monsoons and migrating for the rest of the year, the raika shepherds would be especially hard put to survive without the income yielded by animal herding. What Salzman calls "the multi-resource economy," talking about nomads in Baluchistan and North Africa (1972: 66), is clearly the case for the shepherds as well.[2]

To explore at greater depth the ways in which mobility is connected with sheepherding, this chapter focuses on the economics of migration. In the process, it shows how movement over thousands of kilometers leads to financial profits for the raikas. Although a number of studies have analyzed the significance of migration in the pastoral economy, most of them suffer from a lack of attention to the collective nature of migration. They accept that mobility is essential to survival in environments beset by marked fluctuations. A lively discussion of whether mobility results from environmental causes (Johnson 1969; Stenning 1957), social and political risks (Burnham 1979; Elam 1979; Lee and de Vore 1968; Gulliver 1975; Woodburn 1972), or a complex mix of factors (Ingold 1986; McCabe 1994; Sandford 1983) is available in the works of anthropologists. The debate on the causes of mobility has enhanced our understanding that even if the physical environment presents pastoralists with incentives to migrate, the actual choice of migration is highly dependent on social, economic, and especially political factors. After all, not all people living in western Rajasthan migrate, let alone migrate annually! The raikas have been forced to travel more often as their access to village pastures has declined.

This chapter contributes to discussions on mobility by attending to a different aspect of migrations altogether — their collective nature. In looking at transhumant pastoralism, students of mobility have taken the fact of collective or individual mobility for granted. Few scholars remark on why collective or individually oriented strategies are chosen. Consider, as examples, Brower's careful study of Sherpa pastoralists in Nepal (1987), Burnham's penetrating examination of the relation between political stratification and spatial mobility (1979), Grayzel's evocative essay on the Fulbe pastoral system in Mali (1990), Lancaster and Lancaster's work on camel pastoralism among the Rwala Bedu (1990), and Barth's seminal work on the Basseri (1961).[3] In these accounts, it is difficult even to deduce whether the mobility patterns that are under analysis and are being described are collective or individualized. Yet, if pastoralists migrate both as individual families and in collective camps, it means that for different groups of herders and in different contexts specific social, political, and environmental factors must be operating to make individual versus collective strategies more appealing.

It is not just mobility that allows the raikas to address social, political, and environmental variability; it is *collective mobility* that is critical. If the pastoralists did not migrate together, their migrations would not be viable. Analyses of collective migration that defend it as a preferable strategy must, at a minimum, examine the ways in which moving collectively provides shepherds greater returns in comparison with traveling individually. Collective migration raises other important questions about the mechanisms whereby the shepherds address the hazards of community. In much social-scientific literature, there is vocal advocacy of community. But such efforts on behalf of community are matched by those who believe in the superiority of private markets and property, and by others who find in state initiatives the possibility of overcoming market failures. In each instance, collective action problems must be solved.[4] In the case of the raikas, their collective organization during annual movements is a prime example of communities that self-organize to solve problems of collective action and gain access to resources.

This chapter concentrates on the analytically prior issue of how collective migration leads to higher returns. If collective migration did not provide greater benefits in comparison with individually oriented movement, the question about how shepherds address the hazards of cooperation will not even arise. Greater benefits must accrue to an effective set of politically powerful raika actors. The overall benefits of collective migration for the raikas are higher. In addition, the shepherds must migrate collectively if they are to migrate at all. The argument in this chapter implicitly confirms other accounts, which point to deep-seated problems in policies attempting to sedentarize pastoralists (Ferguson 1994). I defer until chapters 6 and 7 the discussion of how raikas use institutional arrangements within their migrating collectives to solve problems of collective action.

The shepherds yoke collective mobility to another strategy of coping with environmental risks — exchange. Earlier studies of pastoralists often depicted them as relatively autonomous peoples (Evans-Pritchard 1940) or as living in timeless pasts in what Tsing has called "a space of cultural purity and simplicity more 'settled' even than the space of the sedentary" (1993: 150). Recent works have been at some pains to explicate the multiple connections of pastoralists with state officials, markets exchanges, and settled populations (Khazanov [1984] 1994). For the raikas, successful migrations depend crucially on market participation.

EXCHANGE RELATIONSHIPS

Recall that most raikas live in western India in the states of Gujarat and Rajasthan (Davidson 1996; Srivastava 1997) and that their migrations often span distances of more than a thousand miles a year, taking them across provincial borders and bringing them into contact with other shepherds, farmers, and government officials. The shepherds sleep in the open and move their camps, called *dangs*, almost every day. A mobile camp, led by the nambardar, can embrace anywhere between eight and eighteen flocks of sheep. Each flock comprises about five hundred sheep and five camels and is managed by three to eight men, women, and children.

As for Bates's farmers (1981: 3), and indeed, as is true for most household enterprises, the real incomes of pastoralists depend on their performance in three markets. Their revenues result from sales in the market for such commodities as sheep, wool, and animal droppings. Their gross profits are a function of revenues but also of the reigning prices in the markets for inputs — cost of feed and grazing, wool-shearing rates, and veterinary medicines. Their net incomes, finally, are determined by costs they incur in a third major market — that of consumption goods.

Shepherds resemble other peasant producers in that they live in rural areas, rely on land-based resources, and survive at the edge of subsistence. But unlike most peasants, who are presumed to meet a significant proportion of their subsistence needs, the raikas are far more integrally involved with the market.[5] The terms of trade between animal products and food grains forcefully determine their life chances.

Revenues

The raikas sell sheep, wool, and manure.[6] Unlike most nomadic pastoralists, few raikas eat meat.[7] Of the commodities raikas sell, sheep provide the highest proportion of their income (see table 4.1). The proceeds from the sale

Table 4.1   Total Returns for Flocks, 1989–90 (in rupees)

Flock Number	Flock Size	Manure	Wool Sales	Animal Sales	Total
1	95	264	1,705	1,520	3,489
2	107	335	2,100	4,745	7,180
3	110	227	2,295	420	2,942
4	148	396	3,640	2,800	6,836
5	212	396	3,920	10,220	14,536
6	228	335	5,075	7,465	12,875
7	255	396	5,940	6,220	12,556
8	330	396	7,020	9,580	16,996
9	350	791	7,200	12,040	20,031
10	380	791	7,830	1,740	10,361
11	425	791	9,920	21,020	31,731
12	430	396	9,660	10,900	20,956
13	490	791	11,880	17,630	30,301
Average		485	6,014	8,177	14,676
Proportion		3.3%	40.9%	55.7%	100%

Source: Flock survey by the author, 1990.

of manure, earned by folding (penning) sheep in the fields of farmers, is deposited into a common fund managed by the camp leader and used to defray collective migration expenses.

Animal sales. Two types of sheep sales can be distinguished: sale of mature stock (regular sales that take place between January and April) and sale of individual animals to meet short-term cash needs. The sheep are sold to traders and agents who visit the moving camp at regular intervals. The informal market works effectively enough that flock leaders seldom visit urban markets.

The number of sheep a flock leader will sell depends on the rate of lambing, desired size of the flock, labor availability, and the male to female proportion in the flock. The rate of lambing is itself influenced by rainfall and fodder availability and seasonal and annual variations in them. Desired flock size and labor availability are closely related. Raikas consider four to five hundred sheep the ideal size of the flock during migration. To create flocks of this size, a number of families often bring their animals together.

Studies from other contexts have also examined the question of appropriate flock size.[8] Although Spooner suggests that there is an optimum range within which flock size should vary (1973), other writings indicate that pastoralists are more concerned with maintaining particular ratios of herders to animals than with a fixed optimal size related to ecological variables. According to Koster, a Peloponnesian herder can effectively manage no more than 250 goats (1977). Swidler, who studied Brahui shepherds in Baluchistan, suggests that concerns of expediency and convenience set upper and lower limits to grazing units. In her study, the size of the grazing unit ranged between 250 and 500 sheep. More than 500 sheep could not be effectively herded by a shepherd and his dog; when the flock size fell below 250, the sheep did not fare as well (1972).[9] In the case of the raikas economic factors also play a role in determining size — smaller flocks suffer from diseconomies of scale and generate lower surpluses.

The raikas actively manipulate the ratio between male and female adult sheep by culling and selling rams and sometimes gifting ewes. The objective is to increase the proportion of ewes. A minimum number of males must be present for breeding. Once this minimum is satisfied, shepherds try to increase the number of ewes to enhance flock size at the fastest possible rate.

Wool sales. Wool is usually sheared twice a year. The first shearing takes place before migration at the village base of the raikas (in October), the second when the shepherds are on the migration cycle, often during the return leg of the journey. At home, the shepherds may shear the animals themselves with the help of neighbors and relatives. During migration, sheep are sheared by professional migrant shearers called *lavas*.[10] The sale of wool during migration must be coordinated with the shearing since carrying the wool is burdensome. The camp leader coordinates the major tasks associated with the sale of the wool. He establishes contacts with shearers, negotiates a selling price with wool merchants, and selects a site for shearing. He often contacts wool merchants even before the shearing has been arranged.

Distinguish between two types of sales contracts. In the first, wool is sold on the hoof and the merchant advances some cash to the shepherds. In such contracts, the merchant arranges the shearing. Shepherds prefer the second type of contract, in which the shearing is arranged and supervised by the camp leader and payment is received after the shearing. In these cases, the shepherds are usually able to negotiate better prices. The first type of contract, although it improves the household cash flow, also makes the shearers less careful: in an effort to shear very close, they can nick or cut the sheep (FAIR 1980).

Sheep manure. Income from folding (penning) sheep in farmers' fields is an important but generally unrecognized portion of the total income of the migrating camps. Part of the reason is obvious — droppings are presumed to be waste, not an economically valuable commodity. Another part is that the income from the sale of sheep manure is allocated to a common fund shepherds use for covering joint expenses. At the end of the migration, the positive or negative balance in the common fund is shared equally among the different flock leaders.

On the average, the camp leader is able to negotiate a payment for penning the sheep in farmers' fields for a third of the days that the raikas are on the move. The exact amount can vary between Rs 20 and 300. Revenues from folding sheep in the fields of farmers are greater if the number of shepherd camps in the area is small, the sowing season is near, the fields are irrigated, the number of sheep in the migrants' camp is large, and more farmers are competing for the manure.

Table 4.1 shows the total revenues of the shepherds from the sale of sheep, wool, and manure in 1989–90. The highest returns are from the sale of sheep — 56 percent of total revenues. This is nearly half again as much as returns from wool sales. However, the fluctuations in returns from animal sales (Rs 420 to 21,020) are much higher than in the case of wool (Rs 1,705 to 11,880). Most flock leaders earned between Rs 600 and 900 by selling the droppings of their sheep. These earnings scarcely rival the revenues from wool or animal sales. They constitute instead a supplementary income. Yet families that earn less than Rs 5,000 in an average year by no means scoff at Rs 600; indeed, in some cases the amount is as much as 25 percent of the final profit.

Input Expenses

The most important requirement for the survival of the migrating enterprise — grazing for the sheep — is usually available free. But shepherds incur unavoidable expenses on supplemental feed, on medicines, for shearing,[11] to pay labor, and sometimes for grazing. In rare instances, raikas are forced to transport their sheep by truck to areas where fodder can be found (Kavoori 1990: 28–29).[12]

Feed and grazing. Fodder is not available uniformly throughout the migration cycle. In the winter months especially, the raikas must supplement natural fodder with different kinds of purchased feed. Supplementary feed is also bought for pregnant sheep. In addition, the shepherds may incur grazing expenses in two other situations. Camps that migrate throughout the year pay grazing fees to the Forest Department during the monsoon months when almost all private fields are planted and the fodder available in the commons is insufficient even for village animals. Grazing fees vary between states. In

Rajasthan, they were Rs 0.50 per sheep; in Madhya Pradesh, fees were raised tenfold in 1989 to Rs 10.00 per sheep.

Grazing expenses are also incurred in Haryana and Uttar Pradesh — the winter destinations for migrating shepherds. The rent for crop stubble in the fields ranges between Rs 50 to 100 a month for one thousand sheep. The browse in double-cropped, irrigated fields constitutes a new adaptive niche for the raikas, since even thirty years ago few private fields were irrigated. The current situation has reversed earlier exchanges between farmers and shepherds. Prior to the arrival of irrigation and the increasing shortage of fallow fields for the shepherds' flocks, the farmers paid the shepherds for manure from the sheep. The reversal of monetary flows reflects the changing reality of the asymmetrical relationships between the farmers and the shepherds. This changing reality is in part driven by the agricultural and irrigation policies of the Indian state. These policies systematically favor farmers and irrigated agriculture over pastoralists and rainfed cultivation.

Medicines. The shepherds rely on both indigenous and western medicines, but usually they resort to western treatments only when indigenous medicine fails. Vaccines, injections, antibiotics, and deworming medicines are the most important. They are purchased from private traders and used without much supervision (see also Davidson 1996). Government veterinary hospitals are notoriously unreliable for obtaining needed medicines and attention from doctors.

Labor. Seven of the thirteen flocks I studied employed labor during the migration cycle. The salary of the hired hand depends on age, skill, the closeness of the kin relationship with the leader, and the number of sheep he brings into the flock. If the shepherd brings no sheep, he receives between Rs 2,000 and 3,500 as payment during the migration cycle. In addition to the salary, he receives food and a change of clothes as a gift. Food is provided even to those hired shepherds who bring sheep into the flock. But if the number of sheep inducted into the migrating flock is more than one hundred, no salary is paid.

Table 4.2 lists all the expenses the raikas incur in input markets. It is obvious that the largest amounts are spent by groups that are labor deficient and must hire a shepherd.

Consumption Goods Expenses

Consumption expenses are primarily a function of two variables: the duration of migration and the number of people in the group. They can be divided

Table 4.2   Input Expenses Incurred on Sheep, 1989–90 (in rupees)

Flock Number	Flock Size	Feed/ Grazing	Medicines	Hired Shepherd	Shearing	Total
1	95	1,425	475	—	95	1,995
2	107	1,498	642	900	107	3,147
3	110	1,760	605	800	138	3,303
4	148	1,998	814	—	163	2,975
5	212	2,544	1,081	—	233	3,858
6	228	2,508	958	1,200	228	4,894
7	255	2,805	1,020	—	268	3,734
8	330	3,465	1,320	1,200	396	6,381
9	350	3,500	1,330	1,500	333	6,663
10	380	3,724	1,330	1,050	437	6,541
11	425	2,975	1,785	3,500	510	8,770
12	430	2,580	1,290	1,700	559	6,129
13	490	3,430	1,225	—	588	5,243

Source: Flock survey by the author, 1990.

into two categories: those incurred by the shepherds as a collective and those assigned to constituent units of the camp — the flock leaders. Collective funds are spent on guests, information collection, community feasts, fines, and bribes. Flock-related expenses concern food and transport. The largest amounts are spent on food.

Collective expenses. Sheep droppings are the source of collective revenues. General purpose transportation tasks, feasts, and guests are the sinks for collective expenditures. As a proportion of total revenues and expenses, collective sources and sinks seem minor — less than 5 percent. They are immensely important, however, in fashioning the migrating camp into a community. The collective activities that the common fund of the mobile camp facilitates are immensely important to the generation of the belief among the shepherds that they belong to a social entity, are part of a common purpose.

Information about precipitation, fodder availability, and the presence of friendly farmers is the foundation on which daily movements are built. The camp leader undertakes reconnaissance missions every morning by horse or camel. These journeys last two to four hours and span between five and fifteen miles. They help uncover precious details on the best grazing spots, the state of water availability at the usual watering points, and whether farmers are willing to let the shepherds camp in their fields. Interest in early information about rainfall and the state of pastures along migration routes is a common feature of other transhumant groups as well (Doughty 1937; Marx 1978).

Camp leaders also collect information through longer term journeys by public transport. On these trips, which may last several days and in which hundreds of miles may be traversed, they pay closer attention to rainfall and vegetation than to conversations with farmers. Sometimes a number of camp leaders come together for such journeys. The expenses of these trips are met by the collective. In addition, funds spent on periodic journeys to purchase medicines for the sheep are counted as collective expenses.

Food is cooked jointly for the entire migrating camp on such occasions as Holi, Diwali, Akha Teej, Prasaadi, Raakhee, Shivaratri, and Gangaur — Hindu religious festivals that the raikas celebrate. Expenses incurred to feed and welcome guests, even when the visitor is related to only one of the flock leaders in the camp, are a collective responsibility. Finally, all fines and bribes are jointly satisfied. Fines may have to be paid for trespassing, to irate villagers in whose fields the sheep have wandered, or to government officials. Overall, fines are an irregular and relatively small item of expense. Bribes, on the other hand, form an annoying and pervasive cash drain on the mobile economy. They are necessary to cross state borders, graze animals in state forests, procure subsidized medicines from public veterinary hospitals, or mollify police officials. Few raikas can pay the fees fixed by the state. Instead they secure services or avoid trouble by attempting to bribe the officials in charge.[13] The negotiation of the exact amount in each individual case is left to the camp leader, who may seek the advice of elders in the camp, especially if the amounts involved are significant. Fines and bribes constitute the largest proportion of jointly incurred expenses.

Food and transport. Most raika households consume the same food — unleavened bread made from coarse grains (such as millet), onions, red or green chilies, occasional lentil soups and vegetables, sheep's milk, tea, butter, buttermilk, yoghurt, and fresh camel's milk. But adult male members of the richer households consume greater quantities of opium and tobacco than their poorer kinfolk, reflecting their greater purchasing power. The consumption of these two items can cost up to Rs 100 per month. Opium is especially important in the daily lives of the raikas, as it is ritually consumed on most days and is used to welcome visitors.

The main transportation expenses are incurred in maintaining regular

Table 4.3   Consumption Expenses Incurred on Flocks, 1989–90 (in rupees)

Flock Number	Flock Size	Food	Collective Expenses	Transport	Total
1	95	1,040	171	250	1,461
2	107	1,800	326	350	2,476
3	110	1,760	173	400	2,330
4	148	1,600	264	350	2,214
5	212	3,120	264	600	3,984
6	228	3,360	326	750	4,436
7	255	3,600	425	900	4,925
8	330	7,680	314	1,300	9,294
9	350	2,240	575	600	3,415
10	380	4,620	711	800	6,131
11	425	6,480	600	1,500	8,580
12	430	5,400	256	1,200	6,856
13	490	7,440	629	1,600	9,669
Average		3,857	387	815	5,059

Source: Flock survey by the author, 1990.

contact between the camp and the village from which the migration started: shepherds travel home as often as every two months.

Table 4.3 lists all consumption expenses incurred by raika camps in 1989–90.

Flock Economics

Table 4.4 provides a surplus/deficit statement for the shepherds' migrations by comparing the performance of flock owners in three major markets: for commodities, inputs, and consumption goods. For the thirteen different migrant households from which I collected usable data, the figures range from a deficit of about Rs 2,300 to a resounding surplus of more than Rs 15,000. The average surplus for the surveyed flocks is almost Rs 5,000. Flocks 3 and 10 did not earn an excess of income. Recall from table 4.2 that these are also the two flocks that did not manage to sell any of their sheep apart from the few they sold as distress sales. For most flock owners, then, stock sales are essential if they are to stay out of the red. Indeed, for four of the larger flock owners (5, 9, 11, and 13) income from animal sales alone was sufficient to achieve a surplus (see table 4.2). Clearly, the raikas are in a far better position

Table 4.4 Surplus/Deficits for Different Flocks, 1989–90 (in rupees)

Flock Number	Flock Size	Revenue	Consumption Expenses	Factor Expenses	Per Flock	Per Person	Per Sheep
					Surplus or Deficit		
1	95	3,489	1,461	1,995	33	33	.3
2	107	7,180	2,476	3,147	1,557	778	14.5
3	110	2,942	2,330	3,303	−2,691	−2,691	−24.5
4	148	6,836	2,214	2,975	1,647	824	11.1
5	212	14,536	3,984	3,858	6,694	2,231	31.6
6	228	12,875	4,436	4,894	3,545	1,182	15.5
7	255	12,556	4,925	3,734	3,897	1,299	15.3
8	330	16,996	9,294	6,381	1,321	440	4.0
9	350	20,031	3,415	6,663	9,953	3,318	28.4
10	380	10,361	6,131	6,541	−2,311	−385	−6.1
11	425	31,731	8,580	8,770	14,381	2,876	33.8
12	430	20,956	6,856	6,129	7,971	1,993	18.5
13	490	30,301	9,669	5,243	15,389	3,847	31.4
Average		14,676	5,059	4,895	4,722	1,462	17.3

Source: Flock survey by the author, 1990.

than the Chinese peasants Tawney describes as "standing permanently up to the neck in water,"[14] able to survive only when ripples do not disturb the surface. But, if the raika economy seems to be alive and well, it is only because of their operations in markets and their skill at mobility. Or perhaps one should speak of their skill at collective mobility. Movement alone (both in the sense of movement by itself and in the sense of movement that is individual-household oriented) would not help the shepherds enough.

ADVANTAGES OF COLLECTIVE MIGRATION

Whether individual or collective mobility is superior is more interesting as an empirical and theoretical question than a simple comparison of the revenues, expenses, and incomes of the different flocks. The question of whether collective or individual mobility is superior resonates with a range of issues in the social sciences that were opened by Olson's seminal work on the logic of collective action (1965). Why should the shepherds migrate as a group when they can secure the benefit of mobility—access to irregularly distributed grazing—at an individual level also? Group migration results in costs of coordination and organization. It requires institutional investments to resolve possible internal disputes. These problems can be avoided were each shepherd to migrate on his own. The answer lies in the economies of collective migration, economies without which mobility would not be possible.

There are two sources of such economies: those secured through larger flock size and those reaped by migrating with a group of flocks. For shepherds who own between fifty and one hundred sheep, cooperating with other shepherds who have a small number of sheep or migrating with a larger flock owner reduces costs significantly. The smallest flock owners for whose animals the tables present data migrated in combination with other small flock owners to raise the combined size of the migrating flock. This is because almost every aspect of market participation—from the sale of products, to expenditures on consumption, to expenses on inputs—would be affected adversely were the shepherds to migrate alone.

More importantly, however, the political and security risks connected with individual migration mean that if the shepherds are to migrate at all they must migrate collectively. The greatest security benefits flow, of course, from moving as a collective comprising around a hundred humans and thousands of sheep. Collective migration eliminates some kinds of security risks and renders others far more manageable.

Flock-Level Economies

Substantial variations of surpluses are present across different-sized flocks. The trend, however, is clear. If we divide the thirteen surveyed flocks, which ranged in size from 95 to 490 sheep, into three categories, performance improves dramatically as flock size increases. The larger flocks produce a surplus of almost Rs 30 per sheep and Rs 3,000 per person in contrast to the smaller flocks, which earn less than Rs 2 per sheep and Rs 100 per person. The visual representation of the variation across the different flock-size categories is striking (see figures 4.1a and b).[15]

It also seems that once flock size begins to approach 500 to 600 sheep, shepherds either divide their flock into two or sell enough sheep to reduce flock size. Keeping more than 600 sheep in a flock increases diseconomies of scale to the point where the flock size becomes unattractive. Among the more than thirty flocks I encountered, not one had more than 650 sheep and only three had more than 600. The choice between dividing the flock or selling the sheep depends on the availability of labor in the household and on the need for liquidity in cash flow.

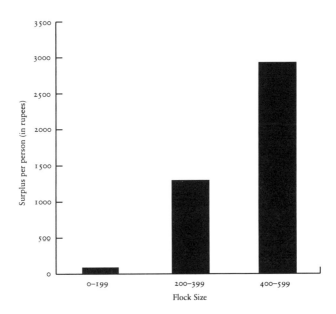

Figure 4.1a   Flock size and economic performance per person

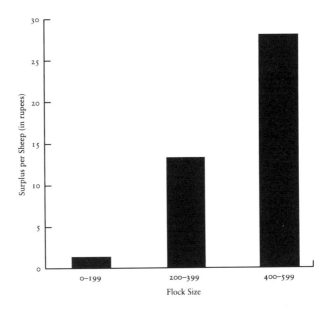

Figure 4.1b   Flock size and economic performance per sheep

Larger flocks enjoy advantages that improve economic performance.[16] The reasons for better performance are easy to discern. The most important lies in the savings on consumption costs. Larger flocks have more sheep per shepherd on the average. When smaller flock owners come together to form a migrating group, at least one shepherd is present for each of the constituent flocks. If a migrating flock unit comprises four smaller flocks of one hundred sheep each, there may be four shepherds managing the grazing. But for a larger flock owner there would seldom be more than two shepherds for a flock of five hundred sheep. Recall from table 4.2 that funds spent on food and transport form the largest proportion of all expenses. It is easy to see why larger flocks would enjoy substantial scale economies. Another reason is that larger flock units can sell more of the male lambs that were added to the flock in the course of the year.

Camp-Level Economies

Economic and political advantages also accrue to shepherds who migrate in groups with their flocks. Of these, economic gains are the easiest to demonstrate. Shepherds ensure themselves at least three sets of economies of scale by collective migration: income from folding sheep in farmers' fields, benefits that stem from the collective purchases of medicines and feed and collective preparation of food for guests and during festivals, and lower payments of bribes and fines to government officials and settled populations.

The manure of a flock of a few hundred sheep would provide a farmer with little motivation to seek out shepherds whose sheep could be penned in his field.[17] But when farmers can get a camp of four to five thousand sheep to spend the night in their fields, the increased fertility becomes worth incurring search, information, and negotiation costs over and above the negotiated price of the manure. Were the flock owners to migrate individually, they would forego approximately Rs 500 each in lost manure sales (see table 4.1).

Shepherds also indicated that because they purchase medicines and feed in bulk for the entire camp's sheep they are able to gain a discount of up to 10 percent. Each flock owner spends approximately Rs 1,000 on medicines and perhaps Rs 500 on supplemental feed. Individually oriented migration would thus lead to a loss of Rs 150 in foregone discounts. Similarly, if shepherds had to cook for their guests and prepare feasts individually, they would spend far more time on these activities than when such tasks are divided sequentially among the ten to twelve constituent households of the camp.

The losses from migrating individually are difficult to quantify in relation to savings on fines and bribes. At present, shepherds spend less than Rs 200 per flock unit on bribes. Additionally, sometimes sheep are stolen from the camp during migration and recovered only because shepherds traveling together can help each other or make a show of force against thieves. Outcomes along these dimensions might change drastically and tragically if the shepherds were to migrate individually. But the economic effects along these dimensions are more difficult to establish quantitatively.

Individual migration may actually turn out to be more attractive where bribes are concerned, not because individual shepherds have any bargaining power but because they are likely to be seen as completely destitute. A single flock may be beneath the notice of government officials because, knowing that the resources of an ordinary shepherd are limited, few officials will attempt to extract bribes.

Security-Related Benefits

If the economic advantages of migrating collectively are significant, the security-related benefits collective migration confers are invaluable. Without the increased ability to protect each other, mobility would be impossible. During the night, the shepherds place their most valuable possessions — the sheep — in the center of their camp and guard them in turn through the night. If shepherds did not travel together, such care in protecting sheep would be impossible. But nighttime security is not the only kind afforded by collective migration.

Other security-related advantages of collective mobility were graphically in evidence during a conflict I witnessed. A raika, whose sheep had congregated around a village pond to drink, became involved in an altercation with a villager who arrived on the scene after the sheep had begun drinking. The villager remonstrated that the water in the pond was not meant for the sheep. As the sheep continued to drink and the discussion became more heated, the villager became increasingly upset. Other villagers gathered. They demanded a fine.

By the time we happened on the scene, the quarrel had taken a physical turn. The shepherd, Hadkaramji, and the farmer had come to blows when the villagers tried to stop the sheep from leaving before the fine was paid. The villagers had tied up Hadkaramji and were threatening to call the police. While their threats may well have been a bluff, the shepherds were in no position to call it. The camp leader sent a number of shepherds to get help from other migrating camps in the vicinity. We settled down to a lengthy process of discussion and negotiation.

Within three hours, nearly forty shepherds had arrived on the scene, some with their flocks. Many of them were from the same camp as Hadkaramji. Information about the fight had spread swiftly and mobilized shepherds to come to the aid of their comrade. Collectively, the shepherds soon outnumbered the villagers.

Initially the villagers had demanded a fine of Rs 1,000 and the cost of treating the wounded villager. The matter ultimately was settled at Rs 150 and the cost of the medicines. Hadkaramji was untied. Slowly the gathered raikas and the villagers dispersed. Without the presence of a large group of shepherds to render help, it is doubtful that the costs to Hadkaramji and his camp mates would have been so low.

The raikas themselves are manifestly aware of the value of migrating collectively in the face of such incidents and therefore seldom travel alone. But contrast the incident with Davidson's description of interactions between farmers and a camp of migrant shepherds in Gujarat. These shepherds were foraging with their sheep close to their home villages in Bhuj:

> One day we had just made camp when a local caste of herders came and began shouting and threatening us. The women placated them . . . [but] the rest of us packed and walked an extra six miles. Every day the farmers told us to move on, threatening both graziers and women with sticks or knives. . . . The mukki [camp leader] of a local Rabari dang came to visit and there was a heated exchange. . . . Phagu [the leader of Davidson's camp] decided that the dang must break up into three groups. Smaller flocks would be less threatening to the locals. (1996: 179–80)

In Davidson's case, larger camp size and a larger group of shepherds appear to pose a threat to villagers. The camp leader decides to divide the larger group into three. The existence of these different strategies of mobility among the raikas, and the depiction of individual household-level mobility by other writers (Brower 1987; McCabe 1985; Mearns 1993) mean that a collective response to spatio-temporal variability requires analysis, not acceptance as a naturalized fact.

From the discussion of the ways in which collective mobility is useful for the raikas, two main factors can be advanced as prompting it. First, collective movement permits pastoralists to secure the benefits of economies of scale and reduces costs that would be far higher under individual migration strategies. Second, group migration is essential to confronting and addressing security risks, especially those related to theft and conflict that a constantly changing social environment presents.

But different pastoralist groups face variable security problems. Security from theft or attack may be of only limited concern when shepherds graze their animals within a short distance of their home villages (as was the case with Davidson's shepherds), when they can appeal to some local group for help, or when their migrations are to specific destinations and are over quickly. When pastoralists migrate through very sparsely populated regions, or when they move along highly defined routes and can spend the nights with households that they have cultivated over time, security problems may again loom small. When government officials respond efficiently to appeals for help and law and order conditions are relatively well organized and un-biased, the need for large groups of relatively autonomous herders, orga-nized for self-protection, may not be significant.

In the case of the raikas, however, most of these conditions are absent. The raikas migrate over long distances, have few local supporters, move con-stantly, traverse highly populated regions with scarce land and grazing, and cannot rely on the police for help. They must help themselves as they migrate.

A Concluding Discussion

This chapter focuses on a critical aspect of mobility among the raika migrant pastoralists in India: its collective orientation. Pastoralists all around the world migrate. But analyses of migration devote rather limited attention to explicating the reasons why migration occurs as a cooperative venture. Nonetheless, the existence of solitary and joint migratory strategies, some-times among the same groups, signifies that neither can be taken as a natu-ralized fact. Both must be explained.

Collective migration among the shepherds leads to significant economic gains, but the more important reasons prompting it lie in security-related concerns. Given the social and political characteristics of the migrants' con-text, security concerns become highly prominent. My account of collective migration uses a kind of functionalist explanation usually considered inap-propriate in the social sciences. But, when the question is one of survival rather than just economic gain, the choice of a functional explanation can be defended (Dore [1961] 1973; Lal 1988).

When collective strategies during migration are prompted because sur-vival is at stake, as in the case of the raika shepherds, economic benefits of migration are primarily a side effect — attractive but less significant as a cause. But collective mobility conceivably could also be prompted by the economic gains it produces. When cooperation takes place primarily or only for economic reasons, individuals acting as agents on behalf of the collective may act, intentionally or out of sheer incompetence, in ways that will neu-tralize the benefits of collective migration.

To minimize abuses of decision-making authority and to prevent dissipation of economic gains attributable to exchange during migration, it would be necessary for the shepherds to devise institutional mechanisms through which they could monitor, detect, and sanction behavior detrimental to the existence of the group. The analysis of such institutional mechanisms can be found in part III of this book, where the focus shifts to the internal organization of the migrating shepherd camps and the construction of community in them (see also Agrawal 1997b). All collectives, after all, require large investments of organizational and institutional capital to address problems of coordination, questions of decision making and the distribution of power, and intragroup conflicts. But before we turn to the ways in which shepherds solve such problems and control their leaders, the next chapter undertakes a more penetrating look at the concepts of markets and exchanges.

5 · Looking at the "Invisible Hand":

Markets and Exchanges

in the Raikas' Livelihood

Politics . . . is what links value and exchange in the social life of commodities.
— Arjun Appadurai, 1986

The marketplace is more than a locus of competition and conflict . . . it is also an instrument of political control. — Robert Bates, 1981

All real markets are in a sense local ones, and the only non-local market is a model of perfection, a moral and economic goal of a particular segment of the population.
— J. Davis, 1985

Participation in market exchanges and collective mobility are critical to migratory success. Migration would not be just inefficient in the absence of markets; it would be impossible. Collective migration allows the shepherds to avail themselves of economies of scale, protect their valuable belongings, and negotiate better prices. Their migration-related earnings might be low, but they are consistently more stable than agricultural incomes and form a critical part of the household budget. The previous chapter underlined these conclusions and simultaneously situated the raikas in the context of the market by presenting some quantitative information on the migration economy. It left unexamined, however, the nature of the markets in which the raikas participate and how much sense it makes to talk about commodity transactions in describing exchanges that yield a livelihood for them.[1] To examine markets, exchange, and value more critically, this chapter focuses attention on perhaps the most intriguing set of exchanges in which the raikas engage: sheep manure for grain and cash.[2]

Through these exchanges, the shepherds realize their desire to camp in private fields for the night and the farmers their need for sheep manure as fertilizer. A brief statistical analysis demonstrates the extent to which obvious factors such as quantity, caste, landholding size, irrigation, or number of buyers and sellers in the market can account for the observed pattern of exchanges. The statistical analysis sets the stage for an examination of current scholarly writings on markets, value, and exchange. In distinction to scholars like Miller and Appadurai, I suggest that the value of a good cannot be located in any specific stage of the process through which articles are finally consumed by human beings.

The grain-manure exchanges I describe raise two major questions. The first is whether these exchanges are best thought of as barter or as monetary exchanges. In other words, how persuasive is it to distinguish between barter and cash exchanges as exemplifying qualitatively different types? I suggest that the usual distinctions made between barter and exchanges involving money are difficult to uphold. Questioning the distinction between barter and commodity exchanges hinging on money has a political effect as well. Usually barter is seen as a characteristic of primitive economies, ones that have not become so specialized as to need money. But showing that there are grounds for questioning the seemingly self-evident distinction between barter and monetary exchanges simultaneously makes it difficult to classify particular groups as primitive and others as developed.

The second issue concerns the problem of price formation. Grain-manure exchanges are highly decentralized. The critical question they raise is: how do decentralized exchanges lead to an aggregate price level that buyers and sellers can take as given? If information on the rate at which goods are exchanged is costly, the emergence of prices in decentralized markets is a phenomenon that cannot be assumed, as it often is in economic theory. It needs investigation. A related problem is the extent to which decentralized markets with voluntary exchanges are, in any compelling sense, "free markets."

MARKETS, VALUE, AND PASTORALISTS

Markets are arenas where transactions to exchange goods and services take place at voluntarily agreed upon prices. Prices may be set, in this formulation, without reference to abstract or contextualized notions of fairness or justice. I use *voluntary* in the rather narrow sense that parties to the exchanges are not obviously coerced into transactions and, if they so desire, can break off negotiations. This definition imposes no special constraints on the identity of actors, the nature of the arena, or the type of transaction. Exchanges can take place between specialized traders or inexperienced novices. They may take place electronically on the floors of stock exchanges or via a computer connected to the Internet. They may be between strangers or involve face-to-face encounters among those who know each other well. They may occur for mundane, mass-produced, and mass-consumed items such as food, grains and clothing or for paintings by Old Masters at exclusive auctions. The manner in which exchanges are organized in different markets may vary according to an enormous range of local, context-specific factors. But all markets have one critical element in common—the exchange of goods and services—to which the above definition directs attention.

This conceptual focus has three related effects, each significant for the argument presented here. First, it allows me to compare gift, barter, or commodity exchanges that are usually presumed to be quite different. Second, bringing together a number of analytical points regarding different types of exchanges is instrumental in understanding grain-manure exchanges between farmers and shepherds. These exchanges fall squarely on the line dividing barter from commodity exchange and contain elements that are usually thought to belong more properly to gift exchanges. Third, the analysis of the exchanges between raika shepherds and farmers creates the opportunity to funnel insights from the discussion back into the larger debate around market, exchange and value, and the relationships among these loaded concepts.

An enormous interdisciplinary scholarly literature has recently begun to focus attention on the "market." Much of this intellectual onslaught stems from anthropologists and sociologists. Their writings express their dissatisfaction with the social-scientific division of labor that, beginning in the late nineteenth century, made economy and markets the sole province of economists.[3] Drawing attention to what gets left out in economists' accounts and highlighting the fact that various features of markets are usually taken for granted in their models, most of these trespassing writers insist on the social moorings of markets and the inescapably sociopolitical nature of all market processes. They further argue that it is necessary to uncover social, cultural, and political aspects of markets in greater detail to understand "real markets" better (Dilley 1992b; Harriss 1993; Haworth 1994; Hewitt de Alcantara 1993).

The writings of these scholars may be seen, in part, as a response to attempts since the mid-1970s by several economists, institutionalists, and political scientists to bridge disciplinary boundaries from the other direction by applying assumptions and analytical techniques from neoclassical economics to nonmarket processes (Alt and Shepsle 1990; Bardhan 1993; Bates 1989; Becker 1976; Ostrom 1992; Popkin 1979; Wilks 1975). The works of these scholars can be taken as a suggestion that models of transactions built on Homo economicus can be used to cut through and explain the complexity of social life. At the minimum, these writings have provoked debate and interdisciplinary conversations, even if such debates, as some would argue, have only muddied the waters rather than clarifying issues.

Nonetheless, critiques of markets and exchange by anthropologists and sociologists and attempts to extend analytical techniques developed for markets to other settings are both moves in a salutary direction. In questioning dualistic oppositions between "primitive" and "modern" economies, they form part of an effort to "restore the cultural dimension to societies that are represented simply as economies writ large, and to restore the calculative dimension to societies that are too often simply portrayed as solidarity writ small" (Appadurai 1986a: 12).[4] Insights from the works of these scholars are indispensable to understanding the nature of markets and the extent to which specific features of markets contextualize exchange and value. This is especially so in this chapter, since part of its burden is to underline the inescapably social and political nature of all economic transactions, even when they seemingly take place voluntarily and among equals.

Value is a notion fraught with tensions. Before a good or service can be deemed valuable, or be consumed by a person, it undergoes a series of stages that can be analytically distinguished. These are usually seen to comprise production, distribution and exchange, and consumption, but they may also include transportation, storage, and appropriation. Where middlemen are involved, or extreme specialization is a pervasive feature of the economy, exchange often takes place for resale, and the stages prior to consumption, especially exchange, may be repeated several times before consumption occurs. In investigating the relationship of value to various processes that render an object fit for consumption, theorists have often focused on a specific stage and attempted to pose it as being the most critical.

The focus of political economists such as Marx and Smith on production is quite well known. Appadurai, on the other hand, drawing upon Simmel to begin his thoughtful analysis, claims that "[e]conomic exchange creates value." He goes on, more assertively, to say that it is "exchange that is the source of value" rather than utility and scarcity (1986a: 3, 4). After a wide-ranging survey of the literature on exchange, he concludes that politics links exchange to value in the "social life of commodities" (57). Exchange in Appadurai's treatment is politicized, but it remains central to the creation and determination of value. In contrast, this chapter defends the position that, although exchange may be a critical part of the series of processes that endow objects with value, the truth of the statement "economic exchange creates value" can only be conceded as a tautology were price made synonymous with value.

But such a gloss would conceal and erase the issues that can be investigated by asking the question in a different form. What creates value? What determines price? In focusing on a particular process that is part of the series through which "things" are finally consumed, one is constrained to answer these questions in an unnecessarily partial fashion. Consider, as another example of such a partial focus, recent work on consumption. In looking to consumption as the critical stage in the economic cycle of value creation, theorists have similarly limited their analytical optic. Miller's polemical assertion, "consumption has become the vanguard of history" (1995: 1), typifies the deliberate narrowing of attention that seeks forcefully to preclude consideration of the contexts in which particular stages in the lives of commodities become critical in influencing value. Indeed, Miller's own argument, insofar as he feels compelled to examine processes of exchange and production in relation to consumption, undermines his assertion.

EXCHANGES BETWEEN THE RAIKAS AND THE FARMERS

Much recent literature on pastoralism recognizes the multiple axes and forms of contact between migrating and settled populations (Fratkin et al. 1994b; Galaty and Johnson 1990; Smith 1992: chap. 8).[5] The role of exchange and markets in the lives of herders thus has begun to receive greater attention. Stereotypes of pastoralists as self-sufficient and able to extract a living from rearing livestock by resorting to mobility in bad years are being questioned (Chatty 1990; Grayzel 1990; Schneider 1990). Pastoral economic strategies counter Sahlins's contention that "underproduction is in the nature of economies organized by domestic groups and kinship relations" (1974: 41). It is important, therefore, to examine how market exchanges yield a surplus in pastoral production.[6] Sahlins sees societies that are organized according to a "domestic mode of production" as suffering from spatial discontinuities that lead to underutilization of resources (98). The case of the raika pastoralists suggests a way out of the general argument Sahlins presents. Although their economic production units during migration are based primarily on kin relations, their participation in the market allows them to produce for exchange and create surpluses. Their mobility allows them to take advantage of grazing resources that are irregularly distributed in space. The economic value of the limited forage by the roadside, in fallow fields, on village commons, and in the liminal spaces between villages would be far lower if the animals of the shepherds did not graze on them.

Recall that sheepherding allows the raikas to tap three main sources of revenue: animals, wool, and manure. Of these, manure disposal yields the lowest amounts in quantitative terms. Transactions over manure, however, bear the potential to yield more interesting and thought-provoking insights regarding markets and exchange. All sheep are owned privately, and the money earned from the sale of animals and wool directly offsets the expenses of the household economy. Exchanges involving sheep manure, however, follow a different path. Because manure is directly deposited in the fields of the farmers there are no intermediaries. Often, the exchanges are not even mediated by money. Farmers offer cash but equally often grain. The revenue from manure disposal is used for collective purposes.

The price of manure is negotiated in long conversations between farmers and the raika leaders (sometimes in the presence of other shepherds).[7] These sorts of face-to-face negotiations, as Polanyi points out, are the hallmark of competitive price setting (1944).[8] The grains or cash earned by exchanging manure are shared equally by members of the camp or consumed in collectively oriented activities such as feasts, care of the camp's visitors, and payment of bribes and fines. Finally, in contrast to the situation in the case of animal and wool sales, where prices are strongly influenced by international movements and the raikas exercise little control, the negotiations over the "price" of manure are far more open. Local markets for manure are not integrated regionally, and a wide range of local factors therefore emerge as critical in influencing the payments the raikas receive.

The exchanges of manure and grains for cash between farmers and raikas may be conceptualized as taking place in a large number of loosely connected local markets. The markets are interesting in that in each case a number of buyers and sellers are usually present, there is a high level of mobility, and the relationship between the buyers and the sellers is short-lived.[9] These conditions approximate those believed to characterize highly competitive markets in economic theory. We find, however, that the exchanges are inescapably influenced by a multiplicity of sociopolitical factors instrumental in constituting the very economic variables seen to be significant in influencing the terms of exchange.

In claiming that social, political, and economic forces are related, I do not go as far as Berry, whose analysis of economic change and exchange proceeds "on the assumption that culture, power and material resources are of equal importance, acting in mutually constitutive ways . . ." (1992: 13). It is, perhaps, impossible to treat culture, power, or material factors equally.[10] But even were it possible to somehow assign a democratically pleasing equal *weight* to these different aspects of livelihood, the *ways* in which these factors influence each other surely differ enormously from one sociohistorical juncture to another. It is difficult, therefore, to support the claim that they are always mutually constitutive, for other factors may help shape them. Whether they should be treated equally or are mutually constitutive must remain under interrogation pending the delineation of the object and span of analysis.

The rate at which the grain-manure exchange takes place is usually determined in negotiations between an individual farmer and the leader of the shepherd camp. Early each morning, long before sunrise, the leader sets out by himself or with his second-in-command (the *kamdar*). The major objective of these early morning "reconnaissance missions" is to discover the direction and location of the best forage and fodder resources. But apart from searching for forage the camp leader is concerned to find a suitable space in which to camp the next night. Several options are available to the shepherds. They can camp in publicly owned forests or uncultivable lands, in common lands owned by village communities, or in privately owned fields. Although shelter for the night may be obtained by camping in communally owned village lands or areas owned by the Revenue or Forest Departments, the shepherds prefer to settle for the night in private fields. They especially prefer fields that have an irrigation well (Agrawal 1992).

Such fields often belong to the larger landowners. The immediate advantage accruing from irrigated fields is that the water from the well can be used for drinking, cooking, washing, and the needs of the sheep. But there are other benefits as well. If the irrigated field belongs to a larger or upper caste landowner, there will be fewer security risks during the night. A more powerful local acquaintance deters casual harassment and theft. The shepherds I interviewed related a number of instances in which farmers in whose fields they penned their sheep would sometimes help them look for culprits when sheep were stolen.

If the raikas prefer spending the night in irrigated fields that belong to powerful landowners, the logic works the other way as well. Farmers welcome migrating shepherds for the manure the sheep deposit. This manure is most effective in irrigated rather than rain-fed fields. Sheep manure is also far cheaper than chemical fertilizers. The popular belief is that it is a more suitable nutrient for the fields than inorganic fertilizers[11] and is better than the dung from other animals.[12] In light of these advantages, it is not surprising that the farmers offer money and grain in exchange for the shepherds spending the night in their fields.

The negotiations, once the camp leader has contacted a farmer, may last anywhere from two to twenty minutes. Some seemingly essential pieces of information are exchanged first — the number of sheep in the camp and whether the field is irrigated.[13] Other important information, including the caste of the farmer and the shepherd, can usually be discerned from the body, dress, and carriage of the person. The farmer and the camp leader also already possess some inkling as to how many other sheep camps might be present in the vicinity.[14]

If the farmer and the camp leader do not believe the conversation will be fruitful, the leader will often leave with a simple good-bye. In that case, he will seek out another farmer to strike a bargain. The process continues until either a farmer and the camp leader arrive at a bargain or the marginal search costs become higher than the need to return with the identity of that evening's camp location. Depending on availability, the camp leader might talk with as many as ten farmers before he reaches an agreement.

If the two parties gauge the probability of a successful exchange as positive, bargaining starts in earnest. At this point, the farmer might offer inducements such as the easy availability of fuelwood in his fields, or he may display indifference to the bargain because other shepherd camps are present around his village. The shepherd may indicate the presence of other animals in the camp, such as camels and horses, whose manure the farmer would receive for free, or he might offer to take a look at a farmer's sick camel or horse. But the actual words and the fluidity with which they are used are as much a feature of the bargain as the substance of what is being offered. While few transactions can equal the vividness and passion of bettors in a Balinese cockfight (Geertz 1973), expressive gestures, changes in tone of voice and facial expressions, and impatient body movements form essential parts of the repertoire of strategies to negotiate a better price. Eloquent and articulate camp leaders can create substantially better deals than those who are reticent or retiring.[15]

The two facts about the markets for manure that impress themselves upon the observer are the unregulated and scattered nature of the markets and the range of variables that influence price. The exchanges are unregulated in the sense that no government authority interferes to constrain or fix the price of manure. Indeed, not only do governments refrain from setting prices but it is difficult even to imagine why or how they might interfere. The amounts that change hands are small; manure is traditionally, if incorrectly, regarded as possessing little value by urban-based (and urban-biased) administrators; and controls would be almost impossible to administer. The markets are scattered in the sense that there is no central or assigned space in which negotiations must take place. The price the raikas receive, therefore, is set through open negotiations between the farmer and the shepherd. Both the farmers and the shepherds are free to break off negotiations at any point they wish and seek a different partner. Given the mobility of raika camps, any formal attempt to coercively fix prices would be destined to fail.

Another way to focus on the nature of these exchanges is to view them in light of the difference Williamson and his coworkers have posited between markets and hierarchical exchanges (Williamson 1975, 1979, 1981; Williamson and Ouchi 1981). Exchanges that are uncertain in outcome, recur frequently, and require substantial transaction-specific investments, they argue, are likely to take place under hierarchical forms of organization. Those that have relatively few uncertainties attached to them, occur infrequently, and possess little asset or transaction specificity are likely to be organized through market institutions. Despite the functional nature of the argument, it fits the raikas' exchanges with farmers quite well. The raikas move frequently, seldom enter into more than one or two transactions with a farmer in the course of the annual migration, possess similar assets and have similar needs, and encounter relatively few uncertainties in any particular exchange.

An obvious question arises here. Why is it that the raikas do not enter stable exchange relationships with specific farmers along their migration routes, especially since the raika camps tend to follow the same general direction from one year to the next? By establishing recurrent exchange relations, perhaps analogous to patron-client relationships, they can reduce their search and negotiation costs, security risks, and the inherent uncertainty surrounding the search for a different farmer/host each day.

In fact, the raikas do try to cultivate particular farmers with whom they might have found their exchanges to be especially productive in an earlier year. When their sheep are sheared, for example, they tend to return to the same one or two farmers from one year to the next. Shearing requires up to a week, and without an understanding and helpful farmer/host it would be difficult to accomplish successfully. Yet the pattern of ecological variability and the logic of migration render impossible the pursuit of stable partners in whose fields the shepherds can camp each night. Because rainfall is highly variable, spatially as well as temporally, and the shepherds must reach their destinations in Haryana, Uttar Pradesh, or Madhya Pradesh in northern India by specific deadlines, it is impossible for them to go to the same farmers each year. In the direction of the fields of their preferred farmer, no rain may have fallen, and there might be no forage for their sheep at all.

The markets for manure, then, are not hierarchically regulated, nor does a centralizing tendency operate in spatial or social terms. A wide variety and range of factors influence the individual exchanges that set the price of manure. In their annual migrations, the raikas cross several agro-climatic zones, soils with varying features, land under different forms of ownership, small and large villages, and irrigated and fallow fields. Because they move to a new location almost every day, their relationships with settled populations are brief and fleeting. Each of these facts can be critical in influencing the value of their sheep manure. Both the raikas *and* their economic partners/ adversaries, the farmers, recognize the subtle ways in which these factors influence prices. The exchanges thus take place under conditions of open and widespread information availability. To the extent that these factors resemble the model of competitive market exchanges, some of the provocations the analysis raises possess wider resonance than just for the raikas.

STATISTICAL ANALYSIS

For the ensuing statistical analysis, I have used data on individual exchanges between shepherds and farmers that took place as the shepherds decided where to camp each night. A total of eighty-three observations constitute the data set. All data were collected between the months of November and May. Table 5.1 presents the basic descriptive statistics on the variables. Some interesting patterns can be discerned in the data about the preference of the raikas for irrigated fields and about the interrelations of irrigation, caste, and landholding as they affect price. For example, of the eighty-three instances in which the raikas camped in private fields, they used irrigated fields thirty-two times (38 percent). In the areas through which the raikas migrate, and where I collected the data (the districts of Jodhpur, Pali, Nagaur, Alwar, Bharatpur, Jaipur, and Ajmer), no more than 2 to 5 percent of the fields were irrigated.[16] It is clear that the shepherds have a strong preference for irrigated fields.

This preference translates into concrete returns. Whether we look at amounts the shepherds earned as a camp or at returns per sheep, irrigated fields led to higher average returns. The average return was Rs 45.1 for camping in fields without irrigation (Rs .89 per hundred sheep) and Rs 62.3 in the case of irrigated fields (Rs 1.17 per hundred sheep).[17] It seems safe to infer, then, that the shepherds demonstrate their preference for irrigated fields by seeking out a higher than average proportion of them. Further, they

Table 5.1   Basic Decriptive Statistics for the Analyzed Data

Variables	Mean	Standard Deviation	Minimum	Maximum
Price of manure per camp	51.77	20.72	15	110
Price per 1,000 sheep	9.97	3.78	3.53	22.73
Number of shepherd camps	2.82	1.05	1	5
Number of farmers	5.88	2.16	2	12
Number of sheep in a camp	5,375.90	1,502.89	2,300	7,300
Caste	.80	.41	0	1
Landholding size	.69	.47	0	1
Irrigation	.39	.49	0	1
Months until sowing	3.00	2.45	1	8

seem to derive the highest returns when they camp in fields of lower caste groups whose holdings are small or medium sized (Rs 1.30 per hundred sheep).

To assess statistically the relative influence of the entire set of variables on price, I use a multiple regression. Data on the dependent variable, "price received by the raikas for folding the sheep in the fields of the farmers," were in the form of either kilograms of grains or cash. Of the eighty-three exchanges on which I collected data, the shepherds received grain fifty-six times (68 percent), which seems to confirm a preference for in-kind exchanges on the part of the farmers as well as the shepherds. Using the prices for grain prevailing at the time of the fieldwork, all data have been converted into cash prices for the ensuing analysis.

I used seven independent variables as proxies for two different kinds of influence on price. Data on three variables, number of shepherd camps, number of farmers with whom the shepherd leader bargained, and the number of sheep in the camp (SHEPHERDS, FARMERS, and SHEEP1, respectively) signify the level of competition and the quantity of the manure being sold. I expect the price to be higher with a larger number of sheep and a higher number of farmers. A higher number of shepherd camps in the area should reduce the amount the raikas receive.

A second set of variables provides information on the participants in the bargaining process. The caste of the farmers, the size of farmers' landholdings, and whether the fields are irrigated are all coded as dichotomous variables. They represent the individual-specific variables for each transaction (the variable names are CASTE, LANDHOLDING, and IRRIGATION, respectively). Higher caste and landholding should help farmers negotiate a lower price for manure; irrigated fields should help the migrating shepherds get a better price since farmers will be more keen to have their fields fertilized. Finally, the number of months until the sowing season (MONTHS) represents seasonal variations in the price of manure that resulted from the individual farmer's desire to fertilize his fields. The greater the time before sowing, I hypothesize, the less the farmer will be willing to pay the shepherds.

Table 5.2 presents the results of the multiple regression. The independent variables were entered into the equation as two sets. First, to examine the influence of variables that were more closely associated with the characteristics of the participants in the individual transactions, the variables MONTHS, CASTE, LANDHOLDING, and IRRIGATION were used. SHEEP1 (number of sheep), SHEPHERDS (number of shepherds), and FARMERS (number of farmers) were entered together as the second block of variables. The first four together explained 28 percent of the variance in price; all the variables collectively explained 53 percent of the variance.[18]

Table 5.2   Results of Multiple Regression for Price

Variable	B	Standard error of B	β	t-value	Sig t
Months	−1.05	.71	−.12	−1.47	.14
Irrigation	9.81	3.94	.23	2.49	.01
Landholding	−7.96	3.81	−.18	−2.09	.04
Caste	−5.78	5.01	−.11	−1.15	.25
Sheep 1	.50	.11	.36	4.47	.00
Farmers	2.98	.79	.31	3.78	.00
Shepherds	−2.90	1.71	−.15	−1.69	.09
Constant	24.87	11.09		2.24	.03

Multiple R .73
R^2 .53 (adjusted R^2 .49)
Standard error 14.82
Analysis of variance

	df	Sum of squares	Mean square
Regression	7	18,740	2,677
Residual	75	16,479	219

$F = 12.18$ Sig F = .00

In terms of their influence on the dependent variable "price of manure" (positive or negative), all the variables have the expected sign. Further, all the variables, except CASTE and MONTHS are statistically significant (see table 5.2). While SHEEP 1 (number of sheep in a camp) has the highest t-value (greatest statistical significance), variables such as LANDHOLDING (holding size) and IRRIGATION (whether the field is irrigated) also emerge as highly statistically significant and as having a strong influence on the amount received by the shepherds. Counter to expectation, CASTE is statistically insignificant. One possible reason is that CASTE has a relatively high correlation with landholding size and irrigation. It is therefore possible that some of the independent effects of CASTE on PRICE might have been captured by the other two variables.

Overall, two aspects of the empirical findings bear reiteration. First, the entire set of independent variables explains just about half of the total observed variance in price. Variables such as the level of competition and quantity are usually presumed to be instrumental in explaining price. But these factors, even together with several others regarding the characteristics of the parties to the negotiations, remain incomplete predictors of why negotiated prices show such a wide range. The observation points to the tremendous diversity, and difficulty, in capturing quantitatively the nature of variables that influence prices. Some of these variables might relate to the different negotiating abilities of the farmers and the shepherd leaders. Other influences may stem from differences in actual or implied obligations that attend a given settlement but remain unexpressed in the selected variables.[19]

Second, variables specific to individual participants, by themselves, account for nearly half of the explained variance in price. While economic theory places great stress on factors such as quantity and competition as the ones most critical in explaining prices, these factors are not the only significant ones in the case of the raikas. Irrigation or holding size seem to be just as important in determining prices as the numbers of sheep, farmers, or shepherds. In part, this points to the overall asymmetry in power relations that characterizes the context in which the raikas and the farmers come into contact.

One indicator of a systematic asymmetry in bargaining relations seems to be the depressed price of manure during migration. During monsoons, when the raikas are back in their villages, they can sell manure at consistently higher rates. According to a number of conversations, nightly droppings from a flock of 200 to 250 sheep can be sold for Rs 5.00 when the raikas are in their own homes (Rs 20.00 for 1,000 sheep). The average return they receive for the same amount of manure during migration is just about half — Rs 9.97 for the nightly droppings of 1,000 sheep.[20]

BARTER OR COMMODITY EXCHANGE?

The description of the exchanges between the raikas and the farmers raises doubts about two orthodoxies regarding barter and commodity exchanges — one the product of anthropological writings, the other resulting from economists' discussions. A large literature in anthropology has attempted to separate barter from other types of exchange (such as redistributive exchanges) but especially from gift and commodity exchange. Independent theories of gift and commodity exchange exist. Barter has attracted far more limited attention. Often barter is seen simply as a precursor to commodity exchange. Economic literature, on the other hand, has taken the difference between barter and commodity exchange as obvious, using as the criterion whether money as a numeraire is involved. This literature has sought, in addition, to demonstrate the inferiority of barter to monetary exchanges.

In the raikas' case, of course, it seems to make no sense to insist on separating barter from commodity exchange. The fact that they seem willing to shift between money and grain for the droppings of their sheep, and that these exchanges are located in a wider political economy that is thoroughly imbued with the influence of money, suggest the pointlessness of such an argument. One might paraphrase Braudel to argue that, while it is all too easy to call one form of exchange barter and the other monetary, in real life exchanges possess characteristics of both (1985: 227). The analytical point, however, remains. Does it make sense to separate barter from monetary exchange on other, more theoretical grounds?

Barter is presumed to take place without the mediating influence of money, between single "buyers" and "sellers." In such exchanges, protagonists, who are essentially free and equal, demand particular goods and services. Their demands result from their interests in the direct consumption value of the objects being exchanged (Humphrey and Hugh-Jones 1992: 1; Simmel 1978). The rate of exchange cannot be assessed with reference to any external criteria of value, and the act itself might be transformative in nature in that it might move objects between "regimes of value" (Appadurai 1986a: 2; Strathern 1992). These features—absence of money or, more generally, of some other external criterion of value; interest in direct consumption; and movement of objects across culturally incongruent spaces—characterize barter "pure and simple"[21] and presumably set it apart from gift and commodity exchange.

Although initially persuasive, the above criteria are not sufficient to set barter apart as a particular form of exchange in its own right, nor do they coalesce into a theory of barter. Of the three features believed to characterize barter, perhaps the most critical is the belief that in barter the terms of trade (and therefore the value of exchanged goods) emerge out of the transaction itself. That is to say, the value of articles that are exchanged in barter is determined in the process of barter since external criteria of value are lacking in contexts where barter is the mode of exchange. But posing the lack of external criteria of value as a characteristic of barter is highly misleading. Without external criteria of value, no exchanges could possibly take place. Objects gain value only in relation to other objects and persons, indeed, only in relation to entire systems of signification, meaning, and value production. While there is a kernel of truth in Appadurai's assertion that it is exchange that creates value by setting the parameters of utility and scarcity, his statement downplays a large part of the picture by suggesting that processes of exchange can be autonomous from those of production and consumption. It would be far more accurate to say that the same matrices of social relations that create scarcity and utility are also the ones that impel exchange.

Within the process of exchange, value may indeed be created depending on the resources participants bring to the transaction, how negotiations unfold, and what influences them — issues that correspond to what Appadurai terms the politicization of exchange. But it is worth keeping in mind that these aspects of exchange are neither independent of the forces whereby participants in the exchange process come to possess the articles they are exchanging nor unrelated to the reasons why particular individuals wish to exchange products. Exchange, then, is neither autonomous of the social contexts in which it takes place nor separable from processes of production and consumption when we think of value.

Analysis is constrained unproductively by the idea that the process of production (even in combination with transportation, storage, and appropriation) infuses an object with a preliminary value, which is finally modified during exchange and consumption. In the case of the raikas and the farmers, the reasons why one group sells manure and the other pays in grain or cash, why one group migrates and the other lives in permanent settlements, why one group actively negotiates but ultimately accepts highly depressed prices while the other succeeds in holding prices down even without collusion are not unrelated historical or empirical accidents. Specific relations of production between animals, land, and humans, implicitly unequal relations of domination and marginalization that describe how the raikas and the farmers connect with centers of political and coercive power, physical aspects of ecological variability that affect the raikas and the farmers differently — all of these help explain the different value placed on manure-grain exchanges in particular transactions.

These relationships, in turn, need to be connected to the location of the raikas in the political economy of agricultural production in a country where irrigated agriculture finds the greatest support from the state and grazing animals and their keepers are presumed a priori to be wasteful resource users. Transactions, by themselves, create value in only a limited sense.

This is worth reiterating. Exchange on its own can be seen as neither the generator of value nor its proximate modifier.[22] Its relation to value can only be assessed together with its connection to production, transportation, storage, appropriation, advertising, consumption, and the other socioeconomic processes that create objects as articles fit for consumption. It might be analytically convenient to designate exchange as the locus of value, but such convenience is bought at a high price. First, it suggests that exchange relations can be extracted from the network of other political, social, and economic relations among which they are located and from which they gain their meaning and value. Second, it marginalizes the importance of the other processes that assist in making objects fit for exchange, whether they be labor or advertising.

Marx's note on this is instructive. He criticized the Gotha Program for defining labor as "the source of all wealth and all culture" ([1875] 1972: 8). But in saying "the man who possesses no other property than his labor power" must of necessity become "the slave of other men who have made themselves the owners of the objective conditions of labor" (9),[23] he moved in a different direction, locating the creation of "value" in the ownership of productive resources: "the objective conditions of labor." Interpreted sympathetically, without interrogating the notion of ownership and its difficult relationship with power, what Marx asserted is obviously correct. But to discuss value we must extend Marx's use of *ownership* beyond merely the ownership of means of production. We must relate ownership to control and include in it the ways in which wants and desires can be manufactured by manipulating signs. Ownership of productive resources generates value only in combination with control over the ability to process, exchange, transport, store, and create new needs and desires.

The point applies to all attempts to locate value in a specific stage of the entire process whereby objects are consumed. Consider, for example, an emerging literature that holds practices and meanings associated with consumption to be the source of value. The focus on consumption is seen to be especially appropriate in a global economy that is increasingly driven by the demands of fashion conscious consumers, by the creation of needs through advertising, and by retail houses that dominate producers (Miller 1995). The end of political economy, production, and labor proclaimed by Baudrillard (1993) leads logically to a focus on the sign value of objects as they are consumed, rendering consumption and its logic the organizing principle of society.[24]

It is possible at specific historical junctures or in given social-spatial contexts, perhaps, that a particular stage leading to consumption might constitute the critical point from which power can be leveraged to manipulate value. But this cannot be taken as a general theoretical conclusion about the significance of that particular stage globally or historically. In the context of the raikas' exchange with farmers, it appears that the fact of their mobility and lack of legally defensible access to pastoral resources diminishes their ability to gain the appropriate value for the products they exchange. As the raikas would say, "the one who owns the land holds the power." Not to respect the specificity of this assertion, and to conclude instead that control over land, or stable, stationary production activities will always be the most significant factor in determining value, would be too quick a jump. It is necessary, if one wishes to gain an understanding of what makes an object valuable, to look at the ensemble of social relations in which production, exchange, consumption, and other related processes are located.

Similarly, money or its lack becomes a measure of the extent to which exchanges can be quantified more or less accurately, especially by an outside observer, rather than constituting a qualitative break between barter and monetary exchange. By the same token, the belief that barter results in the movement of objects across regimes of value does not necessarily set it apart from other forms of exchange. Monetary and gift exchanges can result in similar transfers of objects across culturally incongruous spaces. Indeed, as Humphrey and Hugh-Jones (1992) and Strathern (1992) point out, the same exchange can be viewed by different parties as belonging to separate universes. It is unlikely that there is anything inherent in the exchange itself that marks it as a commodity, barter, or gift exchange.[25] Just as objects gain their value in a web of relations among things and persons, so, too, do exchanges gain a marker from the manner of their social implication. If it does not make sense to ask how many oxen a statue is worth, it also does not make sense to ask how much money a tube of toothpaste is worth. In both instances, a host of contextual factors define "worth."

Economists characterize barter using the important concepts of marginal utility and trust. Three criteria are seen to be especially critical. According to Marshall, the marginal utility of bartered objects diminishes for both parties, but in the case of monetary exchanges the marginal utility of the exchanged object for one of the parties, the one that receives money, is practically constant (1920). According to Anderlini and Sabourian (1992: 100), the differences between barter, monetary exchange, and credit exchange can be viewed as originating in different degrees of trust in an economic system. In the case of barter, no trust is present and therefore traders do not take on commodities they ultimately do not want; in monetary exchanges, traders trust the monetary system, and credit implies that traders trust each other.[26] Finally, many economists have argued that barter is comparatively more inefficient than monetary exchanges.

The arguments above, while commonsensical, are not compelling. It might seem that barter takes place primarily on the basis of the interest in the objects being offered for exchange. But barter participants might also be willing to exchange if they can trade new acquisitions with others. Relatedly, the marginal utility of money may change more slowly than that of objects such as grain or manure! But it does decline for individuals, just as the marginal utility of other objects diminishes. An extra dollar is unlikely to have the same utility for a poor individual after he or she wins the lottery.

Second, to the extent that barter transactions can be deferred, in the sense that an individual delivers goods in exchange for a promise of payment, there is no reason why barter partners cannot have trust in each other (Humphrey and Hugh-Jones 1992). The idea that barter transactions are complete upon the exchange of a given commodity is a misconception no different from the belief that monetary transactions in a supermarket are concluded upon the payment of cash for commodities purchased.[27] In both cases, the negotiating parties cannot avoid a more extended, if implicit and informal, contractual relationship because of uncertainties inherent in all contractual transactions (Kreps 1990). Thus, for the raikas the face-to-face transaction that concludes with the payment of grain or cash by the farmers and the depositing of manure in the fields by the sheep contains additional uncertain obligations as well. Shepherds may call upon farmers for aid if they are harassed or their sheep are stolen. The farmers, similarly, expect and are given the assurance that sheep will not wander from fallow areas nor graze in planted fields. In the case of all transactions, then, there is a lingering trace whose precise outlines depend on the social context in which the transactions take place and on the fact that all commodities possess multiple, only incompletely specifiable attributes.[28]

Finally, while economists tend to focus on efficiency losses resulting from barter, there can be many reasons why different parties to an exchange would prefer barter to monetary exchange and why this might in fact be more efficient for them. For example, the preference for grain on the part of the shepherds as well as the farmers exists for fairly obvious reasons. The shepherds, in receiving grain, are saved the trouble of visiting markets to purchase this bulky item of daily subsistence; the farmers, by paying in the form of grain, raise the value of what they pay. The raikas would pay retail prices, usually 10 to 15 percent higher, for the grain they would purchase in the market. The farmers, if they sold the grain in the market, could charge only wholesale prices. The raikas, therefore, value the grain they receive for manure more highly than the farmers selling it do. Who appropriates the value at the margin depends on the negotiating abilities, existing needs, relative endowments, and political station of the parties to the exchange.

PRICE FORMATION IN FREE MARKETS?

Regardless of whether the grain/cash and manure exchanges are viewed as barter or monetary, they are, nonetheless, market exchanges. The concrete characteristics of these markets are that they are decentralized and unregulated, participation is voluntary, and exchanges are free, competitive, and take place in face-to-face negotiations. Neither the farmers nor the shepherds are under any compulsion to negotiate a deal successfully. Given that it is possible to use money as a numeraire to externally assess the value of transactions, the question automatically raised is the extent to which prices that emerge in these exchanges are formed in a process that might be recognizable as the neoclassical account of price formation.

Prices are central to the operations of markets. According to Polanyi, "[b]y concentrating on price as the economic fact *par excellence*, the formal method of approach offers a total description of the economy as determined by choices induced by an insufficiency of means" (1957: 33). The centrality of prices is demonstrated as well in policy injunctions to "get the prices right." Once appropriate prices prevail, market reformers would assert, not only will the macroeconomy revive but different segments of the population will enjoy greater opportunities. Indeed, the force of economic rationality attributed to right prices is only compounded by the rhetorical and ethical weight attributed to price-making markets.

> Democracy and the market economy have survived the battle of the systems. The recent downfall of communism in many countries has shown the inferiority of the underlying economic system in supplying people with the means of material well-being. (Siebert 1994: v)

Surely there is much that appeals in the exhortation to focus on prices and allow unregulated prices to prevail. But the analytical punch of the simple maxim, "get the prices right," can easily be lost in its usefulness as populist rhetoric. At one level, if prices are simply the products of existing levels of demand and supply, all prices are tautologically "right." But if they are right only in relation to some mix of forces that *should* determine levels of demand and supply, any attempt to practice the maxim is bound to become mired in a tangle of conceptual and practical difficulties. Prices are certainly central to understanding outcomes in an economy. But a focus on understanding their formation must be coextensive with a focus on the wider social and political forces that are critical to the operations of markets. Focusing simply on prices, as shaped by scarcity and choice, can only help resuscitate the sterile formalist-substantivist divide.[29] Instead, even as one examines exchanges, one must trace the manner in which they are shaped by pervasive non-economic forces in order to understand why particular prices prevail.[30]

In this context, opposing views can be elaborated regarding price formation. One holds that the economy is inextricably suffused with power and passions; the other would suggest that prices in unregulated markets are the objective outcome of the forces of demand and supply. Weber articulates the first position as follows:

> Money prices are the product of conflicts of interest and of compromises; they thus result from power constellations. Money is not a mere

"voucher for unspecified utilities," which could be altered at will without any fundamental effect on the character of the price system as a struggle of man against man. "Money" is, rather, primarily a weapon in this struggle. ([1922] 1978: 108, cited in Granovetter and Swedberg 1992: 8–9)

Contrast this position with the one to be found in any standard undergraduate economics textbook, in which prices are determined by the intersection of demand and supply curves and buyers and sellers have little capacity to influence prices unless they are capable of colluding. Shifts and movements of these curves and how multiple buyers and sellers aggregate their desires into demand and supply schedules remain underexamined.

The question of how numerous independent buyers and sellers enter mutually beneficial exchanges that could take place at the same price throughout a market, but without collusion among the market participants, becomes deeply puzzling. One example of how an aggregate level such as a price comes into being as a result of many independent transactions is the process whereby the raika shepherds make deals with farmers.[31] They meet a number of farmers (and the farmers meet a number of shepherds) to negotiate the best price. Negotiations over the appropriate rate of exchange inform the different parties about the range in which returns are likely to lie on a given day. Costs involved in locating buyers (or sellers) contribute to variation in the prices ultimately secured.

But, if prices emerge in real markets as a consequence of negotiations among buyers and sellers, and these buyers and sellers incur search costs in the process of locating a suitable transaction partner, the fiction that market participants are price takers without the capacity to influence the prices they encounter is revealed primarily as a convenient analytical fiction. In the presence of many independent sellers and buyers, and of costs of searching, one is likely to discover multiple local price equilibria that depend on a host of factors specific to the local context. This is precisely what we observe in the case of the raikas. The shepherds and farmers negotiate constantly, their negotiations are as valuable for creating exchanges as for providing information to conduct the best possible exchange, and there is considerable variation in the price at which the transactions take place.

While there is considerable variation in prices and no collusion among buyers and sellers, these facts say little about whether political forces are significant in exerting a systematic or structuring influence on the negotiated prices. A large literature on rural markets documents the importance of social and political forces that shape economic outcomes, including that economic fact par excellence, "price." Fairhead (1993), for example, shows in an African rural context how powerful mercantile or government actors can stand between peasants and wider political-economic arrangements, preventing "right prices" from emerging until relations of domination and hierarchy have been challenged and dismantled. Berry (1992: 11–14), noting the pervasive influence of negotiations in African economic life, questions the separation between economic and political processes. Bates (1981) provides powerful evidence to show the intermeshed nature of political and economic forces in shaping markets as arenas of exchange. The writings of several Indian economists show how private trade might be synonymous with unfree markets (Bhaduri 1986; Sen 1981). Where markets for labor, land, credit, and commodities are interlocked, poor producers may find it necessary to sell a substantial part of their harvest to pay debts when they might have preferred to wait for better prices later in the year. To meet the resulting subsistence gap, they may be forced to buy back basic foods at higher prices later in the year, often after they have been driven deeper into debt.

One might disagree with the precise strategy or rhetoric deployed in these arguments. But they, and other examples, provide persuasive evidence on how collusive practices, intentionally exercised by powerful actors, can systematically structure market outcomes against more marginal social actors. The case of the raikas, however, is somewhat different because of their mobility. Because they are mobile and can negotiate with a number of farmers, they have few long-lasting relationships with specific farmers that must be prolonged to make migration successful. Farmers, similarly, have no special need to complete successful negotiations with a shepherd. The process of negotiation and the articulatory abilities of the participants are critical as well to the actual terms on which the deal is struck. Interlocked markets or specific mercantile/government/feudal actors are not, therefore, the obstacles to the emergence of more favorable prices for the shepherds. But, despite the fact that the transactions among the farmers and shepherds are voluntary, that each group has access to several different negotiating partners, and that neither has a particularly pressing and unavoidable need for what the other is offering, we find that the average price the shepherds are able to charge for their sheep manure is less than half of what they might get if they were selling the same manure at home.

Some elements in the explanation of this asymmetry are obvious. The raikas are away from their homes, moving through the villages and territories of strangers. The farmers, on the other hand, negotiate from a position of greater strength in that they own the land on which sheep graze, are located in their own homes, and are part of local social networks. With the increased availability of chemical fertilizers in recent years, the farmers' need for sheep manure has become less pressing. For the raikas, however, the need to migrate has continued to grow, as grazing land has declined in the entire state but especially in the west. In addition, while the raikas like to camp on the irrigated fields of larger farmers because that choice offers greater security, the decision also implies that they negotiate with the more powerful members of a village community. Finally, there is also a structural asymmetry in the bargaining position of the shepherds versus the farmers.[32] The farmer can afford to wait several days if the bargaining process does not go well. The average of 2.8 shepherd camps that might be present near the fields of the farmer on any given day, then, is somewhat misleading. Over the course of a week, a farmer may come into contact with twenty to twenty-five shepherds. The shepherds, because they are mobile, can travel to and negotiate with a larger number of farmers in a day, but precisely because they set up camp in a new location almost every day they have to negotiate with the set of farmers they can meet in a single day. If their negotiations with farmers fail, they are likely to spend the night on public or common lands where they will not get any returns for manure at all.[33] The ability of the farmers to wait and the need of the shepherds to negotiate a deal every day they move is yet another reason why the farmers hold a somewhat superior hand.

This discussion has attempted to make one major point. Even when participants in a given transaction are jurally and formally equal, even when the transactions are voluntary and free, and even when the actors involved in transactions significantly influence prices through their negotiating abilities, the outcomes are unavoidably and systematically inflected by politics and the everyday social relations and production processes that lead to the transactions. A number of theorists have pointed to the political influence that the state exercises upon the organization of markets and the operation of market forces. But political influences on markets are far more pervasive, subtle, and universal than one can appreciate and understand by considering the impact of state policies alone. Social and political effects need not be explicitly asymmetric in their nature or orientation, nor obviously inequitable. Yet, because economic actors are inevitably ensnared in political and structural relations that cannot be divorced from their economic positions and activities, it would be unimaginative to assume that somehow their economic negotiations are independent of who they are.

Consider, for instance, a different way in which these social and political influences operate upon the exchanges between the raikas and the farmers, in this case to the advantage of the shepherds. Recall that the raikas often prefer to camp in the fields of the better-off, larger, upper caste landowners in a village, despite the fact that this choice yields them somewhat lower prices for their sheep manure. Their expectation, in return, is that they will risk a lower probability of harassment or theft if they are camped in the fields of larger landowners. Further, if harassment or theft does take place, they hope to appeal to the honor of the landlord to seek redress and assistance. Indeed, the landlord's status may be adversely impacted if the shepherds suffer loss, theft, or humiliation while camped on his fields, nominally under his protection. This complex nexus of social, political, and cultural expectations and relationships is inextricably bound to that seemingly autonomous economic figure — price — which is supposed to be governed only by the economic laws of demand and supply.

Summary

The description and investigation of the grain or cash for manure exchanges shows the circumscribed influence of factors that are normally seen to be the most critical in explaining prices: quantity and levels of demand and supply. The statistical exercise indicates the important influence of transaction- and individual-specific factors on price levels: landholding size, irrigation, and negotiating abilities. In addition, the data are highly suggestive of the ways in which multiple aspects of the sociocultural context — the power of different actors, their ability to wait for the opportune moment to strike a bargain, the web of mutual expectations, and asymmetric social relations — emerge as extremely significant in influencing price. The importance of the context becomes starkly obvious in the case of the raikas precisely because there is substantial variation from one negotiating situation to the other. Such variation, because it is mostly absent from what we usually see as markets, tends to be ignored in considerations of price formation. The raikas' exchanges, because they differ in many ways from our usual intuitions about markets even as they resemble competitive markets in important respects, allow us to explore the significance of social and political influences on prices.

The case of the raikas also illustrates the difficulty of separating barter from commodity transactions. Many of the transactions lie on the cusp of this often taken for granted division. More importantly, however, the analysis of these transactions allows a critical exploration of the theoretical reasons usually advanced to justify the separation of barter and monetary exchange. The arguments I offer strengthen other critiques that have questioned a strict separation between gift, barter, and commodity transactions.

Finally, the chapter examines the theoretical ambition in some existing writings to relate value to particular stages in the life of a commodity: production, exchange, and consumption. While exchange is clearly a significant step in the creation of a commodity, it is difficult to accept that it, or other stages, can create value on its own. We must pay attention to the relations within the ambit of which particular commodities are produced, exchanged, and consumed (or transported, stored, and appropriated). Only then can we meaningfully answer the question "What creates value?"

The conditions of rootlessness and mobility that Clifford identifies as the concomitant of modernity (1988: 3) are usually seen to corrode community. After all, our definitions and understandings of community come wrapped in metaphors of stability, continuity, and sympathetic engagement. Some scholars see a community as a group of people who have common beliefs and preferences. Its membership does not change too rapidly, and its members interact over extended time periods about multiple issues (Singleton and Taylor 1992). Such an understanding seems intuitively correct, even obvious. We can note that none of these aspects of community are particular to settled populations. Yet it is hard to imagine how one could live in a community in the absence of links to a place. Settlement seems necessary for community, even if for only instrumental reasons. It potentially reduces the costs of shared beliefs or stable group membership and allows multifaceted interactions to be continuous.

But travel and movement, increasing with modernity, reduce the likelihood of individuals meeting each other over sustained periods. Multistranded relationships that are the presumed hallmark of community begin to change, replaced with unidimensional interactions. Individuals, when they are not part of a given space, are more likely to be exposed to many different ways of doing things, of striving for objectives, of defining what is desirable. They are likely to have fewer grounds for sharing normative beliefs and preferences. Each of these developments connected with movement goes against the grain of conventional understandings of community. It is not surprising that discussions of community take it for granted that it is to be found connected to a place and that its members will have resided in that place for an extended time.

The mobility and the "homelessness" of the raikas exists, however, with an enormously lively sense of community among them. They see themselves as a community of wanderers, but wanderers with a sense of purpose, even pride.

"Our home is under the sky. Our village is the forest. For 300 days out of the 365 we are on the road. Using the motor road, you get to your destination quickly. But we move along the thin, narrow, by-paths in the fields. Others would get lost [on these paths]. Instead of taking us to the end of a journey, these paths always take us to new places. Each new place is a destination. In each new place, we again sleep under the sky, on the ground in the open fields, our staffs our pillows. Our home is the sky. I find it wherever we go." These words of Kanaramji, with their haunting lyrical quality, are marked by a quiet self-assurance that was strangely at odds with other sentiments of deprivation and marginalization that the raikas sometimes expressed. But perhaps the explanation is simple—Kanaramji was speaking about movement, a condition that he has experienced so regularly it is now a part of his very being. Those who lead a settled life might find it hard to imagine how comfort can be gained from a condition of constant movement and newness. Kanaramji, even when he complained about his life and the need to travel more or less every day, did not think it odd that his sense of community grew out of his familiarity with travel.

We often take particular kinds of social collectivities to be synonymous with community—e.g., villages and neighborhoods. The following two chapters on community, however, proceed on the basis of a doubt regarding the naturalness of any community. Rather than taking the existence of community for granted in groups that are attached to a place and seeing place-based attachments as a defining feature of the possibility of community, I explore the idea that a sense of community must always be constructed. The mobility of the raikas and their strong communities make such doubt inevitable but make its exploration satisfying. I examine what is critical for the creation of communities when the gratifying fixity of spatial association dissolves in the uncertainties introduced by movement.

When association with a place becomes difficult owing to constant movement, members of a group must rely on other markers of their shared fate if they are to construct community. Place, perhaps, is always simply a proxy for these other markers, whose existence comes into sharper focus only when we no longer take place for granted. Lacking a familiar geography from one day to the next, shepherds in the mobile camp focus on their shared histories and common activities. Such a focus on the collective and how it is strengthened or undermined leads to a far more conscious investment in the everyday building of community. This investment in community is evident from the enormous range of tasks in the camp that are shared and performed collectively.

Conscious attempts to invest in community become especially critical when groups and individuals possess the mutual ability to disengage from interactions voluntarily. When life is lived in close proximity, it creates interactions that are routine and frequent. The problems involved in building community are of a quite different type when even the proximity and interactions themselves have to be created. The raikas must decide who it is they will meet as they migrate, in whose fields it would be best to spend the night. They must try to recall the pasts in which particular farmers may have helped during some minor crisis. Because the shepherds are not tied to any particular farmer, the community they construct with farmers must be advantageous to both. Mobility, as it opens a plethora of new possibilities for creating community, also makes community harder to achieve.

> My home is with us. My village is the mobile camp. It [the camp] is all my relatives and friends who have left their homes and come with their sheep and with whom I am traveling this year. Every year, my village is in a different place because there is a different group that makes up the camp. Because every year my village is different, I can talk to a lot of different people. It would be the same story in the village also, even if I didn't travel the whole year. Everyone changes — then they become different people. There are other things that are the same between the village and our camp. In the village there is a panchayat. We also have one. Both these panchayats help their people. Villagers have a sarpanch. We have our nambardar. But we are better. We have food for our sheep, we go when we want, wherever we want. Villagers have to stay in one place, and during the famine they follow our example. But, of course, moving all the time is not easy. That is why we move in a group. And as a group we have all the problems that people living in one place face. A kitchen that has many pots and pans will also have the noise of them banging together. But if all the pots and pans were not there, how would you cook?

These compelling words from a young shepherd, comparing the village home with home in the camp, bring to life the social investments raikas make to construct community.

The attempts of the raikas to construct community within their camps and with farmers are based on a solid foundation of common interests. The organization of camp life to meet common goals is part of the story that chapter 6 tells. It describes the everyday practices of decision allocation in the mobile camps. Allocation and delegation of decision making is the fulcrum upon which all collective organization of social tasks hinges. Without effective allocation of the power to make decisions, the lives of the shepherds on the road would be impossible. In the performance of allocated tasks lies the seed of community. It is doubtful whether community leads to common interests, but without common interests there can be no community.

Not only do the shepherds seem to dwell within a community as they move through the landscape, but they also cultivate communities with settled farmers along the way. "My home is back in village Patawal. But it is also here in the dang. And it is also wherever we camp for the night. And sometimes, we become so friendly with farmers along the way that their homes become like our own homes. But none of these come easy. We have to work with each other. We have to give a little if we want a little." Kanaramji's words, using home as the figure signifying community, describe the multiplicity of ways in which shepherds imagine community. To each of these "imagined communities," giving is necessary, he seems to be saying.

In many instances, especially when their sheep are sheared, the shepherds spend several days with a farmer. Often they go out of their way to ensure a visit to a farmer with whom they might have fared well during a previous migration. They remember times shared with farmer friends with fondness and affection. Such relations and recollections are the grist that occupies the interstitial spaces of the social matrices out of which communities emerge. They are especially important for mobile groups. Only through conscious and consistent efforts to reiterate and renew interactions with well-remembered friends can a mobile group create community of any sort.

The raikas' lives can be conceptualized as an image that contests other stereotypical conceptions of migrancy and nomadism as well. In anthropology, as Tsing points out, "nomadism is understood as a repetitive, tradition-bound mobility" (1993: 150). If repetition and tradition figure as counters to reflection and forethought, they describe little of the different aspects of the raikas' mobile lives. Indeed, mobility may be seen as the liquid hammer that shatters tradition conceptualized as binding rules. In this sense, one might even wonder to what extent any migrant or nomadic lifestyle can be described using metaphors of repetition and tradition. If activities in raika mobile camps are to be understood in terms of tradition at all, the meaning of tradition itself must undergo revision. Rather than being the incubus of the past weighing upon the chest of the present, tradition and custom can more appropriately be seen as flexible, discretionary, and dynamic guides to action.

Community is also usually imagined in opposition to hierarchy. That the opposition cannot be sustained should be obvious. Indeed, a number of theorists have remarked on it. But that community might be impossible without hierarchy, and without its successful negotiation, is what the example of the raikas suggests to us. Among the raikas, socially equal members seek subsistence together as a mobile community. But this formal equality is underwritten by subtle hierarchical relations. Hierarchy based upon functional specialization, it might be argued, makes formal equality possible among the raikas. At the same time, to prevent hierarchical relations from becoming exploitative, the shepherds observe and monitor the behavior of their leaders using mechanisms that are integral to daily life (chapter 7).

The use of a simple formal model from game theory to analyze the institutionalized dynamics of authority relations between the shepherds and their leaders illustrates several aspects of hierarchical interactions. Chief among them is the relative weight shepherds place upon monitoring the actions of their leaders ex ante rather than trying to sanction leaders ex post for abuse of authority. Because shepherds and their leaders understand well the expectations embodied in their relationship, the political aspects of their everyday interactions are seldom casually observable. The principal-agent analysis I offer not only explicitly incorporates relations of power, but it politicizes what might otherwise be seen simply as normal social relations. The very terminology of the analysis marks an interpretive break because it forces a different look at the interactions of the shepherds with their leaders. It is this possibility of understanding yet another way in which power works that motivates the use of a game-theoretic analysis in chapter 7.

We have repeatedly been compelled to draw a basic lesson . . . that *nonmarket* institutions are organized to promote *economic* objectives. — Robert Bates, 1989

If there is one rule of conduct whose moral character is undisputed, it is that which decrees that we should realize in ourselves the essential features of the collective type. — Emile Durkheim, 1933

This chapter investigates the construction of community in the raika migrating camps in the absence of their attachment to a specific place. The raikas' camps are constructed afresh each year, and during their annual migrations they move their camps almost every day. Lack of connection to a place introduces uncertainties and irregularities of interaction. The raikas contend with these by delinking community-building efforts from territory toward sociality. Common understandings among raikas about who will make decisions related to the success of migration form the scaffolding around which community is created. The perspective used in this chapter suggests that community requires active attempts at construction rather than existing naturally or being a primordial entity. Further, instead of being different from or opposed to rational calculations of self-interest, the cultivation of community in the raika camps goes hand in hand with the rational calculus over what would be in the material interest of the shepherds.

The distribution of decision-making powers in the migrating camp among different centers of authority and the efficient performance of allocated responsibilities are the concrete means through which community is secured. Allocation is critical to the smooth functioning of the mobile camp as the raikas move through unfamiliar territories.[1] The discussion of decision-making responsibilities is necessary for instrumental reasons. It furthers our understanding of how the raika camp functions. It also provides a basis for understanding the raikas' efforts to construct community. But the discussion is valuable in itself as well. Because mobile pastoralism constitutes a mode of production and livelihood dramatically different from settled agriculture (Kroeber 1948; Sadr 1991; Sandford 1983: 1–3) and because millions continue to depend on it as a source of livelihood, the decision-making institutions of pastoralists retain pertinence for the practically as well as the theoretically inclined.[2] Nonetheless, as Niamir points out in an early comprehensive review of the African literature on pastoralists (1990),[3] few studies treat this issue. The situation has not changed in recent years.

After briefly discussing the relationship between community, place, and decision making, I describe the three groups of decision makers among the raikas and their strengths and weaknesses. Different decisions made in the migrant camps require particular kinds of expertise among those who make decisions. I outline the major types of decisions and the capabilities each set of decisions requires. The discussion sets the stage for explaining why specific types of decisions are made by particular decision makers and how placeless communities come about in the course of migration.

COMMUNITY, PLACE, AND DECISION MAKING

Community can denote a set of feelings shared by a group of people: a community of understanding. It can also stand, more loosely, for a minority group — such as the gay community or the African-American community. Communities of purpose and communities of choice are other ways in which the term has been used (Friedman 1989; Garber 1995; Young 1990).[4] But where *community* refers to a small group of people who interact with each other regularly and along multiple dimensions, and where this group collectively depends on certain resources for its livelihood, the idea of community goes hand in hand with place. Both scholarly analyses and popular understandings of community take its relationship with place as essential to its creation and maintenance[5] to such an extent that without links to some fixed place it becomes almost impossible to imagine a small community.[6]

Political theorists writing about community seldom examine its links with place — either because they take the connections for granted or because they do not consider them critical.[7] But as soon as we consider a group of people, such as the raikas, who do not have a long-term relationship with a given place, even other "self-evident" aspects of community are cast into sharp relief. The raikas move virtually every day en route to their destination and during the return journey.[8] Their camps, however, can exist only because they rely extensively on the many attributes of community: shared meanings and values, regular and multiplex interactions, stable membership, expectations on the part of the members that they will continue to interact for some time to come, and mutual vulnerability (Etzioni 1996: 305; Taylor 1982).[9] Many of these aspects of community, often available to settled groups simply as a side-effect of their existence, become objectives toward which the shepherds must expend some effort. Only through great social effort can they overcome the uncertainties and irregularities of interactions introduced by the lack of connection to a specific place.

The discussion of decision making is critical to the interpretation I offer. Appropriate allocation of decision-making tasks to solve the foreseeable problems of a mobile life facilitates the construction of community. It becomes possible for the ordinary shepherd in the camp to feel secure about the group and his position in it and accept the collective tasks enjoined as part of group membership. The appropriate allocation of decisions not only facilitates the achievement of the normal conditions of community, and thus the internal workings of the camp, but it also helps the raikas to migrate successfully in an indifferent, sometimes hostile environment.

Recall that to unravel problems stemming from environmental risks[10] the raikas employ a number of strategies: diversification, storage (on the hoof), exchange, and, most significantly, mobility (Halstead and O'Shea 1989: 1– 3). Indeed, collective mobility in the face of environmental risks undergirds the survival of the raika pastoralists, as chapter 4 suggests. Successful collective mobility also requires that the shepherds carefully order the division of tasks and decision making in the camp and prevent abuse of authority.

RAIKAS AND THEIR DECISION MAKERS

The decision-making arrangements that exist among the raikas are best conceptualized as informal institutions. They are informal because they are neither codified nor legally incumbent upon different groups. They are institutions because they structure, constrain, facilitate, and create interactions and behavior (Bates 1989; North 1990). The necessary decisions in the shepherd camps are made by one or more of three existing centers of decision making. Of these, the nambardar—the leader of the camp—is the most important. He is an influential shepherd who boasts wide-ranging contacts among other shepherds, farmers, wool and sheep merchants, and on occasion even government officials. He is familiar with a variety of issues relating to migration routes, the movements of other shepherd camps, outsiders such as government officials and farmers, the purchase of supplies, and the sale of pastoral products. His past experience and access to sources of information ensure that decisions will not suffer from a lack of information.

The second in command in the camp is the kamdar. He assumes the duties of the camp leader when the leader is sick or away from the camp. Since both perform the same duties, I will not treat them as different loci of decision making. Usually the second in command plays a role as a member of the Council of Elders in the camp. The council comprises five of the older and more experienced persons in the camp. The members of the council tend to represent the spectrum of different interests in the camp since they often were responsible for mobilizing the shepherd groups that created it. They also may be from different villages. Collectively, they possess information and experience that no other decision maker in the camp can match. Finally, there are the *mukhiyas*, the leaders of the individual flock units that comprise the mobile camp. Each is intimately familiar with his flock and its dynamics.[11]

The choice of particular individuals for any of these leadership roles depends on several factors. Age and experience strongly influence the selection of leaders, especially the mukhiyas and the nambardars. Indeed, age often serves as a proxy for experience. But the most important quality governing the selection of the nambardar is the elusive one: status. Apart from age, status can depend on the number of sheep owned, wealth in other forms, leadership experience, articulateness, and kin relationships with well-known raikas.

Major Types of Decisions

Members of different camps identified sixty decision issues as important for the functioning of the camp (see table 6.1). Using the classification the shepherds themselves suggested, I divide them into six categories: camp formation and dissolution, migration, flock management, camp management, market interactions, and interactions with the government and settled populations.

Table 6.1   Aggregate Data on Decision Making Classified by Issue Area

Issue Area	Number of Decisions	Decision-making unit			
		Mukhiyas	Nambardar	Council	Total
Camp formation and dissolution	(2)	49	9	—	58
Migration	(11)	1	265	48	314
Flock management	(13)	322	55	—	377
Camp management	(16)	53	377	48	478
Market interactions	(10)	71	171	58	300
External relations	(8)	8	175	53	236
Total	(60)	504	1,052	207	1,763

Source: Field survey by the author, 1989–90.

Camp Formation and Dissolution

This category contains two major decisions — selection of the camp leader before the beginning of the migration and the breakup of the camp at the end. To select a new leader, a few flock owners approach an individual they respect and trust. Once selected, the camp leader tends to continue in authority for several annual migration cycles. He initiates camp formation by sending messages to different flock owners to assemble in a mutually convenient location. When flock leaders want to choose a new camp leader, or if they become dissatisfied with their existing leader, they can approach another experienced individual to accept the responsibility. The selection of an effective camp leader is a critical decision since it impinges directly on the survival of the camp.

In the normal course of events, the breakup of the camp occurs after the annual migration cycle is complete. On the return journey, flocks leave the camp at points closest to their villages. They seldom leave before the cycle is over, and the camp leader takes special care to ensure that members do not get so dissatisfied that they leave in midmigration.

Migration

The direction of travel, the timing of migration, the daily distance to be covered, and the setting up of the camp are the central migration issues (see Johnson 1969). The raikas camp in a new location almost every day. Decisions related to setting up the camp and the distance to be traveled each day must therefore be made repeatedly. For these decisions, the necessary information is not easily available to all shepherds. Familiarity with the migration route and information about the villagers are prerequisites for good decisions about where and when to camp.

At the same time, decisions on this subject can be considered routine because they are made often and the risks associated with a wrong decision are low. Thus, a wrong decision is unlikely to impose huge costs on the shepherds because few farmers are hostile and most welcome the manure that the sheep deposit in their fields during the night.[12] Finally, decisions about migration affect all individuals in the camp.

Flock Management

Two subclasses of decisions can be distinguished: household decisions (about cooking, loading and unloading camels, and so forth) and decisions about managing the sheep (grazing, watering, accounting, and so forth). Women perform most of the housekeeping work; men carry out the sheep management tasks. Decision making depends on intimate familiarity with the sheep in the flock and an ability to direct individuals. Few of the tasks, however, require much direction from the decision maker. All the decision maker may need to do is to ask that the evening meal be cooked, suggest that camp be broken, or wake the shepherds to take the sheep out for grazing.

Camp Management

Three issues affect the management of the camp: management of people, allocation of collective tasks, and security. By management of people, I refer to issues such as arbitrating disputes, dividing responsibilities related to the camp, and keeping track of shepherds who leave the camp on various errands. Collective tasks include cooking on festive occasions, taking care of visitors and interacting with them, purchasing medicines, and supervising expenses from the common fund. The decision-making unit that undertakes these tasks must be able to command. To make arrangements for better security and ensure that these arrangements will be honored, the decision maker must also have contacts among the settled population and familiarity with the migration route.

Market Interactions

Shearing, sheep sales, and wool sales lead to the major decisions needed to operate in markets. Most decisions on market interactions affect the entire camp. Some are routine: to whom should wool be sold? Others demand substantial asset-specific knowledge: when are the sheep ready for shearing or sale? High stakes hinge on yet other decisions: at what rate should the sheep be sold? Decisions also entail possession of the latest knowledge about market prices for sheep and wool. Finally, since shearing takes place over a week, the decision maker needs to persuade farmers to furnish space during this time.

External Relations

This last issue area generates the greatest level of uncertainty. Decisions involve interactions with government, the legal system, and settled populations. In addition to low information availability on these issues, shepherds face an additional complication: the stakes are very high. Although shepherds make their decisions only irregularly and infrequently, wrong choices can lead to losses of significant sums of money, expedite grave trouble, and precipitate major fights with farmers. Correct decisions, on the other hand, promise no benefits except that the daily business of the camp will continue as usual. Thus, decisions involve high stakes and asymmetries between returns and losses. The high stakes mean that shepherds will be averse to delegating responsibility for handling external relations to a single individual. The asymmetry between returns and costs implies that the decision maker will receive no special praise for making right decisions yet all the blame if things go wrong.

ALLOCATION OF DECISION MAKING

Table 6.1 presents the data collected on decision making in thirty raika camps. To interpret the table, begin with row 1. The 2 in parentheses implies that there are two decision issues that fall under the general category of "camp formation and dissolution." Respondents in each camp were asked who made the decisions on each of these issues. There were 60 responses, but 2 were invalid (or the respondents did not provide an answer): hence, the figure 58 in the last column. Of these 58 responses, the owners of the flocks were mentioned forty-nine times as the decision-making units, and the camp leader was mentioned as the decision maker in nine instances. Of the total of 1,800 responses for sixty decision issues from thirty respondents, 37 (2 percent) were either invalid or unavailable; thus, 1,763 is the total number of responses.

The flock owners make most of the decisions (85 percent) about camp formation and flock management. The camp leaders have extensive powers to make decisions in all other areas. They make 72 percent of the decisions in the other general categories of decision making. The shepherds have delegated the responsibility for making most of the decisions in the areas of migration and camp management to their camp leader. Together with the Council of Elders, the camp leaders cooperate to make decisions where interactions with outsiders such as farmers and government officials are involved. With the flock leaders, they share authority for decisions related to market interactions. Even in these two areas, they make 65 percent of all the decisions.

The table suggests that the responsibility for decisions is not distributed randomly in the shepherd camps. The observed distribution of decision-making authority can be explained once we pay attention to issues related to economies of scale, control of authority, and information availability with a particular decision maker.

Under each category, a particular decision-making unit seems to be chiefly responsible. For camp formation and dissolution, the flock leaders are the primary decision makers. They select the camp leader and decide the time at which they will leave the camp. To understand the logic behind the allocation of these decisions, recall how a new camp is formed. The flock leaders approach an individual whom they trust to guide them through the migration. Choosing a leader allows them to abdicate the responsibility for making a large number of important decisions. They save a significant measure of time and energy. They must, however, be able to exercise some control over their leader or else he could easily exploit them. So, although they give up the power to make many decisions, they retain the right to choose a new leader and the right to leave the camp if they become dissatisfied. Without these rights, they would exercise little control over the camp leader's overall performance. The selection of a camp leader is akin, in this sense, to selecting a leader democratically. Not all the characteristics of the selected individual match a voter's ideal, but voters evaluate their politicians on overall performance. As one of the shepherds laughingly said: "If the nambardar doesn't work out, we can always pick another person next year. But it is better that we pick correctly this year."

For decisions related to flock management, it is the flock unit leaders who exercise greatest authority. They make 85 percent of the decisions. Their decisions affect only a small number of persons, and there are seldom any economies of scale to be harvested. At the same time, the flock unit leaders have more knowledge about their flock units than anyone else in the camp. A flock unit leader can gain no advantage by allowing another decision maker the right to manage his flock unit. They are well aware of this fact and consider it preposterous to allow someone else to make decisions related to the internal aspects of a flock unit.

The camp leader makes the vast majority of decisions about migration and how to manage the camp. Significant economies of scale accrue from delegating decision making to one individual (particularly for decisions about collective tasks). At the same time, feedback about the manner in which the leader manages the camp is a matter of direct experience for the flock owners. For most of the decisions regarding the management of the camp (see table 6.1), the shepherds can assess the quality of the decisions made by the camp leader without expending significant effort. For decisions relating to migration, information is not easily available but the camp leader is better informed than other members. At the same time, it is relatively easy to maintain informal checks on the camp leader to ensure that he does not defraud the shepherds. Most issues in the areas of camp management and migration require routine decisions (decisions need to be made often and not much is at stake) even if the information needed to make the best decision is not available to all. Again, the shepherds permit their leader to make decisions on these issues because their risks are low unless the decisions are absolutely inappropriate. For instance, even if the camp leader decides that the camp should travel three miles rather than five on a given day, the shepherds do not lose much. As one of the shepherds put it: "Who needs the headaches of making all these decisions? If the nambardar wants prestige, he can have it. That is what he is supposed to do in any case."

For decisions related to market interactions and external relations, however, the camp leader shares decision-making responsibilities with the Council of Elders. For many of the issues in these two categories, neither the leader nor any other shepherd in the camp possesses precise information. The decisions affect a large number of individuals in the camp, and the possibility of an adverse impact on the shepherds owing to a wrong decision is high. The shepherds and their leader, therefore, both prefer that the other elders are involved in making decisions. Involvement of the Council of Elders serves two purposes: it serves the interests of the camp leader because it prevents the responsibility for wrong decisions from being laid entirely at his feet. It also serves the interests of the council because their involvement ensures that the leader cannot manipulate uncertain situations to his personal advantage. Further, collective decision making utilizes all the information available among different members of the camp.

This broad survey of the decision areas shows that the shepherds allocate decision-making responsibility in order to meet three objectives: to reduce costs of coordination and avail themselves of scale economies, to minimize the risks of wrong decisions by taking into account all available information, and to control decision makers. However, if we look at table 6.1 more closely, it is evident that significant deviations exist within each class of decisions. It is true that for a given set of decision issues most of the decisions are made by the "appropriate" locus of decision-making authority. Exceptions, however, remain. For instance, we might expect the camp leader to make decisions regarding migration. But within that class, interviewees mentioned the Council of Elders as the decision maker 48 times out of 314. Similar irregularities mark decisions related to flock management, camp management, and market interactions. A satisfactory explanation dictates a closer look into the types of decisions that comprise each class.

Table 6.2 lists the issues that form the set of migration decisions.[13] It is immediately evident that the timing of the return journey and whether the camp should migrate for the entire year are issues the camp leader does not

Table 6.2   Decision Issues: Migration

Decision Issue	Mukhiya	Nambardar	Council
Direction of migration			
Choice of direction	—	26	4
Choice of destination	—	30	—
Gathering information (short-term decisions)	—	29	1
Gathering information (long-term decisions)	—	27	3
Timing of migration			
When to begin migration	—	30	—
When to begin the return journey	1	16	13
Whether to migrate for the entire year	—	2	12
Distance to be traveled			
Distance to be traveled each day	—	30	—
Setting up camp			
Choice of village for camping	—	30	—
Choice of fields for camping	—	29	1
Total	1	275	38

Source: Field survey by the author, 1989–90.

fully control. The decision on when to return home is made only once during the migration cycle. Thus, it is not a routine decision—in the sense that routine decisions are made often and the losses associated with a wrong choice are low. Second, to make an appropriate decision for the entire camp, information on fodder availability in all the shepherds' villages is necessary. No single individual in the camp possesses this information. Finally, in many of the camps the interests of the shepherds diverge as regards an early or late return. Most shepherds also possess land in their villages, which they wish to cultivate when the rains begin. Shepherds with larger landholdings prefer to get home with the first monsoon showers because if they do not plow in time their agricultural incomes may decline. On the other hand, those owning large flocks prefer to return a few weeks after rains have begun so that the sheep can browse on the common lands in the village. The different interests of the shepherds imply that a delicate balance must be struck between an early and a late return. The Council of Elders, representing a larger set of interests in the camp, also possesses more detailed information about individual shepherds than does the camp leader. It is not surprising, therefore, that it makes decisions on this issue fairly often.

Table 6.3 Decision Issues: Flock Management

Decision Issue	Mukhiya	Nambardar	Council
Household decisions			
Cooking	30	—	—
Gathering water/fuelwood	30	—	—
Buying supplies for cooking	29	—	—
Breaking camp	28	2	—
Setting up camp	27	3	—
Flock management			
Separation of sheep in the morning	30	—	—
Grazing and watering sheep	30	—	—
Grazing and watering camels	6	24	—
Milking sheep and camels	30	—	—
Taking care of young sheep	28	2	–
Maintaining accounts	28	2	—
Order in which members will keep night watch	5	23	—
Helpers' salaries	21	—	—
Total	322	55	—

Source: Field survey by the author, 1989–90.

A parallel account explains why the Council of Elders decides whether the camp should migrate for the entire twelve months. It is an issue that needs to be considered only infrequently — when the rains fail almost entirely, making cultivation an unattractive proposition. Again the information about the amount of rainfall in different villages is not available to the camp leader or to any single individual. Naturally, the council — with its broader representation of interests in the camp — forms the most appropriate unit to make decisions on this issue.

By looking at the individual issues that comprise a set and analyzing the exigencies that drive decision making for that issue, we can explain other observed exceptions. Thus, the flock leaders make most of the decisions pertaining to flock management. But, as shown in table 6.3, the camp leader interferes twice in the right of the flock unit leaders to assign responsibilities to the shepherds in their units. He decides how many people will graze and water camels; he also decides the order in which individuals from different flocks will keep the watch during the night. What explains this interference?

We first analyze the issue of grazing camels. Camels and sheep differ in their grazing habits. While camels can browse on tree branches and consume thorny scrub, the sheep prefer vegetation on the ground. It makes sense, therefore, for camels to be grazed separately from the sheep. The average number of camels in a flock is between four and five. But two herders can graze up to fifty camels. This means that significant economies of scale can be captured by grazing all the camels in a camp together. The leader of the camp can select individuals in rotation from the entire camp, which would obviate the need for each flock unit leader to attempt independently to graze the camels belonging to his flock. On the average, there are twelve flock units and forty-six camels in each camp. If each flock unit leader assigns an individual to graze camels, twelve herders might be needed. If the task is delegated to the camp leader, he can substantially reduce labor requirements by rotating the task among shepherds from different flock units. Only two or three herders will then be necessary. Nine fewer individuals are thus needed to carry out the same task under this arrangement of decision-making responsibility. The shepherds I interviewed confirmed the gains accrued from allowing the nambardar to make decisions regarding camel grazing. "The nambardar knows more about camels. And how can I tell someone from another flock to graze my camels?" remarked a young shepherd.

Two reasons explain why the camp leader decides on the order in which shepherds from different flock units will maintain the night watch. First, this is a routine decision. The Council of Elders need not be involved. Second, the camp leader possesses greater familiarity than any other individual with the migration route and hence has more information about the area through which the camp will move. If the migration is through a region where thieves may be encountered, he can change the order of the watch so that the more alert and reliable members of the camp keep watch when there is a greater possibility of theft.

Several factors influence the suitability of the decision maker for issues comprising the set of decisions about market interactions (see table 6.4). The camp leader makes decisions about the shearing of the sheep and the sale of the wool. Wool is a homogenous commodity, especially because the raikas rarely clean or grade it before it is sold. The camp leader can negotiate a price for the wool of the entire camp without unduly upsetting individual shepherds since there are no significant variations in the quality of wool across flocks. Further, the camp leader is the only person capable of coordinating the operations that must be carried out in quick succession to complete the shearing and wool sale.[14] The range of tasks and the complexity of coordination imply large economies of scale if all the sheep in the camp are sheared at the same time.

The sale of sheep, however, need not be coordinated for the entire camp. Shepherds often sell their sheep one at a time to buyers who visit the camps.

Table 6.4 Decision Issues: Market Interactions

Decision Issues	Mukhiya	Nambardar	Council
When to call sheep merchants	—	10	20
When to call wool shearers	—	12	18
When to call wool merchants	—	17	13
To whom to sell wool	2	26	2
To whom to sell sheep	14	16	—
Rate for wool sales	—	27	3
Rate for sheep sales	28	2	—
Rate for shearing sheep	—	28	2
How much wool to sell	—	30	—
How many sheep to sell	27	3	—
Total	71	171	58

Source: Field survey by the author, 1989–90.

Several factors make this an appropriate course of action. The price of a sheep, in comparison with its wool, is much higher, and the higher stakes make it profitable for the sheep merchants to occasionally come to the shepherds.[15] The ordinary shepherd, therefore, need not rely on the camp leader to either contact the merchants (as in the case of the wool merchants) or coordinate the sale of animals. No scale economies accrue to the shepherds from delegating this responsibility to the camp leader. On the other hand, the camp leader does not possess accurate information on variations in the quality of the sheep from flock to flock. Since differences among the animals can significantly alter their prices, he will be unable to negotiate the best price for different flock leaders. If he does negotiate a lower than best price, they might find it hard to determine whether the negotiation was made in good faith or the camp leader received side payments from the merchants. It is clear that the shepherds would not gain much from delegating the responsibility for this task to their leader, and they stand to lose large sums.

The camp leader and the Council of Elders share responsibility for decisions related to the timing of summoning the shearers and merchants. For the three types of decisions about timing, the camp leader's information about the location and identity of merchants can be combined with the information of the council members on the condition of the sheep to allow the best decisions to be made. The basis on which the shepherds have allocated the rights to make various kinds of decisions is summarized in figure 6.1.

To the extent that the model of decision making represents the way the shepherds allocate decisions, it suggests that the camp leader receives the

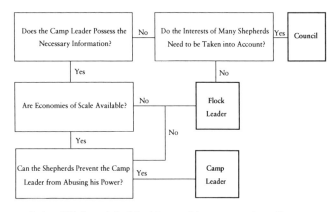

Figure 6.1   A simplified model of decision making among the raikas

power to make particular decisions only after careful consideration by the shepherds. Only when the camp leader possesses information other shepherds do not, *and* when he can create economies of scale, *and* when the shepherds can prevent him from abusing his power to make decisions, does the responsibility for a class of decisions devolve upon him. In other instances, the shepherds either retain the right to make decisions or the council makes them.[16]

The preceding discussion does not explicitly delve into how the observed allocation of decision-making authority came into being: it may have evolved over time, been learned through adaptation, or been chosen ex nihilo with foresight and rational thought. The historical information on the subject simply does not exist. Shepherds suggest that this has always been much the way they have migrated. But the existing arrangements can be understood as "rational" responses to the tasks that must be performed if the camp is to continue as a social unit. They may even be *explained* as rational choices made by shepherds if rationality denotes actions by constrained agents who see themselves choosing over a range of possible actions to achieve a specific goal.[17] There is some variation across the camps and within each camp over time in allocating decision-making authority. When probed, shepherds responded that these variations are an outcome of differences in the decision maker's capacities. Clearly they refine authority allocation to reflect performance.

DECISION MAKING AND COMMUNITY

The judicious distribution of responsibilities for making decisions helps alleviate the anxieties of the shepherds about the material performance of the camp and the flocks to a substantial degree. The previous discussion reveals the manifold ways in which the shepherds have fine-tuned decision making in their camps to extract the greatest material and security benefits from the allocation of decisions. For the vast majority of decisions—timing of the return journey, duration of the migration, who should graze camels, keeping nightly watch over the camp, the sale of sheep—the shepherds have allocated decision making such that it balances the capacities of the decision maker with the needs of the camp.

The final outcome of the migration is, of course, subject to a number of unpredictable events whose source can be either the physical or the social environment. But the observed organization of activities in the camp means that the shepherds reduce uncertainty to the extent it is possible to foresee sources of human error and guard against them. Different members of a migrating camp have clearly assigned roles that take into account their ca- pacities. Secure in the knowledge that they have delegated responsibility to someone who is capable, the shepherds can perform their own tasks with less concern about unpleasant surprises. Without this ability to fulfill the range of diverse tasks within a migrating camp, migration could not become a reality.

The point is not that the shepherds choose to allocate decision-making responsibilities in order to facilitate the creation of community. It is simply that a successful allocation helps generate community. In turn, the emergence of community facilitates the completion of assigned roles in a manner that helps protect the group in its interactions with outsiders. The fact that the shepherds can rely on each other in the face of a multitude of possibly painful surprises confers on the mobile camp the same attributes of community that attachment to a place provides settled groups. Indeed, discussions about communities where members have links to a specific place take for granted exactly those foundations of community that the shepherds must actively construct, even if their activities are not premeditated. Regular and multiplex interactions, stable membership, expectations on the part of the members that they will continue to interact for some time to come, and mutual vul- nerability may be necessary components of a small community. The shep- herds can assume none of them owing to their mobile lives. For social groups that are attached to a place, the landscape and the manner in which group members derive a subsistence from the resources present in the landscape may provide stability to interactions among the group members.[18] The knowledge that they are all dependent on the same resources and the manner in which they use them can create a sense of mutual vulnerability,[19] which the shepherds must generate in alternative fashion. The landscape constantly shifts, and the resources on which they depend change from one day to the next.

Instead of a given territory, then, it is their membership in the group and the manner in which group members perform assigned tasks that become the source for the shepherds of the everyday assurances that settled groups may derive from their connections with a place. The home of a shepherd is the mobile camp, the fellowship of other migrating shepherds (often even in cases when they are not members of the same camp), and the security of interactions with specific farmer friends along the way. The security that would flow from being attached to a place is replaced with a sense of belonging that stems from being a part of the migrating group. This sense of belonging is underlined every day in the songs the shepherds sing around the evening cooking fires. It is affirmed through every negotiation with outsider others over grazing, camping for the night, or the health of the sheep. It comes into play during every moment of crisis: in conflicts with villagers, upon harassment by police or border guards, or when sheep are stolen. The group, formed initially through voluntary acts of choice on the part of each shepherd, is reaffirmed constantly.

The shepherds' experience of making and being a part of a community is rather different from the one most settled villagers undergo. Individuals born into settled communities, possessing fixed assets in land and dwelling, knowing and belonging to the same group from one year to the next, may also confront significant obstacles in building community within their group or in creating new ones. Such difficulties could stem from differences in interests or local politics as influenced by larger political phenomena. Common location in space does not necessarily produce a common locution of interests.

The shepherds, because their assets are in the form of animals and they can exchange membership in one mobile camp with that in another, face an entirely different set of issues in building community. They come together because they have common interests but with no assurances about what may happen if these common interests are not matched by a commonality of striving. Members of spatially fixed social groups can choose not to build solid communities. If the shepherds did not do so, they could not migrate. Their knowledge about who made specific decisions in past migrations and with what result allows the camp to come together as a viable economic unit.

The options that shepherds reserve in terms of exit from and entry into a migrating camp make it difficult to presume that community will emerge in all of them. The shepherds retain the right to form the camp and to leave if they feel the camp leader is not performing his tasks or if they feel exploited in other ways. Similarity in interests and the availability of an exit option are significant in assuring the camp members that their efforts to maintain community will not be abused. The mutual knowledge of what is required of each individual in the camp for the success of the migration and the constant interactions among the camp members help deter free riding.[20] The knowledge that free riding is limited serves as an effective encouragement to community — in its sense of belonging to a group. Material incentives to perform thus contribute significantly to the construction of community.

In the above rendering, the difference between an associative and a communal relationship becomes far less pronounced than a host of writers on community offers as self-evident. Tonnies's enduring distinction between *Gemeinschaft* (community) and *Gesellschaft* (society) has found expression in the works of Weber, Durkheim, Geertz, and other scholars of social change. Whether considered as Weberian ideal types or descriptors of (changing/ desirable) social conditions, the two are supposed to exist in a continual and oppositional tension. Weber's ideal-typical distinction between the two holds that communal relationships spring out of a subjective feeling of the parties that they belong together while associative interactions rest on rationally motivated adjustment of interests ([1922] 1978). Even if the two coexist in a majority of social relationships, they remain as opposing tendencies. Not only are community and society oppositional types, but they also signify a theodicy of change, modernization if you will, as community gives way to associative relations with the passage of time. Questioning the distinction between the two and taking rationally adjusted relations as generative of communal sentiments, then, not only undermines the presumed opposition, but it subverts the notion of modernizing change that is supposed to be accomplished as society replaces community.

Of the two, community is supposed to exist "naturally"; societal relations are the product of artifice. Geertz's discussion of primordiality draws on Shils (1957) to cast communal ties as flowing from "some unaccountable absolute import attributed to the very tie itself," flowing "more from a sense of natural affinity . . . than from social interaction" (1973: 258–61). It is precisely the naturalness of community ties that this chapter questions by examining how material foundations facilitate the creation of community in the migrating camps. It suggests that community among shepherds is integrally linked to an effective distribution of decision making and to the performance of tasks that devolve upon specific decision makers.

If decision making related to the economic functioning of the camp facilitates community, it is also true that the creation of community requires a greater investment than do the everyday interactions over grazing, marketing, or dealing with government officials. To that extent, the primordiality of community can be taken at its face value only because of the enormous amount of artifice that goes into its creation. Because the benefits of routine, material interactions are so clear and specific, explaining them requires far less exploration. The "naturalness" of community is a consequence of our inability often to provide clear explanations of how a sense of belonging comes into being rather than its always-existing existence. In looking at how the material relations of the raikas promote their feelings of belongingness, we take a step toward demystifying the nature of community.

7 · Hierarchy in Community:

Games Shepherds and

Their Leaders Play

In all of man's (*sic*) written record there has been a preoccupation with conflict of interest; possibly only the topics of God, love, and inner struggle have received comparable attention. — R. Duncan Luce and Howard Raiffa, 1957

Strategy . . . is not concerned with the efficient *application* of force but with the *exploitation of potential force.* — Thomas Schelling, 1960

The previous chapter, in analyzing the allocation of decision making and its role in the construction of the raika mobile camps as placeless communities, explored the role of economic motivation in community. But the discussion confined itself to information, economic gain, and efficiency as the relevant aspects of interactions in the camps. Its focus on the relationship between economic gain and the crafting of community, it may be suggested, normalized the politics of the relations between shepherds and their camp leaders by bracketing it. But politics is central in shaping the interactions between the shepherds and their leaders, even if it is hidden under a patina of everyday practices of authority and deference. It is critical to understand politics if we are to grasp more acutely how the shepherds prevent their leaders from taking advantage of their significant powers to make decisions.

The ensuing analysis of these intracamp interactions assumes the form of a simple formal model of principal-agent relations, which views the camp leader as the agent of shepherds, who are the principals. The shepherds delegate to their agent substantial powers to make decisions because of his expertise. But having delegated power, they are then faced with the likelihood that their trust may be abused. The problem shepherds face as principals is how to prevent abuse of the powers they have delegated. The principal-agent framework, thus, helps us analyze how the shepherds negotiate hierarchical relations within their mobile community. The arrangements are effective enough that in the daily interactions in the camp they seldom create differences of opinion, tensions over the exercise of authority, or challenges to the power of the camp leader. If politics describes a gap in the way economic or communal relations unfold, the smoothness with which shepherds' camps function is another reason why politics remains hidden from casual view. My use of a game-theoretic framework in this context is less an attempt to prove that it provides a generally privileged vantage point to uncover politics than a device that can contribute local insights into the moves and countermoves that are a hallmark of all politics. It helps situate more clearly the asymmetric relations between shepherds and their leaders and the possible divergences in their interests.

The use of game theory in this chapter,[1] apart from highlighting the politics of leader-led relations, also ensures that the analysis treats the actions of the shepherds and their leaders as mutually dependent. The approach implicitly engages some of the recent debates on rational choice theory.[2] More specifically, I accept Chong's argument, with which few theorists would disagree, that the value of any theoretical intervention has to be measured by its capacity to engage empirical observations.

The chapter aims to explain observed arrangements that describe the relations between the shepherds and their leaders. A simple principal-agent model helps uncover the logic behind the shepherd-leader relationship. The substantive focus is on the raikas, but the analysis, because it is couched in a generalizable principal-agent framework, has implications for other contexts in which multiple principals hire an agent and problems of moral hazard and adverse selection plague their interactions.[3] To the extent that users of renewable resources in other parts of the world also periodically select new leaders and confront the problem of how to control them, the discussion has wider relevance. Some examples that readily come to mind relate to rural elections; attempts to comanage natural resources in Latin America, Africa, and South Asia; and rural thrift and credit associations whose members periodically select new leaders.

THE ORGANIZATION OF THE MIGRANTS' CAMPS THROUGH A NEW INSTITUTIONAL LENS

With the recognition that transaction costs, information asymmetries, and property rights play exceedingly significant roles in determining economic outcomes, the new institutional literature has burgeoned in the last two decades.[4] Many authors, in addition, have begun to apply insights from the neoinstitutional literature to rural contexts (Bates 1989; Berkes 1989; Cashdan 1990; Ensminger 1992; Ensminger and Rutten 1991; Gibson 1995; Ortiz and Lees 1992; Ostrom 1990; Wade 1988).[5] For most of these theorists, the notion of contracts is fundamental to the analysis (Kreps 1990: 91–93).

The agency literature, launched by the seminal works of Hurvicz (1973), Jensen and Meckling (1976), and Ross (1973), focuses specifically on the divergence in the interests of principals and agents and on the mechanisms that principals may use to tether agents to their will. While earlier theorists (Fama 1980; Fama and Jensen 1983; Jensen 1983) believed that natural selection processes will lead to the most efficient types of contracts between principals and agents, the more recent mathematical literature examines mechanism design at great length to explore how principals may write efficient contracts ex ante (Biglaiser and Mezzetti 1993; Glover 1994; Laffont and Tirole 1987; Lewis and Sappington 1989). Few of these essays, however, consider the situation in which multiple principals engage a single agent.[6] This chapter attempts to understand the effect of information and monitoring in a situation in which multiple principals contract for the services of a single agent.

We can consider the mobile shepherd camp as a congeries of relationships based on contracts between ordinary shepherds (principals) and the camp leader (their agent). According to this set of contracts, the shepherds select a leader for their migration so that they do not each have to perform tasks that would divert their attention from the daily work of sheepherding. In exchange, the camp leader gains social prestige, cultivates political contacts, and garners leadership status.[7] Even a cursory look at the range of issues over which the camp leader makes decisions reveals significant opportunities for malfeasance, graft, and moral hazard (see table 6.1). The camp leader decides upon the course of action in 60 percent of all situations described by the shepherds as important. If we exclude the area of "flock management," which is directly related to issues internal to the management of each flock unit, the camp leader makes decisions for the entire collective in nearly three-quarters of all situations.

Opportunities for graft and exploitation arise from structural differences between the positions of the shepherds and their leader. In turn, these structural differences can be traced to asymmetries of power and information. The camp leader possesses time-, place-, and asset-specific information that is unavailable to the shepherds. Indeed, this is the reason why they select him. But at the same time the asymmetries of power and information place the camp leader in a position rife with the possibilities of adverse selection, moral hazard, shirking, and corrupt behavior.[8]

Each of these — adverse selection, moral hazard, shirking, and corrupt

Leader	Sanction	Does Not Sanction
Cheat	$a_3 - 0\,a_1;\ -a_2 - (a_3/N)$	$a_3;\ -a_3/N$
Does Not Cheat	$-a_1;\ -a_2$	$0;\ 0$

Figure 7.1 The relationship between cheating and sanctions

behavior — can lead to major losses for migrating shepherds. These types of behavior may occur in any situation in which the camp leader interacts with outsiders and goods or sums of money change hands. The leader can misrepresent both the costs and the benefits of actions. Examples of the first type would include bribes negotiated to pay off government officials, payments to settle disputes with farmers, costs of medicine, and costs of supplies bought for feasts and festivals. Benefits might be misrepresented when farmers pay the camp for sheep folded in their fields or merchants pay for pastoral products such as wool and sheep. In response to the wrongdoing of their leader, the shepherds can sanction him in two ways: (1) by returning home in midmigration or (2) by declining to choose him as leader in future migration cycles.[9] The simple game depicted in figure 7.1 represents the choices of the shepherds and their leaders.

If the leader does not cheat and the shepherds do not sanction, neither incurs any costs and the payoffs to each are zero. If the leader cheats, and the shepherds do not sanction, the leader gains an amount, a_3, and each shepherd in the camp loses a_3/N, where N is the total number of shepherds in the camp. If the shepherds choose to sanction the leader, each of them incurs a cost, a_2, as the cost of sanctioning in addition to the cost of the leader's cheating. The cost to the leader is represented by a_1, and his payoff is reduced by that amount. If the leader does not cheat and the shepherds sanction him, the leader suffers the cost of sanctions (a_1) and the shepherds incur the cost of sanctioning (a_2). This schematic specification of costs and benefits to the leader and the shepherds ensures that there is an interdependence between the gains of the leader and the losses to shepherds from wayward behavior on the part of the leader.

The shepherds can impose two types of sanctions on their leader — leave the camp in midmigration and return home or decline to choose him as the leader in future migration cycles. These are strategies that entail high costs, both for the shepherds (principals) and for the camp leader (agent).[10] Leaving the camp in midmigration is a high-cost/high-risk strategy. It defames the camp leader and carries a significant probability of ruining his reputation. In relation to the shepherds, similarly, the migration is risky enough traveling in a group; for a lone shepherd returning home, it would be highly perilous.[11] A shepherd will follow this strategy only under extreme circumstances. The second possibility — to choose a different camp leader or join a different camp after the current cycle concludes — would hurt the camp leader but only defer the current problem of the recalcitrant agent. The costs of inappropriate performance by the leader may continue to be incurred for the remainder of the migration cycle.

The relationships among the payoffs for the leader and the shepherds are summarized in expressions 1 and 2, respectively. The relationships hold regardless of the form of sanction the shepherds choose. For the leader,

$$a_3 > 0 > a_3 - a_1 > -a_1. \tag{1}$$

For the shepherds,

$$0 > -a_3/N > -a_2 > -a_2 - a_3/N. \tag{2}$$

It is easy to verify that under these payoffs there is an equilibrium in pure strategies. In this equilibrium, the leader will cheat and the shepherds will not sanction. This is clearly undesirable from the point of view of the shepherds. More importantly for the analysis, it is not the equilibrium observed during the field research. The dominant strategy for the leader seemed to be seldom to cheat and for the shepherds to sanction rarely. How do we explain the fact that the camp leader seldom cheats?

THE RESTRAINT EXERCISED BY THE CAMP LEADER

The key to understanding the equilibrium that prevails in shepherd camps lies in the significance of information and the dynamics of monitoring in the camp. The shepherds, instead of waiting until their agent has successfully defrauded them, have created reliable mechanisms that monitor their leader and drastically reduce the possibility of "hidden information and hidden actions." Before the camp leader's decision to cheat or not cheat, and the shepherds' response to sanction or not sanction, comes the choice of whether to monitor.[12]

To see how the shepherds monitor and use their information, I discuss four situations: the selection of camping sites; the purchase of medicines and supplies for feasts; dealings with merchants; and the payment of bribes to police, forest, and other government officials. These cases represent the greatest possibility of returns to an unscrupulous decision maker out of all the situations in which decisions are necessitated during the course of the migration. Interactions with outsiders over cash transactions can yield signif-

Table 7.1 Distribution of Decision-Making Responsibilities for Specific Issues

Issue area	Mukhiya	Nambardar	Council
Selection of campsite			
Choice of village	—	30	—
Choice of fields	—	29	1
Purchases			
Medicines	5	25	—
Supplies for feasts	—	28	2
Market interactions			
When to call wool merchants	—	17	13
When to call sheep merchants	—	10	20
When to call sheep shearers	—	12	18
Decision on rate for wool sales	—	27	3
Decision on rate for sheep sales	28	2	—
Decision on rate for shearing	—	28	2
Bribes			
Police officials	—	28	2
Forest officials	5	21	—
Total	38	257	74

Source: Field survey by the author, 1989–90.

icant profits to a person possessing hidden information and undertaking hidden actions. The specific issues related to each of these situations and the distribution of responsibilities for making decisions over these issues is presented in table 7.1. This detailed quantitative information on the distribution of decision-making responsibilities together with the ensuing discussion about each specific situation make it clear that in most situations in which opportunities for "hidden information and hidden action" are present the interactions are primarily between the camp leader and the flock leaders. Among all the listed decisions, the Council of Elders is involved mainly in determining when merchants and shearers should be called—situations in which there is little opportunity for graft.[13]

Selection of Campsites

As we saw in chapter 3, the raikas have a preference for camping in private fields. The leader negotiates with the farmers to select the fields in which the sheep will be penned for the night. The amounts the camp leader receives on

Table 7.2 Income from Folding Sheep and Money Spent on
Bribes and Fines (in rupees)

Flock Number	Income from Folding	Expenditures on Fines and Bribes
1	264.00	107.00
2	335.00	134.00
3	227.00	100.00
4	396.00	150.00
5	396.00	150.00
6	335.00	134.00
7	396.00	154.00
8	396.00	160.00
9	791.00	300.00
10	791.00	300.00
11	791.00	382.00
12	396.00	161.00
13	791.00	350.00
Average	485.00	199.00

Note: U.S. $1.00 was worth Rs 28.00 at the time of the field research.
Source: Field survey by the author, 1989–90.

behalf of the shepherds are sizable — on the average Rs 500[14] for each flock during the year (see table 7.2). The shepherds use a simple mechanism to ensure that the camp leader does not conceal information or siphon off returns from folding: the negotiations between the farmer and the leader usually take place in the open, where some shepherds are present and can monitor payments.[15] In many cases, farmers pay in kind: between fifty and one hundred pounds of grain. The bulk of the grain makes it difficult, if not impossible, for the leader to misrepresent the amount received.

Purchase of Medicines and Supplies

The leader has the opportunity to purchase medicines from vendors known to him personally and skim a commission directly off the price or he can misreport the price he paid. The shepherds guard against the latter possibility by having one or two members of the camp accompany the leader to monitor purchase prices whenever he goes to buy medicines. Generally, on different occasions different individuals go with the leader. This means that if the leader is successfully and systematically to report higher prices for the medicines he buys, he will have to collude with all the persons who go with him.

By patronizing a particular store and buying enough medicine in bulk to meet the requirements of the entire camp, the camp leader could still harvest some gains, yet this opportunity for profit is limited by the fact that the prices he reports should not exceed the prices in other stores. The shepherds use only a few types of western medicines sold in shops and can check prices randomly whenever they happen to be in a town. But because it is time consuming to visit a town regularly, it makes sense for the shepherds to delegate medicine purchases.

To prevent misreporting of prices of supplies for collective feasts, shepherds have created a similar mechanism. The camp leader appoints at least two shepherds to travel to a town to purchase supplies so that an individual cannot exploit the rest of the collective.

Sale of Pastoral Products

Three sets of individuals outside the camp are involved in the sale of pastoral products — the shearers, the wool merchants, and the sheep buyers. The shepherds engage professional shearers to clip the wool. At the same time as the sheep are sheared, wool merchants receive invitations to come and purchase the wool. Individual sheep buyers frequently visit the camps to take advantage of the culling of sheep, which the shepherds are forced to do regularly owing to persistent cash flow problems.

Two factors prevent wrong reports about the rates for shearing. First, the camp leader often makes the decision to invite the shearers in consultation with the Council of Elders. Since he does not have the discretion to call shearers known to him personally, it is difficult for him to engage in price fixing. Second, and this is not an intentional strategy, the entire party of ten to twenty shearers stays with the camp for a week or more, which increases the chances of discovery if collusion has taken place.

The rates for selling sheep are decided by flock owners. This is a response to the possibility of large losses in case the camp leader colluded with the sheep buyers. Many flock owners are so vulnerable that if they did not get a good price in even one or two major sheep sales they would be devastated. The quality of sheep varies widely across and within flocks. Few flock owners trust anyone else to set prices for their sheep. The costs of not delegating remain low, since sheep buyers visit the camp regularly in the hope of buying sheep from cash-poor flock owners.[16]

It is in the case of wool sales that the camp leader finds the greatest opportunities for personal gain. He decides on the merchants to whom the wool should be sold, its quantity, and the price. The wool merchants or their agents stay in the shepherds' camp very briefly, seldom more than a few hours at a time. Finally, since the price of wool fluctuates relatively rapidly in the urban markets, the ordinary shepherds find it difficult to ascertain the best price for their wool at any given time. Misrepresentation of prices, therefore, is a simple matter.

However, the shepherds seem to exercise some control over their leaders through ex post information collection. As they migrate, they constantly exchange information with shepherds in other camps about rates for wool sales. Sometimes new wool merchants visit shepherds' camps and in the process furnish price information. The vigilance of shepherds and the camp leader's awareness of their vigilance keep within limits the commission that the leader can make on wool sales. Most shepherds believe only minor amounts to be at stake. Some of the shepherds with whom I talked even felt that the leader deserved some return for all the tasks he performed for the collective. Using a common metaphor, a shepherd explained to me that everyone had a "stomach to feed." Clearly, as long as their ex-post price monitoring kept his "hidden actions" to a minimum, they were willing to allow him a little leeway,[17] and the efficiency losses from the leader's "corruption" seemed low enough for the shepherds to bear, if not grin while bearing.[18]

Bribes to Government Officials

Few members of the camp have much expertise in the fine art of bribing officials. The "rules of etiquette" that structure interactions with government officials in a rural context, where officials consider themselves superior and gifted, are beyond the ken of shepherds. Even the camp leader possesses the necessary skills for negotiating bribes only to a small degree. He, therefore, enjoys a near monopoly of power in this area of decision making. Yet, as table 7.2 shows, he does not gain much capital from it.

According to the table, flock owners pay Rs 200 in bribes *and* fines on the average during the entire annual migration cycle.[19] As a percentage of total expenses, bribes and fines comprise no more than 3 percent for any of the thirteen flocks surveyed. Even if the leader makes some money for himself in the payment of bribes, it has to be only a small amount, a fraction of the money paid out as bribes. Equally important, the shepherds can do little about it. They have to interact with government officials, and they need someone who can manage side payments when necessary.[20]

Explaining the Camp Leader's Restraint

It is clear that shepherds actively seek information on the behavior of their leader and use a number of mechanisms to control the possibility of graft. In

Shepherd

Leader	Monitor	Does Not Monitor	Probability
Cheat	$-a_5; -a_4$	$a_3; a_3/N$	α
Does Not Cheat	$0; -a_4$	$0; 0$	$1 - \alpha$
Probability	β	$1 - \beta$	

Figure 7.2   The relationship between cheating and monitoring

the various situations in which moral hazard might arise — setting up camp in farmers' fields, purchasing supplies, selling pastoral products, or interacting with government officials — the shepherds monitor their leader closely or collect information after the fact. In most situations in which the camp leader could make money on the side, institutionalized monitoring practices minimize large-scale exploitation. When the camp leader enjoys some discretion in fixing prices and rates, the advantages that accrue to him are quite limited. One can conclude that overall the shepherds monitor most of the time and the leader cheats only infrequently. Figure 7.2 represents the restraint exercised by the leader. According to the figure, if the leader does not cheat and the shepherds do not monitor the payoffs to each are zero. If the leader cheats and the shepherds do not monitor, the leader gains an amount a_3 and each shepherd loses a_3/N (see figure 7.1). If the shepherds choose to monitor and the leader does not cheat, each shepherd incurs a cost a_4 and the payoff to the leader is zero. The costs of monitoring, as the discussion in the previous section reveals, are relatively low for the shepherds since they incorporate monitoring in their everyday interactions with the leader and in the daily routine of their livelihoods.[21] If the shepherds monitor and the agent cheats, then the shepherds gain back the amount a_3/N but still incur the low cost of monitoring. If the shepherds know that their leader is a cheat, it imposes a cost on him equivalent to a_5. This cost is negligible in material terms but high in reputation and prestige. Given the fact that the shepherds monitor the leader closely and live with him in daily contact, systematic and prolonged cheating is likely to be discovered quickly. The ensuing gossip would affect the leader's reputation as well as his chances of selection as a leader in future migration cycles.

The relationships among the payoffs for the leader and the shepherds are summarized in expressions 3 and 4, respectively. For the leader,

$$a_3 > 0 > -a_5. \tag{3}$$

For the shepherds,

$$a_3/N > 0 > -a_4. \tag{4}$$

For these payoffs, there is no equilibrium in pure strategies.[22] There is, however, a Nash equilibrium in mixed strategies, which we can calculate using the expected values of the payoffs for the leader and shepherds.[23] I assign the two strategies of the shepherds (monitor, do not monitor) the probabilities of β and $1 - \beta$, respectively. For the leader, I similarly assign α and $1 - \alpha$ as the probabilities of cheating and not cheating, respectively. In equilibrium, the leader will be indifferent between cheating and not cheating because his payoff from the two strategies would be the same. Therefore,

$$[(1 - \beta)^n a_3 + (1 - (1 - \beta)^n (-a_5)] = 0 \qquad (5)$$

where the left side of the equation represents $E(U_1)$ from cheating and the right-side represents $E(U_1)$ from not cheating. Simplifying, we arrive at the equilibrium value of β as

$$\beta^* - 1 \quad \left(\frac{a_5}{a_3 + a_5} \right)^{1/n} \qquad (6)$$

Similarly, the shepherd will be indifferent between monitoring and not monitoring when his payoffs from the two strategies are the same:

$$[(1 - \alpha)(-a_4) + \alpha(-a_4)] = \alpha[(1 - \beta)^{n-1}](-a_{3/N}) \qquad (7)$$

where the left side of the equation represents $E(U_s)$ from monitoring and the right side represents the $E(U_s)$ from not monitoring. The equilibrium value of α is therefore

$$\alpha^* = \frac{a_4 \cdot N}{a_3 (1 - \beta)^{n-1}} \qquad (8)$$

The derived values of α^* and β^* suggest some interesting interpretations. Two of these merit greater discussion. As a_3 (the payoff to the leader from cheating) increases, the equilibrium probability of cheating declines. Why this should be so can be discovered if we examine the effect of a_3 on β^*, the equilibrium probability of monitoring. It rises especially as it becomes high in relation to a_5, the cost that the shepherd imposes on the leader by monitoring whether he is cheating. The rise in the probability of monitoring swamps the possible effect on the equilibrium probability of cheating. Further, as a_3 rises high in relation to a_5, the probability of monitoring gets closer to 1, but it never reaches 1 unless $a_5 = 0$. Since equation 8 indicates that α^* will always be greater than zero, the game represented by figure 7.2 approximates closely the equilibrium observed among the shepherds, where they monitored most of the time and their agent seldom cheated.[24]

Second, the value of N, the number of shepherds in the camp, plays an important role in determining the equilibrium α^*. As it rises, the value of α^*

also rises. This confirms, perhaps, the "logic of collective action"; as group size rises, it becomes easier for the agent to cheat. Of course, α^* cannot rise above 1, and this imposes a limit on the value of N. Thus, $\alpha^* \leq 1$, if and only if, from equation 8,

$$N \leq \frac{a_3 (1 - \beta)^{n-1}}{a_4} \qquad (9)$$

If N goes beyond this value, then the game will have an equilibrium in pure strategies in which α^* will become 1, the leader will always cheat, and the shepherds will not monitor. The gains from monitoring for each shepherd will be very low, and the losses from not monitoring for each shepherd will also be very low, insignificant enough to make him not wish to incur the costs of monitoring. The other implications of the equilibrium values of α^* and β^* are fairly straightforward and confirm earlier results for noncooperative games that have an equilibrium only in mixed strategies (Tsebelis 1989). These include the results that as the cost of monitoring goes up the equilibrium probability of cheating goes up and as monitoring becomes costless the equilibrium probability of cheating declines to zero; the equilibrium probability of cheating is not affected by the size of the penalty imposed on the wayward agent; and the equilibrium probability of monitoring is not affected by the amount of monitoring costs.

$E(L^*)$ and $E(S^*)$, the expected returns to the shepherds and their leaders, are easy to determine. Since the leader is indifferent between cheating and not cheating in equilibrium, by equation 5 we can say that $E(L^*) = 0$. For the shepherds,

$$E(S^*) = \alpha^*[(1 - \beta)^{n-1}] \left(\frac{-a_3}{N}\right) \qquad (10)$$

Substituting α^* in equation 10, $E(S^*) = -a_4$. Since $a_4 > 0$, the expected returns in equilibrium to the shepherds are negative and a function of the magnitude of their monitoring costs.

A Concluding Discussion

This chapter explicates the political relationship between leaders and ordinary shepherds using a model of interactions between multiple principals and a single agent. It shows that the observed equilibrium between the shepherds and their leaders can be better understood if we take into account the monitoring activities of the shepherds instead of paying attention simply to the range of sanctions the shepherds can impose upon their leaders.

Information, and who possesses it, emerge as crucial in determining whether the leader will cheat. At the same time, the leader's awareness that camp members can impose sanctions upon the discovery of cheating behavior plays a highly significant role in preventing him from mulcting his principals. The fact that the shepherds can choose a new leader for a new migration cycle is critical, then, to keeping the leader's actions within tolerable bounds. The analysis, by focusing on the importance of direct monitoring by the agents, captures an important aspect of the environment in which shepherds operate. Lupia and McCubbins, in their study of bureaucratic accountability (1994), outline three possible methods of information collection for principals. Pointing to the costliness of direct monitoring and the reluctance of agents to reveal information truthfully, they discuss whether third-party information revelation might be efficient. For the shepherds, however, regular and close interactions with the agent and the way in which monitoring is etched into the structure of their daily lives mean that direct monitoring is the most effective means of information gathering.[25] This, perhaps, is a difference that marks the social context of many rural development and environmental projects in comparison with the prevailing situation in urban contexts. In most villages, the fact that the number of households is small and its residents engage in regular, overlapping, and multistranded interactions implies that they possess substantial direct capacities to monitor their leaders. The achievement of the right to a voice in the selection and removal of leaders, together with the existing capacity for direct monitoring, might prove highly useful in enhancing the effectiveness of new rural development and environmental projects.

The analysis presented some counterintuitive findings in addition to confirming some of the principal results of two-person, noncooperative games without an equilibrium in pure strategies. The most important of these is that as gains from cheating increase for the agent a higher probability of cheating behavior can be swamped by the increase in the probability of monitoring. The result stems from several factors, which may be common to community settings in a large proportion of the rural areas of the developing world: (1) the payoffs to the agent from cheating are related to the losses of the principals;[26] (2) the costs of monitoring, in relation to the losses from cheating, are low for the principals; and (3) the loss the principals can impose on their agents by monitoring are relatively low compared to the loss they suffer from cheating, but they still possess the capacity to impose significant costs through sanctions.[27] The end result is an argument in favor of greater authority to principals to monitor their agents.

In light of these observations, the practical implications of the analysis are normatively attractive, if obvious. Policy provisions that stress greater accountability and permit higher monitoring levels of leaders by followers, especially when there are regular and frequent contacts among them, are likely to reduce a host of principal-agent problems. When unprincipled actions of leaders directly reduce the benefits of their followers, extending greater authority to followers to hold leaders accountable is even more likely to reduce cheating behavior.

The second implication of the model, because of the explicit incorporation of the number of shepherds in the camp as a variable to address the existence of multiple principals, is the expected increase in the probability of cheating behavior with group size. The relationship can be interpreted in terms of the free-rider problem. A larger number of shepherds in the group weakens incentives to monitor because the losses owing to cheating are spread over more people. If the effect of a larger number of principals is to be overcome, institutional design must aim at lowering the costs of monitoring and collecting information.

One of the limiting assumptions throughout the analysis is that the shepherds are homogenous in their endowments and preferences. Although the assumption is not far-fetched in the case of the raika camps, an extension to other settings would require consideration of the heterogenous nature of principals. The literature on common agency contains some directions for analysis on this issue (Baron 1984; Braverman and Stiglitz 1982).

In conclusion, I return to the issue of hierarchy in community. In terms of both asset endowments and authority held, heterogeneities among the shepherds are limited. Few shepherds possess sheep in disproportionately high numbers, with most of the migrants owning between one hundred and four hundred sheep. Wealth disparities among shepherds are therefore limited. Yet for the collective to work effectively the shepherds need to allocate substantial powers to their leaders. Role specialization by camp leaders effectively reduces the costs of migration, contributing to the emergence of community in the raikas' migrant camps. Without the allocation of powers to the camp leader, so that he can guide migration, the shepherd camps would incur substantially higher costs and migration might well be impossible.

But this role specialization also has subtle effects in furthering intracamp hierarchical relationships between the ordinary shepherds and their leader (Taylor 1982: 33–38). Such hierarchies are often the instruments through which leaders exploit their followers. This chapter showed how the shepherds mitigate the effects of hierarchies present in their camps and are able to prevent the camp leader, who is in a superior position, from exercising his authority unduly. Their ability to do so is predicated upon effective monitoring and regular dissolution of the camp at the end of the annual migration cycle. Monitoring creates disincentives to the camp leader in the everyday life of the camp. The fear of losing his reputation and not being selected as the leader in fresh migration cycles forms the ultimate threat against open and voracious cheating.

The play of influence and power between the shepherds and their leaders, obscured in chapter 6 because of its focus on showing the relationship between community and economic gain, emerges here as a critical element in understanding the mobile lives of the shepherds. The analysis shows that (1) relations of community that seem to hinge upon cooperation might be founded nonetheless on the pursuit of self-interest and (2) divergent objectives of subgroups within a collective require attention if group dynamics are to be understood. More concretely, the focus on politics provides an answer to the question of how shepherds solve the problem of collective action in the pursuit of a mobile livelihood.

8 · An Ending

Sometimes, I too sought expression. — Jorge Luis Borges, 1961

The myth of the noble savage has been a persistent theme in thinking about nonwestern peoples. It assumes different forms, and its subjects are endowed with varying qualities. But what seems constant across accounts are assertions about the uniqueness of these peoples and yet their similarity to what the reader might consider familiar. Accounts of the lives of Gadulia-Lohars in India, the *kula* voyagers among the Trobrianders,[1] or the Yanomami in Brazil,[2] their marginality to currents of modernity notwithstanding, invariably move beyond the depiction of the specific peoples to offer perspectives on the author's own context. The objective of the fieldworker/researcher becomes the identification of a group of people who are not only different, or have undergone quite remarkable experiences, but also, somewhat paradoxically, possess the capacity to generate insights with "general relevance."

For pastoralists, the application of the myth of the noble savage generates accounts that speak of their courage and independence in relation to the outside world and egalitarianism and democratic organization internally (Beckwith and Fisher 1990; Goldschmidt 1971; Jedrej 1991; Lewis 1961; Riefenstahl 1982).[3] As Dyson-Hudson and Dyson-Hudson sardonically suggest, one reason prompting studies of nomadic peoples is the romantic notion that they are "brave, independent, fierce men, freely moving with their herds and not having to deal with the constraints and frustrations that we ourselves face in day-to-day 'civilized' living" (1980: 15).[4] The raikas do not fit this mold. They are neither exotic nor perfectly common, despite a recent attempt in the *National Geographic* to present them as aesthetic creatures whose beauty can be appropriated and alien nature regurgitated.[5] Located somewhere in the nowhere land between the "courageous nomad" and the "ordinary peasant," the stories of their misfortunes seem hardly different from those of a million other rural families who suffer daily deprivations measured only in rather unremarkable events like missed meals, small humiliations, verbal dismissals (or abuses), and everyday injustices — measured, that is to say, not at all. Suffering a double marginality, in the sense of possessing relatively little power and the sense of not being too exotic, their story seems deserving of sympathy but hardly worth telling.

This book, in telling the story of the raikas and in talking about their marginalization from power as well as from the imagination that exoticizes nonwestern peoples, suggests that these kinds of marginalizations are insufficient to preclude a story from being told. Telling a story or carrying out an analysis is always an act that contests different forms of marginalization. This is what the raikas suggested implicitly when they gave me their time and words.

But providing a narrative or telling a story is simultaneously a statement of what stories should be about. The narratives in this book are neither simple descriptions of what I found nor mere reconfigurations of my fieldwork experiences. Nor, yet, are they simply an engagement with other texts and theorists about other peoples in other places. Rather, they are an attempt to negotiate the tensions across these different meanings of telling a story.

I use the term *negotiation* in Bhabha's sense, as denoting the possibility of an iterative movement among agonistic and oppositional positions without assuming the redemptive rationality of transcendence (1994: 26), that is, without the guarantee of arriving at some greater and better truth. The task in writing about other peoples is to resist the desire to cleave to any of the three pure positions: representing others as they "are," finding in them reflections of oneself or one's own culture, or using them simply as means to extend theory.

In this vein, each of the chapters has provided a vignette from the lives of the raikas, often deploying different rhetorical strategies. The substantive attempt in the book has been to explain a set of interlinked puzzles. Why do the raikas migrate? Why do they migrate collectively? How do they address problems of collective action inherent in all joint action? But simultaneously the arguments have sought to make broader points about the nature of politics between the raikas and their neighbors, the kinds of markets from which they make profits, and how they construct placeless, hierarchical communities in the process of migration.

It is obvious, then, that the perspectival gesture through which I have set the context for the arguments in the book is the focus on choices made by the shepherds. Recall the ways in which I have indicated their agency. We encounter them in chapter 2 contesting local elections and attempting to gain a more secure toehold in village politics. Although they could not meet their aims entirely, they focus on and investigate future possibilities for change. In chapter 3, they appropriate and give their own meanings to the development that state actors attempt to bring to them. In large measure, it is such attempts at resistance by marginalized groups around the world that have mitigated the worst effects of poorly conceived development policies.

A similar vantage point frames the discussions about the interactions of the raikas in markets and as communities. We find them using markets to derive the best possible terms of exchange for their products. Their bargains with wool merchants, sheep buyers, and farmers help them produce a surplus from a social and physical environment that is at best neutral and often hostile. Their negotiations in markets reveal them to be wily negotiators, intent on and able to realize whatever concessions circumstances afford. Again, their resistance to the existing distribution of power and resources is what affords them a better existence, even if sometimes it is only marginally better. In the discussion of community, the focus of the analysis is deliberately on that most basic of human actions — decision. I use the allocation of decision-making power in the mobile camps to make certain points about the emergence of community in the absence of place and about how the shepherds limit abuses of authority within the camp. But the unit of analysis — decisions — explicitly brings to center stage attempts by the shepherds to shape and extend the limits on their lives, to resist the emergence of strong hierarchies in the migrating camp.

Difficult as it is to occupy this position in the face of the spate of recent work that has questioned the meaning of personhood and the possibility of the self, it is a necessary position to negotiate for all who concern themselves with the lives of marginal peoples. It may be appropriate that at the end of this book I elaborate in a small way these central if implicit motifs of intent and resistance.

Stripped to its essentials, the question is whether intentions are necessary to resistance. Scott, in his magisterial work on the subject, *Weapons of the Weak*, provides an initial answer that sees them as closely linked. He suggests that "*any* act[s] by member[s] of a subordinate class that is or are *intended* either to mitigate or deny claims made on that class by superordinate classes or to advance its own claims vis-à-vis those superordinate classes" can be seen as resistance (1985: 290). After a wide-ranging, thoughtful, and authoritative discussion, he modifies the initial definition by limiting the role of intentions (302). Haynes and Prakash understand resistance as "those behaviors and cultural practices by subordinate groups that contest hegemonic social formations, that threaten to unravel the strategies of domination; 'consciousness' need not be essential to its constitution" (1992b: 5).

While both these definitions are useful in that they suitably broaden the range of actions that can be seen as resistance, they do so only at the cost of reducing the role of the resister in resistance. Without intentioned action, one is left with individuals and groups who are unwitting dupes (of history, of macrosocial forces, of elite machinations), not agents (of their own or others' lives). In accepting that the resistance of marginalized groups does not require intent, scholars of resistance give up one of the most important parts of their agenda — the politically progressive project to recuperate subordinated groups as human agents, as creators of history.

Of all the different aspects of resistance — consequences, strategies and organizational forms, intentions of actors, and perceptions of those against whom resistance occurs — the subjective aspects must count as the most critical. In thinking about whether resistance is taking place, without considering whether those who resist aim to resist, the observer/analyst effectively introduces his or her own interpretation of what takes place upon the acts observed. To resist, one must possess an intent — whether it be a principled or a self-interested intent. Else, the notion of human resistance is no different from the resistance of geographical features, inanimate and enduring, that in Braudel's view are critical to the history of the *longue durée*.

Note that the point is logical, not empirical. Intentions, one must concede, are unknowable. But their unknowability does not lead to the conclusion that the relationship I am suggesting — intentions are necessary for resistance — is invalid. To say that for some acts to count as resistance they must be willed as resistance is very different from trying to say that a particular act is one of resistance.

To say that intentions are critical to resistance is not to buy whole hog into the rhetoric of an autonomous, independent consciousness. It is simply to assert that in the gaps between the power relations that characterize different experiences lies the possibility of emerging with a critique of the domination one suffers. Such a critique is dependent neither on a theory of history nor a working out of one's place in history. To believe that agency can only exist depending on the extent to which the agent is complicit in a metanarrative or in history is to argue for a modernist notion of agency. That is a kind of agency that, one may argue, the raikas certainly lack. It is one that only winners possess.

The kind of agency I have described is different in nature. It is what might be called fragmented agency, based on life experiences that one can only apprehend in a fragmented fashion. It is based less on an evaluation of their place or of their actions historically than on their ability to reflect on what they are attempting to do and their own assessments of what they are doing.

Take, for example, what is most obvious about the lives of the raikas — their mobile lifestyle. Analogous to Oldenberg's discussion of the courtesans of Lucknow (1992), their mobility can be seen as constituting a livelihood that is centrally organized around a strategy of resistance. Even if the very fact of mobility cannot be seen as resistance, it permits them to move beyond village politics and hegemonic structures,[6] it creates the space from which they can negotiate exchanges with many different farmers and merchants, and it allows them to create informal institutions during migration that are also instrumental when they attempt to participate in a democratic polity. That is, mobility permits experiences in different fields of social relations that may be inflected by power as much as those within a village but possess a very different character and require very different negotiations. It is in the differences in political and social relations that raikas experience from village to village that they find the resources to engage recalcitrantly the asymmetries that affect them adversely. Even if their migration is not specifically a product of the desire to resist, it allows them to construct an ideology and practice of difference that other village castes might find more difficult. Their fragmented agency finds birth in precisely those practices that in their minds are differently constituted from those of their neighbors.

When it came time to leave all the friends I had come to know among the shepherds, none of us had the right words. We avoided talking about it. Sometimes when the subject came up, we pretended my impending departure this time was no different from the numerous times I had left with one of the shepherds on some small errand. At other times when someone inadvertently talked about my leaving, we would deliberately change the subject. But, of course, there was no avoiding the fact ultimately.

What will you do when you go back to America? What will you remember about us? Will you forget us? Sleeping on the ground, grazing sheep, eating food cooked on open fires, riding camels, walking with our animals: you have done many things with us. Did you do such things before? Have you spent time with other people who move all the time? Does this happen in America? Even in India, in your home, your life must be very different. What will remind you of us once you have left, about our life of constant travel?

You said you will write a thesis on our life and our ways. And this thesis will become a book. Will this book be published only in America? How will this be of use to us? And when will you return? Writing a book must take such a long time.

Perhaps there are no right words for conclusions or to say good-byes. One assumes a distance. One talks of the things that happened and imagines a future that might still be shared in some fashion. One summarizes what one has done and tries to find new words for it. One focuses on the memorable and the mundane and speaks even of what is best forgotten. One observes old rituals and tries to create new ones. But in the back of the mind is the nagging thought that these are just words used only to ease the separation, words uttered in the anticipation that there will be another opportunity, soon, to look for similar words. That next time, I must continue to hope, the words I find will be more appropriate.

Notes

INTRODUCTION

1 Two large bodies of literature, on subalternity and resistance, exemplify the ways in which marginality has become central. The recent attention given to indigenous knowledge and peoples similarly underlines the voice marginal peoples have found, at least among academic representatives.

2 See Srivastava 1997: 7 and Westphal-Hellbusch 1975: 124.

3 See the detailed analysis of the epic of Pabuji (Smith 1991) in which Hariya (also Harmal) raika helps Pabuji steal camels to keep a vow Pabuji had made to his niece at her wedding.

4 As Leach and Mearns (1996) point out for Africa, and Ostrom (1990) points out more generally, particular perceptions about processes of environmental change, even when incorrect, lead to policy prescriptions that may be equally inappropriate.

5 Recall in this context Saint-Simon's dictum that modern society would pass "from the government of men to the administration of things" (cited in Rabinow 1989: 1).

6 Jodhpur had six tehsils in the mid-1980s: Bilara, Bhopalgarh, Jodhpur, Osian, Phalodi, and Shergarh.

7 Behnke and Scoones have extended the point made by Sandford by considering seasonal variations as well (1993: 12–15).

8 See the introduction to Agrawal and Sivaramakrishnan 1997 for a discussion of the hybrid term *agrarian environments*.

9 See Calvert 1995 for the connection between Durkheim's use of "institutions" and its use by rational choice theorists.

10 See Netting 1981 for an exposition of the position that as resources become more valuable, owing to higher levels of demand, property rights to those resources will become more precisely defined. See also Dahlman 1980.

11 "Against the egalitarian order of persuasion stands the authoritarian order which is always hierarchical. If authority is to be defined at all, then, it must be in contradistinction to both coercion by force and persuasion through arguments" (Arendt 1993: 93).

1 MOBILITY, IDENTITY, LOSS

1 Ethnographic texts on pastoralists have used several strategies of representation. Some examples are found in Asad 1970, Barth 1961, and Stenning 1959. The literature on the

crisis of representation in ethnography is too large to be reviewed here. For some discussions and reviews, see Clifford 1988 and the collected essays in Clifford and Marcus 1986 and Marcus 1992.

2 The relationship between different ways of expressing these themes in the lives of the raikas could itself be further elaborated and discussed. See Radhakrishnan 1993 and Sangari 1990 on related questions, as they speak of double coding in the context of postcolonial writings.

3 The exchange rate at the time of the fieldwork was Rs 28 to the dollar.

4 The letter was written by Balkavi Bairagi, a provincial-level legislator from Mandsaur, Madhya Pradesh (cited in CSE 1985: 11–12), following criticisms in the press over the mass killing of sheep by forest officials in Dahinala in September 1983.

5 Khazanov's magisterial work ([1984] 1994) provides a persuasive argument to show why nomadic pastoralism could not have formed an intermediate stage of development between hunting-gathering and settled agriculture.

6 Halstead and O'Shea present a discussion of these aspects of variability and how mobility can address these variations. See especially the introduction to their edited volume (1989).

7 A number of different bundles of rights may be necessary for full ownership. Among them may be rights of access, use/withdrawal, exclusion, management, and transfer (Schlager, Blomquist, and Tang 1994; Schlager and Ostrom 1992). Alchian and Demsetz (1973) also talk of bundles of property rights and their divisibility. It can safely be asserted that the complete specification and enforcement of property rights would be prohibitively expensive if not impossible. For related discussions, see Buck 1988 and Johnson and Libecap 1982. Even if such a complete set of rights were allocable, this may not prevent resource degradation (Cordell and McKean 1987; Larson and Bromley 1990; van Ginkel 1989).

8 An impressive literature explores the relationship between property relations and sustainable management. Voluble protagonists defend the three main analytical forms of organizing resource use: private, state, and common. See Agrawal 1996, McKean 1992, and Ostrom 1990 for useful analyses. The papers in Marcussen 1993 provide a useful review of related issues for sub-Saharan Africa.

9 For a truculent restatement with minor adjustments, see Hardin 1986.

10 For similar assessments of the relationship between mobility, resource use, and property rights arrangements, see Smith 1991 and Ellis and Swift 1988.

11 For a discussion and classification of different forms and patterns of mobility, see Johnson 1969 and Krader 1959. Ingold (1986), Ingold et al. (1988), and Khazanov ([1984] 1994) critique these earlier attempts and present other ways of looking at mobile societies.

12 To maintain stock at desired levels, herders often move out of their accustomed areas of grazing and also in and out of the wage labor market. The alarmist notion of "ecological collapse," which some theorists use to justify sedentarization or exclusion of humans from protected lands, is based upon the view that a given pasture has a stable and predictable carrying capacity. But, where pasture and range are characterized by major variations in growing conditions, "carrying capacity" may be too dynamic for population tracking (Ellis and Swift 1988: 453–54). Under such conditions, open access to resources and mobility of stock may be far more conducive to efficient resource use.

13 Another interpretation of the shepherds' mobility is that it makes them less able to form

community in their home villages. This is often true, but the more important reason for their inability to create a community with their settled village neighbors is the divergence of interests in locally available grazing resources rather than the plain fact of mobility (see chapter 2).

14 See, for example, Halstead and O'Shea 1989.

15 Shiva, one of the three major gods in the Hindu trinity of Brahma, Vishnu, and Shiva, is supposed to be carefree, have a generous disposition, and possess a terrible temper. He also, incidentally, is followed by a train of ghosts, demons, and similar entities whom he tolerates and with whom he plays and dances.

16 A number of other, historical texts also provide scattered information on the raikas (Crooke [1896] 1975; Cross 1912; Enthoven 1920; Ibbetson 1914). Randhawa (1996), Smith (1991), and Srivastava (1997) provide discussions of some of these sources.

17 Srivastava (1997: 16–17) lists thirty-six subcastes. The numbers differ depending on informants, and a full listing is one of the ways in which ethnographies often freeze living histories of which *tradition* is one name.

18 South Asian scholarship provides a number of examples where members of lower castes use originary myths that underscore an initially high status for the caste. The current low social position in the hierarchy may be explained by some act of pollution or sin. See, for example, Cohn 1955, Mandelbaum 1970, Prakash 1991, and Rowe 1968.

19 Because externally introduced and imposed classificatory projects can produce the effects they purport to mark, classified individuals may feel strongly that they do not just belong to a sociological category but they *are* that category. In this regard, see the parable of the "Mpongwé and the Ethnohistorian" recounted by Clifford (1986: 116).

20 See the collection of essays in Casimir and Rao 1992, especially that of Mirga (1992). The redefinition of a mobile lifestyle as home, instead of fixing home spatially, can be done by the group itself or by state and sedentarist neighbors.

21 Gochar (*Go* + *char*) lands are literally *cow* + *grazing* lands: pastures on which cows can graze. Supposedly set aside for cows, such lands form the mainstay of grazing for most village animals, especially during the monsoons when other lands are under cultivation.

22 This works out to approximately forty U.S. cents per kilogram.

23 But see Denbow and Wilmsen (1986), who, through their work on the Kalahari, suggest that herding might have appeared before farming in a number of areas.

24 Thus, in contrast to ethnographies of pastoralists produced in the 1970s and 1980s, which emphasized their vulnerability and fragility, McCabe, writing about the Turkana, notes that they "remain an economically viable, physically healthy, and for the most part happy group of people. . . . Others have chosen to focus their research on groups unable to maintain a pastoral existence, the failures in the pastoral system. These studies are certainly important, but they do not characterize African pastoralists as a whole, and we still have much to learn from viable pastoral communities" (1994: 85–86).

25 The mushrooming literature on indigenous knowledge and institutions argues the need for special protection if they are to be saved from the pressures of modernization and state making. Recent case studies are collected in issues of the *Indigenous Knowledge and Development Monitor*. See Agrawal 1995 for a critical but sympathetic review of the concept of the indigenous.

26 See Wickham 1990 for a critique of generalizing tendencies in postmodernism that

applies more generally. A similar point is explicit in the scholarship produced by historians belonging to the subaltern school. For an introduction, see the papers in *Subaltern Studies*, vols. 1–9 published by Oxford University Press. Volume 1 of *Subaltern Studies* provides a pragmatic statement for subaltern studies in the shape of Ranajit Guha's essay, "On Some Aspects of the Historiography of Colonial India."

2   I Don't Need It but You Can't Have It

1   See Eggertsson 1990 for a discussion of new institutionalism and neoinstitutionalism. The difference hinges, in Eggertsson's view, on the extent to which analysts retain the basic postulates of neoclassical economics.

2   The word *oran* (also *auran*) derives from the Sanskrit word *aranya*, which literally means "forest" or "wilderness." Orans are sacred groves of trees, often set aside during the feudal period in Rajasthan for religious purposes. Villagers regard the oran as a sacred space, investing even the trees with some religious significance. It is thus possible to see orans littered with dead trees — a startling sight in a landscape where dry organic matter is seldom visible owing to its utility as fuel. However, today, for the most part, *oran* simply denotes common land with trees and some grass cover on it. In administrative terms, there are several other forms in which village common lands can exist: *gauchar, nadi, agor,* or *pahar.* Gauchar signifies a common area specifically set aside for grazing; it seldom has trees. A nadi is a water hole, which fills during the monsoon months and contains some moisture for three to ten months during the year. An agor is the catchment area of a nadi. A pahar is hilly common land.

3   The division of the village between animal owners and landowners is the most appropriate classification for the political dynamic I describe. The political struggles around the benefits derived from the village commons were also influenced by local electoral processes in which caste and economic class played a determining role.

4   See Bates 1996 for a discussion, in another context, that treats institutions as investments.

5   A district is an administrative division in India below the provincial level. Districts comprise approximately one thousand villages and have an average population of two million.

6   The terms *oran* and *village common* are used interchangeably here.

7   Scheduled castes are so called because they are listed in the Indian Constitution as oppressed and disadvantaged castes. The Indian state has undertaken to target specific programs — for example, affirmative action and job reservations — to improve their socioeconomic status.

8   Salzman 1986 describes the declining access of pastoralists to all land. His discussion also makes it evident that few agro-pastoralists have much land.

9   I use *household* and *family* as equivalent terms in this chapter.

10   The same pattern of inequality in landholding is revealed if we consider the village as a whole. The bottom 50 percent of the households own less than 15 percent of the cultivated land in the village, but the top 20 percent own 56 percent of the cultivated land.

11   See Dahlman 1980 for an analysis of the reasons why it makes economic sense to treat grazing resources as open-access land and cultivated fields as private property. The

argument hinges on transaction and enforcement costs that would be incurred in policing the boundaries of each field. See also Agrawal 1996.

12 The lower castes own 39 percent of the private cultivated land and 36 percent of the
cattle. The upper castes own 47 percent of the privately owned land and 58 percent of
the cattle.

13 During the monsoons, approximately 30 percent of the fodder needed for the cattle
comes from the oran and the rest from private stocks. After the monsoons are over, cattle usually graze on the fallow and are stall fed. Pregnant and lactating cows are always
stall fed. In addition to the usual hay, they are fed green fodder, some enriched cattle
feed, and traditional medicines to improve milk yield (Household survey, 1989–90).

14 See Jodha 1985, 1990.

15 Villages directly controlled by the crown were known as khalsa villages. Villages
granted to nobles were called *jagir* villages, and the nobles themselves were called
jagirdars.

16 See Upadhyaya 1973 for a description of several such conflicts between the crown and
the nobility. Root 1987 describes similar tensions between the crown, nobility, and
peasantry in prerevolutionary France.

17 I refer to the informal panchayat comprised by village elders as simply the panchayat or
the informal panchayat. The formal, legal, elected body of villagers, on the other hand,
is called the Village Council or just the council.

18 These figures are available in the Village Council's accounts. Daily wages for unskilled
labor were typically between Rs 10 and 15 per day in 1980. Thus, Rs 15,000 created
about twelve hundred days of employment in the village.

19 I am indebted to Brara 1987 for the discussion in the following two paragraphs.

20 *Charagah* literally means an "area for grazing."

21 Chanakya was prime minister under the first Indian emperor, Chandra Gupta Maurya,
who ruled from 323 to 300 B.C. As his adviser, Chanakya gained the reputation of
being the greatest diplomat in Indian history. His reputation has not yet faded.

22 Indeed, in many parts of Rajasthan the Forest Department has stopped recording survival rates of trees because of its abysmal performance in protecting planted seedlings.
The department only records the number of trees it plants as a performance indicator.

23 See, for example, Alchian 1950 and Nelson and Winter 1982. These theorists present
different mechanisms for the emergence of institutions, but the underlying logic is
evolutionary.

24 For some of the best statements of these deficiencies and discussions of an approach that
highlights the importance of politics and distributional conflicts, see Bates 1989, Knight
1992, Levi 1988, and North 1990.

25 For institutionalist accounts that invoke Pareto optimality, see Schotter 1981 and
Sugden 1986.

3 GETTING OUT FROM UNDER
THE VISIBLE FOOT

1 The balance of this chapter does not employ quotation marks to indicate the problem-
atic status that concepts like rationality, state, and development have come to occupy as
a result of intensive interrogation. The aim is primarily to promote fluency in reading
and should not be taken to signify a complicity in naturalizing these concepts.

2 To this extent, the raikas are no different from other mobile pastoralist groups whose interactions with settled populations are critically affected by state policies.

3 The literature on unintended consequences of state initiatives that may run counter to the interests of marginal groups is large. See especially Ferguson's discussion of unintended consequences of development projects (1994: 20–21), for which he draws heavily on Foucault's work on the prison (1979) and Paul Willis's work on schools and working-class children (1981). For a related example from a pastoral context, see the discussion on boreholes by Peters (1994). For an elaboration of how the dynamics of natural systems might defeat well-intentioned policies, see Behnke, Scoones, and Kerven 1993 and Holling 1973.

4 See Sayer's interesting discussion about how the state exists only through the lived performances of individuals as they enact the "lie that is 'the state'" (1994: 374). His discussion echoes some of the points made by Abrams (1988) in his essay on the difficulty of studying the state when he advocates abandoning it as a material object of study. Mitchell (1991) makes substantially similar points when he documents the difficulty of separating the state from society and suggests that the state is a structural or metaphysical effect of discursive practices.

5 It is also noteworthy that the new fees for sheep and goats were five times higher than those for cattle in spite of their smaller size. Forest officials see goats and sheep as far more destructive to existing vegetation and inimical to new growth.

6 In the often cited words of then Indian prime minister I. K. Gujaral, uttered in his Independence Day address to the nation in 1997, corruption is so widespread in India that it has "seeped into the veins of the nation."

7 For a review of the tremendous ecological costs of this canal irrigation project, see Goldman 1994. A brief description of the Rajasthan Canal Project is also available in Sinha 1996: 5–11.

8 Cultivated areas with a cropping intensity of 100 percent typically yield one crop each year.

9 While sedentarization is the most common "solution" that government and early scholarly efforts offered for the pastoralist problem, other blueprints have not been lacking. See Goldschmidt 1975 for a description of an institutional device intended to "rationalize" the economy of pastoralists.

10 The ensuing information on the program is based on documents and interviews with shepherds and government officials and outlines its performance between 1974–75 and 1983–84.

11 See the report prepared by the Jodhpur team (Jodhpur Spearhead Team 1985: 1–2).

12 Jain, speaking about the same project, asserts that the "ecological condition of the common pastures improved much more than expected because of proper technological inputs and timely rains. Forage production increased almost four times. The problems of soil erosion were controlled and water holding capacity of the soil increased substantially" (1993: 60).

13 At prevailing exchange rates, Rs 105 lacs (one lac equals 100,000) would be close to 600,000 dollars.

14 None of them, thankfully, went to the extent of what local farmers did in retaliation against the alienation of their lands in the Basotho Pony Project described by Ferguson (1994). Shortly after the project began, "unknown parties broke into the fenced pastures, took the entire herd of ponies, and, using dogs, drove them all off a precipice to their deaths" (244).

15 See Varshney 1995 for a discussion of how the democratic political structure in India has helped the emergence of the peasantry as a political force. Bratton (1987) examines the formation of agricultural policy in Zimbabwe in relation to existing political equations as well.

16 See, for example, Bates 1981 and Moore 1966. Mitrany 1961 provides a stinging account of Marx's bias against peasants.

17 See Agrawal 1992 for an explanation of why shepherds owning larger flocks are more likely migrants. The explanation hinges on the need for more forage than is available in the villages where the shepherds reside. See also Kavoori 1996.

18 In part, his familiarity with most of the shepherds in the camps we visited might be the result of selection bias: we often visited those camps in which he knew the nambardar. But we visited more than thirty camps in the course of the fieldwork. In many instances, he simply guided us to the closest group of shepherds visible on the horizon as we traveled on the road. These facts indicate that he has an impressive record of contacts among the ordinary migrant shepherds.

19 The description of these programs relies substantially on Gaiha 1991. See also Saith 1990.

20 See critiques of development by Escobar (1995) and Ferguson (1994).

21 States around the world have attempted to sedentarize mobile groups. For some examples, see Hedlund 1971 and Ndagala 1982.

22 For an early treatment of the relationship between territory and property, see Godelier 1978.

23 Evans, Ruschemeyer, and Skocpol thus suggest that the state is "a set of organizations invested with the authority to make binding decisions for people and organizations juridically located in a particular territory" (1985: 46). Similarly, according to Michael Mann, the state engages in "centralized, institutionalized, territorialized regulation of many aspects of social relations" (1986: 26).

24 See Sack 1986: 19, cited in Thongchai 1994: 15.

25 Contrast the current consensus on the social nature of territoriality with earlier writings that often saw territorial behavior as an innate drive among humans or animals (James 1892; Malmberg 1980). For a discussion, see Taylor 1988, Thomas 1981, and Wilmsen 1973.

26 Ingold (1986: 130) provides a discussion of the relationship between territoriality and tenure and the view that the difference between them corresponds to that between social and material dimensions of human existence. This conception would seem to suggest that material dimensions are without their social referents, that they are constituted without sociality.

27 The raikas, for example, in creating their camps follow specific strategies for locating sheep, camels, household belongings, and guards in concentric circles. When women are present in the camp, they, with the household belongings, form the innermost ring, circled by the sheep, the camels, and finally the guards. When there are no women in the camp, the sheep lie in the inner ring, circled by the camels and the household belongings. The guards form the outer ring. See Cashdan 1983 for a discussion of different attempts at territoriality among foragers. While the raikas fit that category only uneasily, Cashdan's discussion raises interesting parallels.

28 Dearlove (1989), Rose and Miller (1992: 176), Sangmpam (1992), Williams (1996), and Zhao and Hall (1994) are some other recent authors who have, at least in passing, commented on the territorial nature of the exercise of state power.

29 Cited in Harvey 1989: 227.

30 See Thongchai's useful discussion of mapping (1994), especially in chapters 6 and 7.

4 PROFITS ON THE MOVE

1 For an examination of the sociopolitical factors behind the need of the raikas to migrate, see Agrawal 1994 and Robbins 1998.

2 Rural populations around the world resort to an enormous range of adaptive strategies for their subsistence. One of the major items in their repertoire is diversification into multiple resources whose production is characterized by differing levels of output and variability. For a theoretical discussion of various strategies, see Halstead and O'Shea 1989. See also the work of Hayami and Ruttan (1971) and Wade (1988, 1992) for empirical discussions of how social and environmental risks influence the creation of institutions to mitigate losses. Bovin and Langer 1990, Campbell 1984, Clay 1988, Forbes 1989, Fratkin et al. 1994a, Hahn 1982, Massey 1987, and O'Shea 1989 present work that discusses the dependence of pastoral and other mobile populations on multiple resources.

3 See also the review of Central and Southwest Asian pastoral nomadism by Bacon (1954), the historical study of the Navajo by Bailey (1980), Bencherifa and Johnson 1990, Fratkin's discussion (1991) of cooperative herding groups within settlements (rather than during mobility), Gooch's study of transhumant gujars (1992), Kelly's examination of different types of mobility (1992), Kuznar's study of goat pastoralism in the Andes (1991), Mearns 1993, Prasad's comprehensive investigation of pastoral nomadism in arid zones of India (1994), Smith 1978, and Swallow 1994. In these studies, the issue of collective versus individual mobility is seldom addressed. Despite the differences that must lead some pastoralists to move in groups and others to move as families, scholars of pastoralism seldom ask why this difference exists.

4 For useful insights into the nature of community organizations that might help solve problems of collective action related to resource use, see Berkes 1989, Bromley 1992, Ostrom 1990, Peters 1994, and Wade 1988. See Lichbach 1996 for a comparative assessment of different rational-choice-based attempts to solve collective action dilemmas.

5 Recent research, especially by historical ecologists and revisionist cultural anthropologists, has begun to undermine the presumption that rural dwellers are primarily subsistence oriented. Fox (1969), Morris (1977), and Parker (1909) presented early evidence on contact and exchange between local groups and outsiders. Bailey et al. (1989) and Wilmsen (1989) present similar arguments more recently.

6 Milk from the sheep is processed into yoghurt, butter, ghee, and buttermilk but is seldom sold. Camel's milk is almost never sold, and many raikas do not even milk their camels, preferring to leave all the milk for the calves.

7 Cf. Davidson 1996. Even if some of them do sometimes eat meat, they deny it. Their public posture can be seen as a part of ongoing attempts to gain higher ritual status in the caste hierarchy.

8 According to Orlove, who studied cameloids in southern Peru, animal behavior can significantly influence the effective size of a herd. Llamas and alpacas have a strong flocking tendency and dominance hierarchy. A trained herder in this context can manage up to a thousand animals (1977).

9 See also Tribe 1950.

10 According to some raikas, it has become necessary to shear the sheep up to three times a year owing to short-term financial pressures and the need for ready cash.

11 The arrangements for shearing are already discussed in the section on revenue earned from wool. The average cost of shearing lies between one and two rupees per sheep.

12 See the work of Chatty (1976, 1980, 1987), who details how nomadic pastoralists use mechanized transport in another context (on the Syria-Lebanon border in West Asia) to transport pastoral products.

13 A vast literature explores the relationship between scarcities and corruption. See Becker and Stigler's seminal theoretical treatment (1974) and Banfield 1975. More recent general reviews are available in Alam 1989 and Scleifer and Vishny 1993.

14 Tawney 1966, cited in Scott 1976: 1.

15 Part of the reason why the difference across categories is so striking is that the owners of flocks 3 and 10 were unable to sell sheep during the cycle of migration. Had they sold even a few sheep at the regular price, the difference in surplus per sheep, or per person in the different categories, would be far smaller, especially between the first two categories.

16 But see Kavoori (1990), who did not find a notable difference between the performance of small and large flocks in his study of migrant shepherds in Rajasthan. Part of the reason may be that in his sample most of the flocks were smaller than two hundred sheep and none were larger than four hundred. A second reason may be that the leaders of only half the flock groups managed to sell animals at regular rates. Far more sheep were sold at the lower, "distress sale" rates.

17 The shepherds estimated that a large basket of manure — which is what a flock of three to four hundred sheep will produce during a night — would fetch possibly Rs 5. For a camp of five thousand sheep — the average for my sample — the value of the manure would be approximately Rs 80.

5   LOOKING AT THE "INVISIBLE HAND"

1 Commodities, by some authors, are seen to be associated with the capitalist mode of production or to refer to only a special subclass of primary goods as in neoclassical economics. Yet, as Appadurai points out, even in Marx "there is the basis for a much broader, more cross-culturally and historically useful approach to commodities" (1986a: 8). I follow Appadurai in his highly nuanced discussion of a "commodity," where he abandons the search for the magic distinction between commodities and other types of things in favor of the view that various things may or may not be defined as a commodity depending on the situation: "[E]xchangeability (of the 'thing') (past, present, or future) for some other thing is its socially relevant feature" (13; italics in original).

2 The issues raised by grain for manure exchanges can be seen in other types of exchanges as well. But the special nature of grain-manure exchanges makes the elaboration of a number of theoretical issues more tractable.

3 Despite arguments offered by such important theorists as Weber ([1922] 1978) and Durkheim ([1915] 1982), and later Schumpeter ([1942] 1975), Parsons and Smelser (1956), and Mills (1959), about the need to prevent a sharp separation between economic and other social theorizing, it is only recently, and then in response to a perceived economic imperialism, that scholarship from other social sciences has renewed efforts

to work across disciplinary lines. See, for example, the collection of articles in Grano-vetter and Swedberg 1992 and Dilley's collection of anthropologists' writings (1992b).

4 See also Bates 1983, Bates and Weingast 1995, Baudrillard 1981, Tambiah 1984, and Sahlins 1976.

5 Bates and Lees 1977 provides an early discussion of exchange in the lives of nomadic pastoralists.

6 See also Spencer 1990 for an attempt to situate pastoralism in relation to capitalist accumulation.

7 These face-to-face exchanges in which manure is sold for cash as well as grain would seem to indicate that there is no particular reason why only nonmonetary modes of valuation lead to what Firth calls "exchange by private treaty." Negotiations over price are far more common than might be supposed (cited in Appadurai 1986a: 19).

8 Thompson (1971) would also view in face-to-face exchanges a moral economy in which profit is not the dominant motif. Because of the personal nature of exchanges, cer-tain types of outcomes that threaten subsistence provisioning become more difficult to achieve. This moral economy of the market is lost with the emergence of middlemen, who purchase goods only to sell them again rather than for personal consumption. I am grateful to James Scott for pointing this out.

9 As noted earlier, the raikas move almost every day to a new location.

10 On the issue of whether concepts in the social sciences can be treated equally, see the nuanced discussion by Orlove and Rutz (1989) as they analyze the relationship between production, exchange, and consumption.

11 See Gupta 1998. He describes the beliefs of farmers about different types of fertilizers and the superiority of animal manure in another north Indian context.

12 According to the shepherds, chemical fertilizers improve fertility for one year, cattle dung increases the capacity of the fields to yield a higher product for two years, but sheep manure has a yield-enhancing effect that lasts five years. James Scott, a sheep farmer in Connecticut, suggests another reason why farmers might prefer sheep ma-nure: because sheep move around more, they distribute their manure more evenly in the field (personal communication).

13 Fields, if they are irrigated, are also more likely to be plowed by tractors and therefore less likely to possess trees and fuelwood. But the farmer might possess contiguous rain-fed fields or have trees along the boundary of his fields from which fuelwood might be gathered.

14 The exchange of information is costly, and both parties recognize it. For a discussion of the significance of information costs in exchange, see Dahlman 1979, Furubotn and Richter 1991, and Hurvicz 1973.

15 See Stewart 1992 for an engaging discussion of the role words play in bargaining. His de-scription of horse sales and swaps captures some of the subtleties involved in bargaining.

16 Rainfall and subsurface water resources are quite poor in these districts. It is not sur-prising that so few of the fields were irrigated.

17 The t-tests for these differences in average values are statistically significant at the .001 level.

18 Adjusted R^2 for the first set of variables was .25; it was .49 for the entire set.

19 Recall Appadurai's discussion regarding the "endlessly shifting (and potentially infinite) scenario of variables that affect price" (1986a: 51). Even with consistent improvements in the technical basis and data base for analyzing and playing the commodities market,

one of the most researched markets, there is no fail-safe formula for knowing what prices will be like from one period to the next.

20　The difference in price between home and migration seems unrelated to seasonality. One of the factors explicitly incorporated in the statistical analysis was MONTHS, which represents the "time until sowing" for a given farmer. This turns out to be statistically not very significant.

21　A curious tension inhabits recent anthropological writings on barter. On the one hand, some authors suggest that "it is not useful to analyze barter as an isolated phenomenon" (Humphrey and Hugh-Jones 1992: 6; see also other papers in their edited volume). But at the same time they wish barter were an important theoretical concept in its own right (7), one that, they believe, "creates social relations in its own mode" (8). The analytic features of barter they cite are not, however, barter specific. A more consistent theoretical analysis, it would seem, must abandon the ambition to confer an analytical purity on barter or, for that matter, gift or commodity exchanges. See Bourdieu 1977 and Tambiah 1984 for a questioning of Mauss's ([1925] 1954) discussion of gift. Parry and Bloch (1989) and Dilley (1992) provide useful interrogations of the "market."

22　The argument holds equally well against attempts to localize value in any other specific stage of the process whereby objects are made ready for consumption and are consumed.

23　In questioning what Marx said, I obviously do not endorse the sentiment of the Gotha Program that "the proceeds of labor belong undiminished with equal right to all members of society" (Marx [1875] 1972).

24　See the volume edited by Kellner (1994), especially essays by Gottdiener, Cook, and Schoonmaker, for discussions on the valorization of consumption practices in Baudrillard's work.

25　See Appadurai's brilliant analysis on this score (1986a).

26　These quickly sketched points drawn from the work of economists and anthropologists obviously do not do justice to the full discussion presented by their authors. I trust, however, that I have captured the main thrust of their arguments.

27　See Fischer 1986, Gell 1992, and Orlove 1986 for evidence of deferred obligations in barter.

28　See Barzel 1989 for an insightful discussion of the multiple attributes of all commodities.

29　See Dilley 1992b and Stewart 1992 for a discussion of Polanyi's contribution to originating the debate between formalists and substantivists.

30　As the Alexanders argue, value is not determined necessarily in exchange alone (1995a: 191–92).

31　See Alexander 1987; Alexander and Alexander 1995b; Geertz 1973, 1979; Gray 1984; and Stewart 1992 for other descriptions of processes through which buyers and sellers successfully meet and arrive at bargains.

32　See Alexander 1992 for the argument that such structural asymmetry between parties to exchanges is always present. To the extent that asymmetric power is unavoidable in any bargaining situation, as Foucault would argue (1983; see also Gordon 1980), the case of the raikas is only an example of what is a universal phenomenon, albeit an example that brings out these differences clearly.

33　One method of gaining revenue from the manure deposited on public or common lands would be to gather it in sacks in the morning before leaving for the next camp. This procedure, feasible as an outside option, would provide the shepherds with some flexibility in negotiations. But it would require at least an extra half hour of labor and could not be continued for more than two to three days since the weight of the manure would hamper mobility.

6 COMMUNITY OUT OF PLACE

1 Although the camp leader is familiar with the paths traversed during migration and knows many farmers as well, individual shepherds know few features of the migration route.

2 As institutional and popular faith in top-down development policies erodes, studies valorizing local knowledge and institutions are gaining ground. An impressive body of research now stresses that the goal of securing an improved life for the poor will be better served if we first appreciate their desires, knowledge, and institutions (Chambers, Saxena, and Shah 1989; Croll and Parkin 1992; Oldfield and Alcorn 1991; Posey and Balee 1989; Schmink and Wood 1984). In consequence of these emerging trends in "development science," new studies on local knowledge and institutions have become increasingly available (Brokensha, Warren, and Werner 1980; Warren 1991; Warren, Slikkerveer, and Brokensha 1991; McKean 1992; Ostrom 1990).

3 Exceptions are available in the works of anthropologists, who have produced several studies on decision making and organization among nomads and hunter-gatherers. See, for example, Abel and Blaikie 1990, Barth 1961, Mithen 1989, and Weissleder 1978. See also Barlett 1980, Gladwin 1979, Ortiz 1967, and Quinn 1975 for anthropological studies of decision making. The vast literature on decision making by game theorists and management scientists suggests possible future directions for research but few current applications. See, for example, Bell et al. 1990 and March 1988.

4 For a discussion of the multiple ways in which the term community is deployed, see Poplin 1972: 3–26 and Gusfield 1975: 20–21.

5 In a review of community undertaken in 1955, Hillery discovered more than ninety definitions and identified three central characteristics: social interaction, shared ideas and beliefs, and common territory. Most later definitions of small communities see place as central in defining them.

6 Weber refers to community simply as "a sense of belonging together" ([1922] 1978: 40). Brow, drawing upon Weber's authority, differentiates between community as denoting either a place (as in local community or community development) or a subjective state (1990: 1). What such a quick dichotomization of the meanings of community avoids, however, is precisely what I wish to examine. What is the relationship between the "subjective state of being in community" and "community as a place"? What transformations does the task of constructing community undergo when links to a place are unavailable?

7 See the discussion in Corlett 1989.

8 See Boer and Prins 1989 for an analysis of optimal foraging strategies in an African context and the amount of time foraging groups might find profitable to spend in one place.

9 See also Singleton and Taylor, who discuss the different elements that are signified by the use of *community* (1992: 315).

10 Environmental risks include those in the physical and ecological as well as the social and the political environment.

11 Rarely, if ever, do women hold positions of formal authority among the raikas. Thus, in

none of the thirty camps surveyed was a woman the leader. Nor was a woman ever a flock unit leader.

12 Much has been made of the hostility between settled populations and the migrating shepherds. For the raikas, at least, such conflicts are the exception; mutual accommodation the rule.

13 Table 6.2 can be interpreted much like the previous table. Begin with row 1. Of the thirty respondents who were asked who makes the decisions related to the direction in which the camp should travel, twenty-six mentioned the nambardar and four said it was the Council of Elders.

14 Recall from the discussion in chapter 4 that these tasks include contacting the shearers, negotiating prices for the shearing and the sale of the wool, selecting a farmer who will host the shepherds during the shearing, finding space for the shearing and water for washing the sheep, storing the wool after shearing if it is not immediately taken to the market, and finding a way to transport the wool to the market.

15 The wool on a sheep is worth no more than Rs 20, often less. The price of a sheep, however, is approximately Rs 400.

16 The last part of figure 6.1 needs further analysis. How, precisely, do the shepherds ensure that their leader will not misuse the power that is delegated to him? The shepherds seem to be caught in a dilemma. On the one hand, they stand to gain substantial economic benefits by delegating to their leaders the power to make decisions in a wide variety of situations. But they also face the risk that their leaders, especially the nambardar, may abuse delegated powers. In response, the shepherds use a comprehensive set of preventive and corrective measures that help guard against opportunistic behavior. The analysis of these mechanisms is of more general interest and forms the subject of chapter 7.

17 Neither is it necessary nor is this the place to launch into a discussion of rationality — surely one of the most debated concepts in the social sciences. I use the term somewhat provocatively, but also narrowly, with recognition of the many pitfalls awaiting attempts to establish intent, agency, and cause.

18 As Hirschon and Gold (1982) point out in their study of territoriality in an urban community in Greece, space forms a foundational part of the everyday lives of community members — providing a framework as well as a basis for communication. See also Edney 1976.

19 See Horowitz 1972 for a discussion of the relationship between ecological niches and a sense of ethnicity among pastoralist and farmer groups in Sudan.

20 The greatest incentives and opportunities for free riding, moral hazard, adverse selection, and corruption exist in the relationship between the camp leader and the average shepherd (see chapter 7).

7 HIERARCHY IN COMMUNITY

1 In an important paper, Ferguson (1985) examines the "bovine mystique" and the reasons why the Basotho place a high emphasis on cattle keeping. He contests alike attempts to view pastoralists through the lenses of "tradition" and "rational choice." According to him, explanations based on tradition are unfounded and misunderstand the changing nature of pastoralist activities and contexts; rational choice explanations are ad hoc and do not really explain much (648–49). His solution is to incorporate more context and pay greater attention to the cultural aspects of the situation. Fer-

guson's engagement with rational choice approaches, I suggest, may itself be somewhat misplaced. His explanation can be connected with rational choice approaches if the reason cattle are not sold lies in their greater utility in times of acute shortage rather than some "cultural fact" particular only to the Basotho livestock owners. This chapter, specifically focusing on the cultural context in which the expectations of shepherds and their leaders are formed, shows that the use of rational choice approaches is not irreconcilably in conflict with cultural explanations.

2   See Green and Shapiro 1994, the debate in *Critical Review* (vol. 9, nos. 1–2), and O'Neill 1995. The strategy of developing the discussion also addresses those who see new institutionalism as possessing a potential relevance to development issues (Nabli and Nugent 1989).

3   The chapter shows that it is possible to derive useful insights even through easily accessible game-theoretic models in contrast to some recent literature on principal-agent relationships that increasingly deploys highly complex reasoning and models. While my treatment simplifies the empirical situation I observed, it still incorporates the most significant aspects of the social context through the payoff structure of the game I use.

4   Bromley (1989), Eggertsson (1990), North (1990), and Williamson (1985) provide useful introductions.

5   Among anthropologists, Baily (1965, 1988, 1991), Barth (1966, 1967), and Colson (1974) are among the earliest exponents of approaches that are either compatible with or presage the current institutionalist approaches to the study of rural or "traditional" societies.

6   But see Li 1993. Several works on multiple agents and single principals are, of course, also available (Demski and Sappington 1984; Mookherjee 1984; Tirole 1986). See also Krepps 1992.

7   Economic considerations seem to play only a small role in the desire to be the leader. The power to make decisions for a group of followers is perhaps the primary force impelling some individuals to seek status as a leader.

8   I refrain from a description of the concepts of adverse selection, moral hazard, shirking, and corruption, as they are relatively well discussed elsewhere. See, for example, Baiman 1982, Ostrom et al. 1993, and Williamson 1985. See Kiser and Tong 1992 for a discussion of different types of corruption and Shleifer and Vishny 1993 for the relation of corruption to efficiency.

9   A third alternative is logically possible — that the camp will split into two or more parts as a result of dissension between the principals and the agent. I did not observe, nor could the shepherds recall, such fissioning.

10   None of the shepherds I interviewed felt that the camp leader would be removed *during* a migration cycle even if he proved incompetent or corrupt.

11   Few shepherds leave a camp in the middle of the migration cycle, but the fact that they possess this choice remains an ultimate restraint on hasty, thoughtless, or arbitrary decisions. The extent to which the leader can impose his will is thus limited by the shepherds' freedom to express their preferences through exit and voice. The shepherds use voice not by protesting directly. Instead they use voice to talk with other shepherds and thus affect the reputation of a camp leader and the possibility of his continued selection (see Hirschman 1970). In a rare conversation, a group of shepherds remembered one instance in which a flock leader, disgusted with the camp leader, left the camp in midmigration. The flock leader was universally condemned by other camp leaders

and shepherds as having behaved in a capricious and willful fashion. "It is like a father deserting his son in the wilderness" was a common expression used by shepherds to describe the errant leader's behavior. When the shepherd left the camp, his leader lost status and respect.

12 One of the earliest theorists to stress the necessity of monitoring in principal-agent relationships was Max Weber, who discussed how factors such as complexity and diversity of tasks and ease of communication and transportation affect the possibility of monitoring effectively ([1922] 1978).

13 The camp leader and the Council of Elders are each responsible for roughly half of the cases requiring a decision on the time at which sheep shearers and wool merchants should be called. The most important factor governing who should make the decision seemed to be the size of the camp—in smaller camps, the camp leader was far more likely than the council to make this decision. The reason behind this distribution seems to relate to the increasing amount of information needed to make decisions (as the camp grew in size) about when the entire camp's sheep would be ready for shearing.

14 At rates of exchange current during the fieldwork, U.S. $1.00 equaled Rs 28.00.

15 As the raikas say: "Even your enemy does not cheat you while looking you in the eye."

16 For a detailed explanation of why sheep buyers often visit the camps, see Agrawal 1992.

17 See Crèmer 1995 and Frey 1993 for discussions of how tighter monitoring may turn out to be counterproductive. Frey examines the role of trust and loyalty in principal-agent relationships, while Crèmer discusses how more information might make threats of punishment less credible. Holmstrom (1979), of course, provides the classical statement regarding the benefits of gaining and using all available information. Lewis and Sappington (1993) discuss how ignorance might introduce discontinuities into the performance of the agent.

18 Cf. Alam 1989 and Shleifer and Vishny 1993.

19 Usually the fines paid to settle disputes with villagers are negotiated openly. Thus, all shepherds know the amount. The negotiations for bribes are carried out more covertly and seldom anyone other than the camp leader is involved. An elder member of the camp may contribute his expertise, but most of the time the leader alone decides the amount of the bribe.

20 In a colorful phrase, one shepherd explained to me that government officials absorb bribes like the parched earth sucks rain.

21 Collectively the shepherds spend perhaps no more than three or four hours monitoring the camp leader each day since the rest of the leader's day is filled with innocuous tasks. Individually each shepherd need spend no more than ten or fifteen minutes in the course of the daily routine on monitoring tasks. Thus, during the approximately three hundred days of migration, when shepherds work twelve to fifteen hours per day, they spend no more than four or five days on monitoring tasks. This implies in monetary terms an expenditure of about Rs 100 to 150 per shepherd in labor time (see also note 22).

22 The cost of monitoring is very low for the shepherds because they constantly engage their agent in face-to-face interactions. If the cost of monitoring, a_4, were to rise to a point where it is greater than a_3/N, the losses suffered by the agent's cheating, then there would be an equilibrium in pure strategies. In this case, the shepherds will never monitor and the leader will always cheat.

23 I follow the standard procedure for calculating equilibrium in mixed strategies (see Ordeshook 1986 and Rasmusen 1989).

24 See the exchange between Bianco (1990), Ordeshook (1990), and Tsebelis (1990) for the relative merits and problems of using a mixed strategies game model.

25 As North (1993) suggested, direct monitoring and sanctioning, when feasible, avoids the additional principal-agent problems that third-party involvement can introduce.

26 Cf. Tsebelis 1989, 1990.

27 There are relatively low variations in income, wealth, and asset ownership among migrating raikas. The lessons I draw from their example may not, therefore, be easily applicable to groups that are highly stratified. See Frantz 1975 and Irons 1971. See Flanagan 1989 for an extensive review of hierarchies and inequalities in simple "egalitarian" societies.

8   AN ENDING

1 See, for example, Leach and Leach 1983, Malinowski 1922, and Weiner 1976.

2 See Chagnon 1983 and Lizot 1985.

3 See also Fratkin, Roth, and Galvin's introduction to their edited volume (1994b: 2–4) and Waller and Sobania as they condense, discuss, and contest "coffee-table book stereotypes" of nomadic pastoralists: "[T]hey are instantly recognizable by their exotic and romantic dress and bearing and by their obsessive concern for livestock . . . they themselves collude in this external definition of the 'noble savage' because they resist change and disdain the modern world" (1994: 46).

4 See Bolton et al. (1976), who attempt to show that the personality traits of pastoralists make up a coherent and self-consistent type. Even pastoralists' children, according to them, are more independent, self-reliant, and responsible than those of farmers! Ekvall makes some similar points about pastoralist culture in Tibet (1974).

5 See the thirty-page spread in the September 1993 issue of the magazine by the "Australian adventurer" Robyn Davidson. A later, more extended treatment by Davidson of her stay among the raikas is insightful. For a discussion of the use of stereotyped constructions to facilitate aesthetic appropriation, see Little 1991 and Galaty and Bonte 1991. For a telling account of the ways in which the *National Geographic* produces nonwestern peoples for an American audience, see Lutz and Collins 1993.

6 See O'Hanlon 1992: 62–64 for a criticism of Oldenberg's position.

Bibliography

Abel, N., and P. Blaikie. 1990. Land degradation, stocking rates, and conservation policies in the communal rangelands of Botswana and Zimbabwe. Pastoral Development Network Papers, no. 29a. London: Overseas Development Institute.

Abrams, Philip. 1988. Notes on the difficulty of studying the state. *Journal of Historical Sociology* 1(1): 58–89.

Abu-Lughod, Lila. 1990. The romance of resistance: Tracing transformations of power through Bedouin women. *American Ethnologist* 17(1): 41–55.

Adams, Robert M. 1978. Strategies of maximization, stability, and resilience in Mesopotamian society, settlement, and agriculture. *Proceedings of the American Philosophical Society* 22:329–35.

Adas, Michael. 1981. From avoidance to confrontation: Peasant protest in precolonial and colonial Southeast Asia. *Comparative Studies in Society and History* 23(2): 217–47.

Agrawal, Arun. 1997a. *Community-in-Conservation: Beyond Enchantment and Disenchantment.* Conservation and Development Forum Working Paper 5, no. 1. Gainesville: University of Florida.

Agrawal, Arun. 1997b. Shepherds and their leaders among the raikas of India: A principal-agent perspective. *Journal of Theoretical Politics* 9(2): 235–63.

Agrawal, Arun. 1996. The community vs the market and the state: Forest use in Uttarakhand in the Indian Himalaya. *Journal of Agricultural and Environmental Ethics* 9(1): 1–15.

Agrawal, Arun. 1995. Dismantling the divide between indigenous and scientific knowledge. *Development and Change* 26(3): 413–39.

Agrawal, Arun. 1994. *I don't need it but you can't have it.* Pastoral Development Network Papers, no. 36a, 36–55. London: Overseas Development Institute.

Agrawal, Arun. 1993. Mobility and cooperation among nomadic shepherds: The case of the raikas. *Human Ecology* 21(3): 261–79.

Agrawal, Arun. 1992. Risks, resources, and politics: Studies of institutions and resource use from village India. Ph.D. diss., Duke University.

Agrawal, Arun, and K. Sivaramakrishnan, eds. 1997. Agrarian environments. Mimeo.

Alam, M. Shahid. 1989. Anatomy of corruption: An approach to the political economy of underdevelopment. *American Journal of Economics and Sociology* 48(4): 441–56.

Alchian, Armen. 1950. Uncertainty, evolution, and economic theory. *Journal of Political Economy* 58(3): 211–21.

Alchian, Armen, and Harold Demsetz. 1973. The property rights paradigm. *Journal of Economic History* 33 (March): 16–27.

Alexander, Jennifer. 1987. *Trade, Traders, and Trading in Rural Java*. Singapore: Oxford University Press.

Alexander, Jennifer, and Paul Alexander. 1995a. Commodification and consumption in a Central Borneo community. *BKI* 151(2): 179–93.

Alexander, Jennifer, and Paul Alexander. 1995b. Markets, gender, and the state in rural Java. Paper presented in the Program in Agrarian Studies Colloquium Series, Yale University, November.

Alexander, Paul. 1992. What's in a price? In Roy Dilley, ed., *Contesting Markets: Analyses of Ideology, Discourse, and Practice*, 79–96. Edinburgh: Edinburgh University Press.

Almond, Gabriel. 1988. The return to the state. *American Political Science Review* 82:853–74.

Alt, James E., and Kenneth A. Shepsle, eds. 1990. *Perspectives on Positive Political Economy*. Cambridge: Cambridge University Press.

Althusser, Louis. [1969] 1996. *For Marx*. Trans. Ben Brewster. London: Verso.

Anantram, K. 1988. Economic analysis of harnessing common property resources for livestock development in arid zones of Western Rajasthan. Ph.D. thesis, University of Jodhpur.

Anderlini, Luca, and Hamid Sabourian. 1992. Some notes on the economics of barter, money, and credit. In C. Humphrey and S. Hugh-Jones, eds., *Barter, Exchange, and Value: An Anthropological Approach*, 75–106. Cambridge: Cambridge University Press.

Anderson, D., and Richard Grove, eds. 1987. *Conservation in Africa*. Cambridge: Cambridge University Press.

Anderson, Benedict. 1983. *Imagined Communities: Reflections on the Origin and Spread of Nationalism*. London: Verso.

Appadurai, Arjun. 1986a. Introduction: Commodities and the politics of value. In Arjun Appadurai, ed., *The Social Life of Things: Commodities in Cultural Perspective*, 3–63. Cambridge: Cambridge University Press.

Appadurai, Arjun, ed. 1986b. *The Social Life of Things: Commodities in Cultural Perspective*. Cambridge: Cambridge University Press.

Appiah, Kwame Anthony, and Henry Louis Gates Jr., eds. 1995. *Identities*. Chicago: University of Chicago Press.

Arendt, Hannah. 1993. *Between Past and Future*. New York: Penguin.

Arhem, Kaj. 1985. *Pastoral Man in the Garden of Eden: The Maasai of the Ngogongoro Conservation Area, Tanzania*. Uppsala: University of Uppsala.

Arnold, David. 1985. Bureaucratic recruitment and subordination in colonial India. In R. Guha, ed., *Subaltern Studies IV: Writings on South Asian History and Society*, 1–53. New Delhi: Oxford University Press.

Arora, Sushil, and A. K. Haldar. 1994. Economy of the nomadic communities of India. *Man in India* 74(2): 181–91.

Asad, Talal. 1970. *The Kababish Arabs*. London: Hurst.

Avineri, Shlomo, ed. 1969. *Karl Marx on Colonialism and Modernization*. New York: Anchor.

Bacon, Elizabeth E. 1954. Types of pastoral nomadism in Central and Southwest Asia. *Southwest Journal of Anthropology* 10:44–68.

Bailey, Fred. 1991. Why is information asymmetrical? Symbolic behavior in asymmetrical organizations. *Rationality and Society* 3(4): 475–95.

Bailey, Fred. 1988. *Humbuggery and Manipulation: The Art of Leadership*. Ithaca: Cornell University Press.

Bailey, Fred. 1965. Decisions by consensus in councils and committees with special reference to village and local government in India. In M. Gluckman and F. Eggan, eds., *Political Systems and the Distribution of Power*. New York: Praeger.

Bailey, Lynn R. 1980. *If You Take My Sheep. . . : The Evolution and Conflicts of Navajo Pastoralism, 1630–1868*. Pasadena: Westernlore.

Bailey, Robert C., et al. 1989. Hunting and gathering in the tropical rain forest: Is it possible? *American Anthropologist* 91:59–82.

Baiman, S. 1982. Agency research in managerial accounting: A survey. *Journal of Accounting Literature* 1:154–213.

Banfield, Edward. 1975. Corruption as a feature of government organization. *Journal of Law and Economics* 18:587–605.

Bardhan, Pranab. 1993. Analytics of the institutions of informal cooperation in rural development. *World Development* 21(4): 633–39.

Barlett, P., ed. 1980. *Agricultural Decision-Making: Anthropological Contributions to Rural Development*. New York: Academic.

Baron, D. 1984. Noncooperative regulation of a non-localized externality. *Rand Journal of Economics* 16:553–68.

Barraclough, Solon. 1991. *An End to Hunger? The Social Origins of Food Strategies*. London: Zed.

Barth, F. 1967. On the study of social change. *American Anthropologist* 69:661–69.

Barth, F. 1966. *Models of Social Organization*. Occasional Papers, no. 23. London: Royal Anthropological Institute.

Barth, F. 1961. *Nomads of South Persia*. Oslo: Oslo University Press.

Barthes, Roland. 1977. *Image Music Text*. New York: Hill and Wang.

Barzel, Yoram. 1989. *Economic Analysis of Property Rights*. Cambridge: Cambridge University Press.

Barzel, Yoram. 1977. An economic analysis of slavery. *Journal of Law and Economics* 20(1): 87–110.

Bates, Daniel G. 1971. The role of the state in peasant-nomad mutualism. *Anthropological Quarterly* 44(3): 109–31.

Bates, Daniel G., and Susan H. Lees. 1977. The role of exchange in productive specialization. *American Anthropologist* 79:824–41.

Bates, Robert H. 1996. *Institutions as Investments*. Development Discussion Papers, no. 527. Cambridge: Harvard Institute for International Development, Harvard University.

Bates, Robert H. 1989. *Beyond the Miracle of the Market: The Political Economy of Agrarian Development in Kenya*. Cambridge: Cambridge University Press.

Bates, Robert H. 1988. Contra contractarianism: Some reflections on the new institutionalism. *Politics and Society* 16:387–401.

Bates, Robert H. 1983. *Essays in the Political Economy of Rural Africa*. Berkeley: University of California Press.

Bates, Robert H. 1981. *Markets and States in Tropical Africa: The Political Basis of Agricultural Policies*. Berkeley: University of California Press.

Bates, Robert H., and Barry R. Weingast. 1995. *A New Comparative Politics: Integrating Rational Choice and Interpretivist Approaches*. Working Papers, no. 95-3. Cambridge: Center for International Affairs, Harvard University.

Baudrillard, Jean. 1993. *Symbolic Exchange and Death*. London: Sage.

Baudrillard, Jean. 1981. *For a Critique of the Political Economy of the Sign*. St. Louis: Telos.

Baudrillard, Jean. 1975. *The Mirror of Production*. Trans. Mark Poster. St. Louis: Telos.

Becker, Gary. 1976. *The Economic Approach to Human Behavior*. Chicago: University of Chicago Press.

Becker, Gary, and George J. Stigler. 1974. Law enforcement, malfeasance, and the compensation of enforcers. *Journal of Legal Studies* 3:1–19.

Beckwith, C., and A. Fisher. 1990. *African Ark*. New York: Abrams.

Behnke, Roy, Jr. 1994. Natural resource management in pastoral Africa. *Development Policy Review* 12(1): 5–27.

Behnke, Roy H., Jr., and Ian Scoones. 1993. Rethinking range ecology: Implications for rangeland management in Africa. In Roy H. Behnke Jr., Ian Scoones, and Carol Kerven, eds., *Range Ecology at Disequilibrium: Pastoral Adaptation in African Savannas*, 1–30. London: Overseas Development Institute, International Institute for Environment and Development, and Commonwealth.

Behnke, Roy H., Jr., Ian Scoones, and Carol Kerven, eds. 1993. *Range Ecology at Disequilibrium: Pastoral Adaptation in African Savannas*. London: Overseas Development Institute, International Institute for Environment and Development, and Commonwealth.

Bell, D., H. Raiffa, and A. Tversky, eds. 1990. *Descriptive, Normative, and Prescriptive Interactions*. New York: Cambridge University Press.

Bencherifa, Abdellatif, and Douglas L. Johnson. 1990. Adaptation and intensification in the pastoral systems of Morocco. In John G. Galaty and Douglas Johnson, eds., *The World of Pastoralism: Herding Systems in Comparative Perspective*, 394–416. New York: Guilford.

Bendix, John, Bartholomew H. Sparrow, Bertell Ollman, and Timothy Mitchell. 1992. Going beyond the state. *American Political Science Review* 86(4): 1007–21.

Benjamin, Walter. 1978. *Illuminations*. New York: Schocken.

Berkes, Fikret, ed. 1989. *Common Property Resources: Ecology and Community Based Sustainable Development*. London: Belhaven.

Bernheim, B., and M. Whinston. 1986. Common agency. *Econometrica* 54(4): 923–42.

Bernheim, B., and M. Whinston. 1985. Common marketing agency as a device for facilitating collusion. *Rand Journal of Economics* 16:269–81.

Bernstein, H. 1989. *Agricultural Modernization in the Era of Structural Adjustment*. Development Policy and Practice Discussion Papers. Milon Keynes: Open University.

Berry, Sara. 1992. *No Condition Is Permanent: The Social Dynamics of Agrarian Change and Sub-Saharan Africa*. Madison: University of Wisconsin Press.

Bhabha, Homi. 1994. *The Location of Culture*. London: Routledge.

Bhaduri, Amit. 1989. Employment and livelihood: The rural labor processes and the formulation of development policy. *International Labour Review* 128(6): 685–701.

Bhaduri, Amit. 1986. Forced commerce and agrarian change. *World Development* 14(2).

Bianco, W. 1990. Crime and punishment: Are one-shot, two person games enough? *American Political Science Review* 84(2): 569–73.

Biglaiser, G., and C. Mezzetti. 1993. Principals competing for an agent in the presence of adverse selection and moral hazard. *Journal of Economic Theory* 61:302–30.

Block, F. 1990. *Postindustrial Possibilities: A Critique of Economic Discourse*. Berkeley: University of California Press.

Block, W., G. Brennan, and K. Elzinga, eds. 1985. *Morality of the Market*. Vancouver: Fraser Institute.

Bolton, Charlene, Ralph Bolton, Lorraine Gross, Amy Koel, Carol Michelson, Robert L. Munroe, and Ruth H. Munroe. 1976. Pastoralist and personality: An Andean replication. *Ethos* 4(4): 463–81.

Bonte, Pierre, and John Galaty. 1991. Introduction to John Galaty and Pierre Bonte, eds., *Herders, Warriors, and Traders: Pastoralism in Africa*, 3–22. Boulder: Westview.

Bourdieu, Pierre. 1977. *Outline of a Theory of Practice*. Cambridge: Cambridge University Press.

Bovin, Mette, and Leif Langer, eds. 1990. *Adaptive Strategies in African Arid Lands: Proceedings from a Seminar at the Scandinavian Institute of African Studies*. Uppsala: Scandinavian Institute of African Studies.

Braidotti, Rossi. 1994. *Nomadic Subjects: Embodiment and Sexual Difference in Contemporary Feminist Theory*. New York: Columbia University Press.

Braithwaite, Edward K. 1971. *The Development of Creole Society in Jamaica, 1770–1820*. Oxford: Oxford University Press.

Brara, Rita. 1987. Shifting sands: A study of rights in common pasture. Jaipur: Institute of Development Studies. Mimeo.

Bratton, Michael. 1987. The comrades and the countryside: The politics of agricultural policy in Zimbabwe. *World Politics* 39(2): 174–203.

Braudel, Fernand. 1985. *Civilization and Capitalism, 15th–18th Century*. Vol. 2, *The Wheels of Commerce*. London: Fontana.

Braverman, A., and G. Stiglitz. 1982. Sharecropping and the interlinking of agrarian markets. *American Economic Review* 72:695–715.

Brokensha, D., D. Warren, and O. Werner, eds. 1980. *Indigenous Knowledge Systems and Development*. Lanham, MD: University Press of America.

Bromley, Daniel, ed. 1992. *Making the Commons Work: Theory, Practice, and Policy*. San Francisco: Institute for Contemporary Studies.

Bromley, Daniel. 1989. *Economic Interests and Institutions: The Conceptual Foundations of Public Policy*. Oxford: Blackwell.

Brow, James. 1990. Notes on community, hegemony, and the uses of the past. *Anthropological Quarterly* 63(1): 1–6.

Brower, Barbara. 1987. Livestock and landscape: The Sherpa pastoral system in Sagarmatha (Mt. Everest) National Park, Nepal. Ph.D. diss., University of California, Berkeley.

Buchanan, James M. 1986. *Liberty, Market, and State: Political Economy in the 1980s*. Brighton, Sussex: Wheatsheaf.

Buck, Susan J. 1988. Inter-jurisdictional management in Chesapeake Bay fisheries. *Coastal Management* 16:151–86.

Burnham, Philip. 1979. Spatial mobility and political centralization in pastoral societies. In L'Equipe Ecologie et Anthropologie des Societes Pastorales, ed., *Pastoral Production and Society*, 349–60. Cambridge: Cambridge University Press.

Butler, Judith. 1995. Collected and fractured: Response to *Identities*. In K. Anthony Appiah and Henry Louis Gates Jr., eds., *Identities*, 439–47. Chicago: University of Chicago Press.

Calvert, Randall L. 1995. The rational choice theory of social institutions: Cooperation, coordination, and communication. In Jeffrey S. Banks and Eric A. Hanushek, eds., *Modern Political Economy: Old Topics, New Directions*, 216–67. Cambridge: Cambridge University Press.

Campbell, David J. 1984. Response to drought among farmers and herders in Southern Kajiado District, Kenya. *Human Ecology* 12(1): 35–64.

Cashdan, Elizabeth A., ed. 1990. *Risk and Uncertainty in Tribal and Peasant Economies.* Boulder: Westview.

Cashdan, Elizabeth A. 1985. Coping with risk: Reciprocity among the Basarwa of northern Botswana. *Man* (n.s.) 20:454–74.

Cashdan, Elizabeth A. 1983. Territoriality among human foragers: Ecological models and an application to four Bushmen groups. *Current Anthropology* 24(1): 47–66.

Casimir, Michael J. 1992. The determinants of rights to pasture: Territorial organization and ecological constraints. In M. J. Casimir and Aparna Rao, eds., *Mobility and Territoriality: Social and Spatial Boundaries among Foragers, Fishers, Pastoralists, and Peripatetics*, 153–204. New York: Berg.

Casimir, M. J., and Aparna Rao, eds. 1992. *Mobility and Territoriality: Social and Spatial Boundaries among Foragers, Fishers, Pastoralists, and Peripatetics.* New York: Berg.

Chagnon, Napoleon A. 1983. *Yanomami: The Fierce People.* New York: Holt, Rinehart and Winston.

Chambers, R., N. Saxena, and T. Shah. 1989. *To the Hands of the Poor: Water and Trees.* London: Intermediate Technology Publications.

Chatty, Dawn. 1990. The current situation of the Bedouin in Syria, Jordan, and Saudi Arabia and their prospects for the future. In Carl Salzman and John Galaty, eds., *Nomads in a Changing World*, 123–38. Naples: Instituto Universitario Orientale.

Chatty, Dawn, 1987. The Harasiis: Pastoralists in a petroleum exploited environment. *Nomadic Peoples* 24:14–22.

Chatty, Dawn. 1980. The pastoral family and the truck. In Philip Carl Salzman, ed., *When Nomads Settle: Processes of Sedentarization as Adaptation and Response*, 80–94. New York: Praeger.

Chatty, Dawn. 1976. From camel to truck: A pastoral adaptation. *Folk* 18:113–28.

Cheung, Steven. 1970. The structure of a contract and the theory of a non-exclusive resource. *Journal of Law and Economics* 13:49–70.

Chong, D. 1995. Rational choice theory's mysterious rivals. *Critical Review: Rational Choice Theory and Politics* (special issue) 9(1–2): 37–58.

Clay, E. J., C. Benson, B. Harriss, and S. Gillespie. 1988. *Food Strategy in India.* 2 vols. London: Relief and Development Institute.

Clay, Jason. 1988. *Indigenous Peoples and Tropical Forests: Models of Land Use and Management from Latin America.* Cambridge, MA: Cultural Survival.

Clifford, James. 1988. *The Predicament of Culture: Twentieth-Century Ethnography, Literature, and Art.* Cambridge: Harvard University Press.

Clifford, James. 1986. On ethnographic allegory. In James Clifford and George Marcus, eds., *Writing Culture: The Poetics and Politics of Ethnography*, 98–121. Berkeley: University of California Press.

Clifford, James, and George E. Marcus, eds. 1986. *Writing Culture: The Poetics and Politics of Ethnography.* Berkeley: University of California Press.

Cohn, Bernard. 1955. The changing status of a depressed caste. In McKim Marriott, ed., *Village India.* Chicago: University of Chicago Press.

Colburn, F., ed. 1989. *Everyday Forms of Peasant Resistance.* Armonk, NY: M. E. Sharpe.

Colson, E. 1974. *Tradition and Contract: The Problem of Order.* Chicago: Aldine.

Connolly, William E. 1988. *Political Theory and Modernity.* New York: Blackwell.

Cooper, Frederick. 1994. Conflict and connection: Rethinking colonial African history. *American Historical Review* 99(5): 1516–45.

Cooper, Frederick, Florencia E. Mallon, Steve J. Stern, Allen F. Isaacman, and William Roseberry. 1994. *Confronting Historical Paradigms: Peasants, Labor, and the Capitalist World System in Africa and Latin America*. Madison: University of Wisconsin Press.

Cordell, John C., and Margaret McKean. 1987. Sea tenure in Bahia, Brazil. In National Research Council, ed., *Proceedings of the Conference on Common Property Resource Management*, 85–114. Washington, DC: National Academy Press.

Corlett, William. 1989. *Community without Unity: A Politics of Derridean Extravagance*. Durham: Duke University Press.

Crèmer, J. 1995. Arm's length relationships. *Quarterly Journal of Economics* 110(2): 275–95.

Croll, E., and D. Parkin, eds. 1992. *Bush Base, Forest Farm: Culture, Environment, and Development*. London: Routledge.

Crooke, H. E. [1896] 1975. *The Tribes and Castes of the North-West Provinces and Oudh*. Delhi: Cosmo.

Crosby, Christina. 1991. *The Ends of History: Victorians and "The Woman Question."* New York: Routledge.

Cross, H. E. 1912. *The Camel and Its Diseases*. London: Balliere, Tindall and Cox.

CSE (Center for Science and Environment). 1985. *The State of India's Environment, 1984–5: The Second Citizen's Report*. New Delhi: Center for Science and Environment.

Dahlman, Carl. 1980. *The Open Field System and Beyond: A Property Rights Analysis of an Economic Institution*. Cambridge: Cambridge University Press.

Dahlman, Carl. 1979. The problem of externality. *Journal of Law and Economics* 22:141–62.

Dalton, Melville. 1959. *Men Who Manage*. New York: Wiley.

Dasgupta, Partha. 1985. *Epochs of Economic Theory*. London: Blackwell.

Davidson, Robyn. 1996. *Desert Places*. London: Viking.

Davidson, Robyn. 1993. Wandering with India's rabari. *National Geographic* (September): 62–92.

de Alessi, Louis. 1983. Property rights, transaction costs, and X-efficiency: An essay in economic theory. *American Economic Review* 73(1): 64–81.

de Alessi, Louis. 1980. The economics of property rights: A review of the evidence. *Research in Law and Economics* 2:1–47.

Deane, P. 1978. *The Evolution of Economic Ideas*. Cambridge: Cambridge University Press.

Dearlove, John. 1989. Bringing constitutions back in. *Political Studies* 37(4): 521–39.

de Boer, W. F., and H. H. T. Prins. 1989. Decisions of cattle herdsmen in Burkina Faso and optimal foraging models. *Human Ecology* 17(4): 445–64.

de Certeau, Michel. 1984. *The Practice of Everyday Life*. Berkeley: University of California Press.

de Lauretis, Teresa, ed. 1986. *Feminist Studies/Critical Studies*. Bloomington: Indiana University Press.

Demsetz, Harold. 1967. Toward a theory of property rights. *American Economic Review* 62:347–59.

Demski, J., and D. Sappington. 1984. Optimal incentive contracts with multiple agents. *Journal of Economic Theory* 33:152–71.

Denbow, James, and Edwin Wilmsen. 1986. Advent and course of pastoralism in the Kalahari. *Science* 234:1509–15.

DiIulio, J. 1994. Principled agents: The cultural bases of behavior in a federal government bureaucracy. *Journal of Public Administration Research and Theory* 4(3): 277–318.

Dilley, Roy, ed. 1992a. *Contesting Markets: Analyses of Ideology, Discourse, and Practice*. Edinburgh: Edinburgh University Press.

Dilley, Roy. 1992b. Contesting markets: A general introduction to market ideology, imagery, and discourse. In Roy Dilley, ed., *Contesting Markets: Analyses of Ideology, Discourse, and Practice*, 1–34. Edinburgh: Edinburgh University Press.

Domhoff, G. William. 1971. *The Higher Circles*. New York: Random House.

Dore, R. P. [1961] 1973. Function and cause. *American Sociological Review* 26.

Doughty, C. M. 1937. *Travels in Arabia Desert*. New York: Random House.

Dumont, Louis. 1986. *Essays on Individualism: Modern Ideology in Anthropological Perspective*. Chicago: University of Chicago Press.

Dumont, Louis, 1977. *From Mandeville to Marx: The Genesis and Triumph of Economic Ideology*. Chicago: University of Chicago Press.

Durkheim, Emile. [1915] 1982. *The Rules of Sociological Method*. New York: Free Press.

Dyson-Hudson, R., and N. Dyson-Hudson. 1980. Nomadic pastoralism. *Annual Review of Anthropology* 9:15–61

Easton, David. 1981. The political system beseiged by the state. *Political Theory* 9:303–25.

Eckstein, H. 1979. On the "science" of the state. *Daedalus* 108:1–20.

Edney, Julian. 1976. Human territories: Comment on functional properties. *Environment and Behavior* 8(1): 31–47.

Eggertsson, Thrainn. 1990. *Economic Behavior and Institutions: Principles of Neoinstitutional Economics*. Cambridge: Cambridge University Press.

Ekvall, Robert B. 1974. Tibetan nomadic pastoralists: Environments, personality, and ethos. *Proceedings of the American Philosophical Society* 118(6): 519–37.

Elam, Yitzchak. 1979. Nomadism in Ankole as a substitute for rebellion. *Africa* 49(2): 147–58.

Ellis, J. E., and D. M. Swift. 1988. Stability of African pastoral ecosystems: Alternate paradigms and implications for development. *Journal of Range Management* 41(6): 450–59.

Elster, Jon. 1989. *Nuts and Bolts for the Social Sciences*. Cambridge: Cambridge University Press.

Engels, F. [1884] 1942. *The Origins of the Family, Private Property, and the State*. New York: International.

Ensminger, Jean. 1992. *Making a Market: The Institutional Transformation of an African Society*. Cambridge: Cambridge University Press.

Ensminger, Jean, and A. Rutten. 1991. The political economy of changing property rights: Dismantling a pastoral commons. *American Ethnologist* 18(4): 683–99.

Enthoven, R. E. 1920. *The Tribes and Castes of Bombay*. Vols. 1–3. Bombay: Government Press.

Escobar, Arturo. 1995. *Encountering Development: The Making and Unmaking of the Third World*. Princeton: Princeton University Press.

Etzioni, Amitai. 1996. Positive aspects of community and the dangers of fragmentation. *Development and Change* 27:301–14.

Etzioni, Amitai. 1993. *The Spirit of Community: The Reinvention of American Society*. New York: Simon and Schuster.

Evans, Peter, Dietrich Ruschemeyer, and Theda Skocpol, eds., 1985. *Bringing the State Back In*. Cambridge: Cambridge University Press.

Evans-Pritchard, E. E. 1940. *The Nuer: A Description of the Modes of Livelihood and Political Institutions of a Nilotic People*. Oxford: Oxford University Press.

FAIR (Foundation to Aid Industrial Recovery). 1980. A study of migrant shepherds. Report submitted to All India Handicrafts Board, Ministry of Commerce, New Delhi, India.

Fairhead, James. 1993. Paths of authority: Roads, the state, and the market in Eastern Zaire. In Cynthia Hewitt de Alcantara, ed., *Real Markets: Social and Political Issues of Food Policy Reform*, 17–35. London: Frank Cass.

Fama, E. 1980. Agency problems and the theory of the firm. *Journal of Political Economy* 88:288–307.

Fama, E., and M. Jensen. 1983. Separation of Ownership and Control. *Journal of Law and Economics* 26:301–26.

Fanon, Frantz. 1963. *The Wretched of the Earth*. New York: Grove.

Ferguson, James. 1994. *The Anti-Politics Machine: "Development," Depoliticization, and Bureaucratic Power in Lesotho*. Minneapolis: University of Minnesota Press.

Ferguson, James. 1985. The bovine mystique: Power, property, and livestock in rural Lesotho. *Man* (n.s.) 20:647–74.

Fine, Bob. 1984. *Democracy and the Rule of Law*. London: Pluto.

Fischer, J. F. 1986. *Trans-Himalayan Traders*. Berkeley: University of California Press.

Flanagan, James G. 1989. Hierarchy in simple "egalitarian" societies. *Annual Review of Anthropology* 18:245–66.

Forbes, H. 1989. Of grandfathers and grand theories: The hierarchised ordering of responses to hazard in a Greek rural community. In Paul Halstead and John O'Shea, eds., *Bad Year Economics: Cultural Responses to Risk and Uncertainty*, 87–97. Cambridge: Cambridge University Press.

Foucault, Michel. 1982. Afterword: The subject and power. In Hubert L. Dreyfus and Paul Rabinow, *Michel Foucault: Beyond Structuralism and Hermeneutics*, 208–26. 2d ed., with afterword by and interview with Michel Foucault. Chicago: University of Chicago Press.

Foucault, Michel. 1979. *Discipline and Punish: The Birth of the Prison*. New York: Vintage.

Foucault, Michel. 1978. *The History of Sexuality*. Vol. 1. New York: Random House.

Foucault, Michel. 1977. *Language, Counter-Memory, Practice: Selected Essays and Interviews, edited, with an introduction by Donald F. Bouchard*. Ithaca: Cornell University Press.

Fox, Richard. 1969. "Professional primitives": Hunters and gatherers of nuclear South Asia. *Man in India* 49:139–60.

Frantz, Charles. 1975. *Pastoral Societies, Stratification, and National Integration in Africa*. Research Reports, no. 30. Uppsala: Scandinavian Institute of African Studies.

Fraser, Nancy. 1992. Rethinking the public sphere: A contribution to the critique of actually existing democracy. In Craig Calhoun, ed., *Habermas and the Public Sphere*, 109–42. Cambridge: MIT Press.

Fratkin, Elliot. 1991. *Surviving Drought and Development: Ariaal Pastoralists of Northern Kenya*. Boulder: Westview.

Fratkin, Elliot, Kathleen Galvin, and Eric Roth, eds. 1994a. *African Pastoralist Systems: An Integrated Approach*. Boulder: Lynne Rienner.

Fratkin, Elliot, Kathleen Galvin, and Eric Roth, eds. 1994b. Introduction to Elliot Fratkin, Kathleen Galvin, and Eric Roth, eds., *African Pastoralist Systems: An Integrated Approach*, 1–16. Boulder: Lynne Rienner.

Frey, B. 1993. Does monitoring increase work effort? The rivalry with trust and loyalty. *Economic Inquiry* 31 (October): 663–70.

Friedman, Milton. 1989. Feminism and modern friendship: Dislocating the community. *Ethics* 99:275–90.

Friedman, Milton. 1953. *Essays in Positive Economics*. Chicago: University of Chicago Press.

Friedman, Milton, and Rose Friedman. 1980. *Free to Choose: A Personal Statement*. New York: Harcourt Brace Jovanovich.

Furubotn, E., and S. Pejovich, eds. 1974. *The Economics of Property Rights*. Cambridge, MA: Ballinger.

Furubotn, Eirik, and Rudolph Richter. 1991. The new institutional economics: An assessment. In Eirik Furubotn and Rudolph Richter, eds., *The New Institutional Economics*, 1–32. College Station: Texas A&M University Press.

Fuss, Diana. 1995. Look who's talking, or if looks could kill. In K. Anthony Appiah and Henry Louis Gates Jr., eds., *Identities*, 424–33. Chicago: University of Chicago Press.

Fuss, Diana. 1989. *Essentially Speaking: Feminism, Nature, and Difference*. New York: Routledge.

Gaiha, Raghav. 1991. Poverty alleviation programmes in rural India: An assessment. *Development and Change* 22(1): 117–54.

Galaty, John G., and Pierre Bonte, eds. 1991. *Herders, Warriors, and Traders: Pastoralism in Africa*. Boulder: Westview.

Galaty, John G., and Douglas L. Johnson, eds. 1990. *The World of Pastoralism: Herding Systems in Comparative Perspective*. New York: Guilford.

Galbraith, J. 1977. *The Age of Uncertainty*. Boston: Houghton Mifflin.

Garber, Judith. 1995. Defining feminist community: Place, choice, and the urban politics of difference. In Judith A. Garber and Robyne S. Turner, eds., *Gender in Urban Research*, 24–43. Thousand Oaks, CA: Sage.

Gates, Henry Louis, Jr., and Kwame Anthony Appiah. 1995. Editors' introduction: Multiplying identities. In K. Anthony Appiah and Henry Louis Gates Jr., eds., *Identities*, 1–6. Chicago: University of Chicago Press.

Geertz, Clifford. 1979. Suq: The bazaar economy in Sefrou. In C. Geertz et al., eds., *Meaning and Order in Moroccan Society*. Cambridge: Cambridge University Press.

Geertz, Clifford. 1973. Deep play: Notes on the Balinese cock-fight. In *The Interpretation of Cultures*, 412–53. New York: Basic Books and Harper Collins.

Gell, Alfred. 1992. Inter-tribal commodity barter and reproductive gift-exchange in old Melanesia. In Caroline Humphrey and Stephen Hugh-Jones, eds., *Barter, Trade, and Value: An Anthropological Approach*, 142–68. Cambridge: Cambridge University Press.

Gellner, Ernest. 1994. Foreword to Anatoly M. Khazanov, *Nomads and the Outside World*, ix–xxv. 2d ed. Madison: University of Wisconsin Press.

Gellner, Ernest. 1981. General introduction: Relativism and universals. In B. Lloyd and J. Gay, eds., *Universals of Human Thought*, 1–20. Cambridge: Cambridge University Press.

Genovese, Eugene. 1974. *Roll, Jordan Roll: The World the Slaves Made*. New York: Pantheon.

Gilles, Jere Lee, and Jerome Gefu. 1990. Nomads, ranchers, and the state: The sociocultural aspects of pastoralism. In John Galaty and Douglas Johnson, eds., *The World of Pastoralism: Herding Systems in Comparative Perspective*, 99–118. New York: Guilford.

Gladwin, C. 1979. Production functions and decision models: Complementary models. *American Ethnologist* 6(4): 653–74.

Glover, J. 1994. A simpler mechanism that stops agents from cheating. *Journal of Economic Theory* 62:221–29.

Godelier, Maurice. 1978. Territory and property in primitive society. *Social Science Information* 17(3): 399–426.

Goldman, Michael. 1994. "There's a snake on our chests": State and development crisis in India's desert. Ph.D. diss., University of California, Santa Cruz.

Goldschmidt, Walter. 1975. A national livestock bank: An institutional divide for rationalizing the economy of tribal pastoralists. *International Development Review* 17(2): 2–6.

Goldschmidt, Walter. 1971. Independence as an element in pastoral social systems. *Anthropological Quarterly* 44(3): 132–42.

Gooch, Pernille. 1992. Transhumant pastoralists in northern India: The Gujar case. *Nomadic Peoples* 30:84–96.

Gordon, Colin. 1980. *Power/Knowledge: Selected Interviews and Other Writings.* New York: Pantheon.

Gorra, Michael. 1995. Response to *Identities.* In K. Anthony Appiah and Henry Louis Gates Jr., eds., *Identities,* 434–38. Chicago: University of Chicago Press.

Gramsci, Antonio. 1971. *Selections from the Prison Notebooks.* New York: International.

Gramsci, Antonio. 1959. *The Modern Prince and Other Writings.* New York: International.

Granovetter, Mark, and Richard Swedberg, eds. 1992. *The Sociology of Economic Life.* Boulder: Westview.

Gray, John. 1984. Lamb auctions on the borders. *European Journal of Sociology* 25(1): 59–82.

Grayzel, John Aron. 1990. Markets and migration: A Fulbe pastoral system in Mali. In John G. Galaty and Douglas Johnson, eds., *The World of Pastoralism: Herding Systems in Comparative Perspective,* 35–68. New York: Guilford.

Green, Donald, and Ian Shapiro. 1995. Pathologies revisited: Reflections on our critics. *Critical Review: Rational Choice Theory and Politics* (special issue) 9(1–2): 235–76.

Green, D., and I. Shapiro. 1994. *Pathologies of Rational Choice Theory.* New Haven: Yale University Press.

Gregory, C. A. 1988. Village moneylending, the World Bank, and landlessness in village India. *Journal of Contemporary Asia* 18:47–58.

Grossman, S., and O. Hart. 1983. An analysis of the principal-agent problem. *Econometrica* 51(1): 7–45.

Guha, Ranajit. [1982] 1988a. The prose of counter-insurgency. In Ranajit Guha and Gayatri C. Spivak, eds., *Selected Subaltern Studies,* 45–88. New York: Oxford University Press.

Guha, Ranajit. [1982] 1988b. On some aspects of the historiography of colonial India. In Ranajit Guha and Gayatri C. Spivak, eds., *Selected Subaltern Studies,* 37–44. New York: Oxford University Press.

Guha, Ranajit. 1983. *Elementary Aspects of Peasant Insurgency in Colonial India.* Delhi: Oxford University Press.

Gulliver, P. H. 1975. Nomadic movements: Causes and implications. In Theodor Monod, ed., *Pastoralism in Tropical Africa,* 369–81. Oxford: Oxford University Press.

Gupta, Akhil. 1998. *Postcolonial Developments: Agriculture in the Making of Modern India.* Durham: Duke University Press.

Gusfield, Joseph. 1975. *Community: A Critical Response*. New York: Harper and Row.

Habermas, Jurgen. 1989. *The Structural Transformation of the Public Sphere*. Cambridge: MIT Press.

Hahn, Steven. 1982. Hunting, fishing, and foraging: Common rights and class relations in the postbellum South. *Radical History Review* 26(1): 37–64.

Hall, John A., ed. 1986. *States in History*. Oxford: Blackwell.

Hall, Stuart. 1977. Culture, media, and the "ideological effect." In J. Curran, M. Gurevitch, and J. Woollacott, eds., *Mass Communication and Society*, 315–48. London: Edwin Arnold.

Hall, Stuart, and T. Jefferson, eds. 1976. *Resistance through Rituals: Youth Subcultures in Post-war Britain*. London: Hutchinson.

Halstead, Paul, and John O'Shea, eds. 1989. *Bad Year Economics: Cultural Responses to Risk and Uncertainty*. Cambridge: Cambridge University Press.

Hardin, Garrett. 1986. Cultural carrying capacity: A biological approach to human problems. *Bioscience* 36(9): 599–606.

Hardin, Garrett. 1978. Political requirements for conserving our common heritage. In H. P. Bokaw, ed., *Wildlife and America*. Washington, D.C.: Council on Environmental Quality.

Hardin, Garrett. 1968. The tragedy of the commons. *Science* 162:1243–48.

Harriss, Barbara. 1993. Real foodgrain markets and state intervention in India. In Cynthia Hewitt de Alcantara, ed., *Real Markets: Social and Political Issues of Food Policy Reform*, 61–81. London: Cass.

Harriss, Barbara. 1984. *State and Market*. New Delhi: Concept.

Harvey, David. 1989. *The Condition of Postmodernity: An Enquiry into the Origins of Cultural Change*. Cambridge, MA: Blackwell.

Haworth, Alan. 1994. *Anti-libertarianism: Markets, Philosophy, and Myth*. London: Routledge.

Hayami, Yujiro, and Vernon Ruttan. 1971. *Agricultural Development: An International Perspective*. Baltimore: Johns Hopkins University Press.

Hayek, Friedrich. 1960. *The Constitution of Liberty*. Chicago: University of Chicago Press.

Haynes, Douglas, and Gyan Prakash, eds. 1992a. *Contesting Power: Resistance and Social Relations in South Asia*. Delhi: Oxford University Press.

Haynes, Douglas, and Gyan Prakash. 1992b. Introduction: The entanglement of power and resistance. In Douglas Haynes and Gyan Prakash, eds., *Contesting Power: Resistance and Social Relations in South Asia*, 1–22. Delhi: Oxford University Press.

Hebdige, D. 1979. *Subculture: The Meaning of Style*. London: Methuen.

Hedlund, H. 1971. *The Impact of Group Ranches on a Pastoral Society*. Institute of Development Studies Papers, no. 100. Nairobi: University of Nairobi.

Herskovits, M. 1926. The cattle complex in East Africa. *American Anthropologist* 28:230–72, 361–88, 494–528, 633–64.

Hewitt de Alcantara, Cynthia. 1993. Introduction: Markets in principle and practice. In Cynthia Hewitt de Alcantara, ed., *Real Markets: Social and Political Issues of Food Policy Reform*, 1–16. London: Cass.

Hillery, George A., Jr. 1955. Definitions of community: Areas of agreement. *Rural Sociology* 20(June): 111–23.

Hindess, B. 1988. *Choice, Rationality, and Social Theory*. London: Unwin Hyman.

Hindess, B. 1986. *Freedom, Equality, and the Market*. London: Tavistock.

Hirschman, Albert O. 1986. *Rival Views of Market Society and Other Recent Essays*. Cambridge: Harvard University Press.

Hirschman, Albert O. 1970. *Exit, Voice, and Loyalty: Response to Decline in Firms, Organizations, and States*. Cambridge: Harvard University Press.

Hirschon, Renee B., and John Gold. 1982. Territoriality and the home environment in a Greek urban community. *Anthropological Quarterly* 55(2): 63–73.

Hitchcock, Robert K., and John D. Holm. 1993. Bureaucratic domination of hunter-gatherer societies: A study of the San in Botswana. *Development and Change* 24:305–38.

Hogg, Richard. 1992. Should pastoralism continue as a way of life? *Disasters* 16(2): 131–37.

Holling, C. S. 1973. Resilience and stability of ecological systems. *Annual Review of Ecology and Systematics* 4:1–23.

Holmstrom, B. 1979. Moral hazard and observability. *Bell Journal of Economics* 10:74–91.

Homewood, K., and W. Rodgers. 1991. *Maasailand Ecology: Pastoral Development and Wildlife Conservation in Ngorongoro, Tanzania*. Cambridge: Cambridge University Press.

Homewood, K., and W. Rodgers. 1984. Pastoralism and conservation. *Human Ecology* 12(4): 431–41.

Horowitz, Michael M. 1972. Ethnic boundary maintenance among pastoralists and farmers in the western Sudan. *Journal of Asian and African Studies* 7(1–2): 105–14.

Humphrey, Caroline, and Stephen Hugh-Jones. 1992. Introduction: Barter, exchange and value. In Caroline Humphrey and Stephen Hugh-Jones, eds., *Barter, Exchange, and Value: An Anthropological Approach*, 1–20. Cambridge: Cambridge University Press.

Hurvicz, L. 1973. The design of mechanisms for resource allocation. *American Economic Review* 63:1–30.

Ibbetson, D. 1914. *A Glossary of the Tribes and Castes of the Punjab and North-West Frontier Province*. Vol. 3. Lahore: n.p.

Ingold, Tim. 1986. *The Appropriation of Nature: Essays on Human Ecology*. Manchester: Manchester University Press.

Ingold, Tim. 1980. *Hunters, Pastoralists, and Ranchers*. Cambridge: Cambridge University Press.

Ingold, Tim, David Riches, and James Woodburn, eds. 1988. *Hunters and Gatherers*. Vol. 1. Oxford: Berg.

Irons, William. 1971. Variation in political stratification among the Yomut Turkmen. *Anthropological Quarterly* 44(3): 143–56.

Jain, H. K. 1993. The institutional environment and its relationship to sustainable development. In Richard Cincotta and Ganesh Pangare, eds., *Pastoralism and Pastoral Migration in Gujarat*, 59–64. Anand, India: Institute of Rural Management.

James, William. 1892. *Textbook of Psychology*. London: Macmillan.

Jameson, Frederick. 1990. *Postmodernism or the Cultural Logic of Late Capitalism*. London: Verso.

Jedrej, M. C. 1991. The role of rainmakers. In Jeffrety C. Stone, ed., *Pastoral Economies in Africa and Long-Term Responses to Drought*, 54–61. Aberdeen: Aberdeen University African Studies Group.

Jensen, M. 1983. Organization theory and methodology. *Accounting Review* 50:319–39.

Jensen, M., and W. Meckling. 1976. Theory of the firm: Managerial behavior, agency costs, and capital structure. *Journal of Financial Economics* 3:305–60.

Jodha, Narpat. 1990. Rural common property resources: Contributions and crisis. *Founda-*

tion Day lecture, Society for the Promotion of Wasteland Development, New Delhi, May 16. Mimeo.

Jodha, Narpat. 1988. Population growth and common property resources: Micro-level evidence from selected areas. Paper presented at the conference Expert Consultation on Population and Agricultural Development: Institutions and Policies, Food and Agriculture Organization, Rome, June 29–July 1.

Jodha, Narpat. 1987. A Note on contribution of CPRs to PPR-based farming systems in dry tropical regions of India. Paper presented at the Common Property Resources Workshop, Sariska, Rajasthan, India.

Jodha, Narpat. 1985. Population growth and the decline of common property resources in Rajasthan, India. *Population and Development Review* 11:247–63.

Jodhpur Spearhead Team. 1985. Short note on Pasture and Sheep Development Programme, under DPAP, Jodhpur (1974–75 to 1983–84). Mimeo.

Johnson, Douglas L. 1973. *Jabal al-Akhdar, Cyrenaicia: An Historical Geography of Settlement and Livelihood.* Research Papers, no. 148. Chicago: Department of Geography, University of Chicago.

Johnson, Douglas. 1969. *The Nature of Nomadism.* Research Papers, no. 118. Chicago: Department of Geography, University of Chicago.

Johnson, Ronald N., and Gary D. Libecap. 1982. Contracting problems and regulation: The case of the fishery. *American Economic Review* 72(5): 1005–22.

Joseph, Gilbert. 1990. On the trail of Latin American bandits: A reexamination of peasant resistance. *Latin American Research Review* 25:7–53.

Joseph, Gilbert, and Daniel Nugent, eds. 1994. *Everyday Forms of State Formation: Revolution and the Negotiation of Rule in Modern Mexico.* Durham: Duke University Press.

Kaul, M. 1996. Two centuries on the commons: The Punjab. Manuscript.

Kavoori, Purnendu. 1996. Pastoralism in expansion: The transhuming sheep herders of western Rajasthan. Ph.D. diss., The Hague, Institute of Social Studies.

Kavoori, Purnendu. 1990. Pastoral transhumance in western Rajasthan: A report on the migratory system of sheep. Jaipur, Institute of Development Studies. Mimeo.

Kellner, Douglas. 1994. *Baudrillard: A Critical Reader.* Oxford: Blackwell.

Kelly, Robert L. 1992. Mobility/sedentism: Concepts, archaeological measures, and effects. *Annual Review of Anthropology* 21:43–66.

Khazanov, Anatoly. [1984] 1994. *Nomads and the Outside World.* 2d ed. Madison: University of Wisconsin Press.

Khazanov, Anatoly. 1990. Pastoral nomads in the past, present, and future: A comparative view. In Paul A. Olson, ed., *The Struggle for Land: Indigenous Insights and Industrial Empire in the Semiarid World,* 81–99. Lincoln and London: University of Nebraska Press.

Kiewiet D., and M. McCubbins. 1991. *The Logic of Delegation: Congressional Parties and the Appropriations Process.* Chicago: University of Chicago Press.

Kirzner, Israel M. 1994. The ethics of competition. In Horst Siebert, ed., *The Ethical Foundations of the Market Economy,* 101–14. Tubingen: Mohr.

Kirzner, Israel M. 1979. *Perception, Opportunity, and Profit: Studies in the Theory of Entrepreneurship.* Chicago: University of Chicago Press.

Kirzner, Israel M. 1973. *Competition and Entrepreneurship.* Chicago: University of Chicago Press.

Kiser, E., and X. Tong. 1992. Determinants of the amount and type of corruption in state fiscal bureaucracies: An analysis of late imperial China. *Comparative Political Studies* 25(3): 300–31.

Knight, Jack. 1992. *Institutions and Social Conflict*. Cambridge: Cambridge University Press.

Kohler-Rollefsson, I. 1992. The raika camel pastoralists of western India. *Research and Exploration* 8(1): 117–19.

Kohli, Atul. 1987. *The State and Poverty in India: Politics of Reform*. New York: Cambridge University Press.

Koster, Harold A. 1977. The ecology of pastoralism in relation to changing patterns of land use in the Northeast Peloponnese. Ph.D. diss., University of Pennsylvania.

Krader, L. 1959. The ecology of nomadic pastoralism. *International Social Science Journal* 11:499–510.

Krepps, M. 1992. *Bureaucrats and Indians: Principal-Agent Relations and Efficient Management of Tribal Forest Resources*. Discussion Papers, no. 1,601. Cambridge: Harvard University, Institute of Economic Research.

Kreps, D. 1990. Corporate culture and economic theory. In J. Alt and K. Shepsle, eds., *Perspectives on Positive Political Economy*, 90–143. Cambridge: Cambridge University Press.

Kroeber, A. 1948. *Anthropology*. New York: Harcourt Brace.

Kuznar, Lawrence A. 1991. Transhumant goat pastoralism in the high Sierra of the south central Andes: Human responses to environmental and social uncertainty. *Nomadic Peoples* 28:93–104.

LaBianca, Oystein Sakala. 1990. *Sedentarization and Nomadization: Food System Cycles at Hesban and Vicinity in Transjordan*. Berrien Springs, MI: Institute of Archaeology and Andrews University Press.

Laffont, J., and J. Tirole. 1987. Using cost observation to regulate firms. *Journal of Political Economy* 94:614–41.

Lal, Deepak. 1988. *The Hindu Equilibrium: Cultural Stability and Economic Stagnation*. Vol. 1. Oxford: Clarendon.

Lamprey, Hugh. 1983. Pastoralism yesterday and today: The overgrazing problem. In F. Bouliere, ed., *Tropical Savannahs*, 643–66. Amsterdam: Elsevier.

Lancaster, William, and Fidelity Lancaster. 1990. Desert devices: The pastoral system of the Rwala Bedu. In John G. Galaty and Douglas Johnson, eds., *The World of Pastoralism: Herding Systems in Comparative Perspective*, 177–94. New York: Guilford.

Larson, Bruce A., and Daniel Bromley. 1990. Property rights, externalities, and resource degradation: Locating the tragedy. *Journal of Development Economics* 33:235–62.

Leach, J. W., and E. Leach. 1983. *The Kula: New Perspectives on Massim Exchange*. Cambridge: Cambridge University Press.

Leach, Melissa, and Robin Mearns. 1996. Challenging received wisdom in Africa. In Melissa Leach and Robin Mearns, eds., *The Lie of the Land: Challenging Received Wisdom on the African Environment*, 1–33. London: International African Institute.

Lee, R., and I. De Vore, eds. 1968. *Man the Hunter*. Chicago: Aldine.

Lefebvre, Henri. [1947] 1991. *Critique of Everyday Life*. London: Verso.

Lenin, V. I. [1917] 1976. *State and Revolution*. Peking: Foreign Languages Press.

Leshnik, L., and G. Sontheimer. 1975. *Pastoralists and Nomads in South Asia*. Wiesbaden: Harrassowitz.

Levi, Margaret. 1988. *Of Rule and Revenue*. Berkeley: University of California Press.

Lewis, I. M. 1961. *A Pastoral Democracy: A Study of Pastoralism and Politics among the Northern Somali of the Horn of Africa.* London: Oxford University Press for the International African Institute.

Lewis, T., and D. Sappington. 1993. Ignorance in agency problems. *Journal of Economic Theory* 61:169–83.

Lewis, T., and D. Sappington. 1989. Countervailing incentives in agency problems. *Journal of Economic Theory* 49:294–313.

Li, S. 1993. *Competitive Matching Equilibrium and Multiple Principal-Agent Models.* Discussion Papers, no. 267. Minneapolis: Center for Economic Research, University of Minnesota.

Libecap, Gary. 1989. *Contracting for Property Rights.* Cambridge: Cambridge University Press.

Lichbach, Mark. 1996. *The Cooperator's Dilemma.* Ann Arbor: University of Michigan Press.

Little, I. 1957. *A Critique of Welfare Economics.* Oxford: Clarendon.

Little, K. 1991. On safari: The visual politics of a tourist representation. In David Howes, ed., *The Varieties of Sensory Experience: A Sourcebook in the Anthropology of the Senses.* Toronto: University of Toronto Press.

Lizot, Jacques. 1985. *Tales of the Yanomami: Daily Life in the Venezuelan Forest.* Cambridge: Cambridge University Press.

Lubasz, Heinz. 1992. Adam Smith and the invisible hand — of the market? In Roy Dilley, ed., *Contesting Markets: Analyses of Ideology, Discourse, and Practice,* 37–56. Edinburgh: Edinburgh University Press.

Ludden, David. 1992. India's development regime. In Nicholas B. Dirks, ed., *Colonialism and Culture,* 247–88. Ann Arbor: University of Michigan Press.

Lupia, A., and M. McCubbins. 1994. Designing bureaucratic accountability. *Law and Contemporary Problems* 57(1): 91–126.

Lutz, Catherine A., and Jane L. Collins. 1993. *Reading National Geographic.* Chicago: University of Chicago Press.

Macaulay, Stewart. 1963. Non-contractual relations in business: A preliminary study. *American Sociological Review* 28(1): 55–67.

Malinowski, B. 1922. *Argonauts of the Western Pacific.* London: Routledge.

Mallon, Florencia E. 1994. The promise and dilemma of subaltern studies: Perspectives from Latin American history. *American Historical Review* 99(5): 1491–515.

Mallon, Florencia E. 1993. Dialogs among the fragments: Retrospect and prospect. In Frederick Cooper, Florencia E. Mallon, Steve J. Stern, Allen F. Isaacman, and William Roseberry, eds., *Confronting Historical Paradigms: Peasants, Labor, and the Capitalist World System in Africa and Latin America,* 371–401. Madison: University of Wisconsin Press.

Malmberg, Torsten. 1980. *Human Territoriality: Survey of Behavioral Territories in Man with Preliminary Analysis and Discussion of Meaning.* The Hague: Mouton.

Mandelbaum, David. 1970. *Society in India,* vol. 2. Berkeley: University of California Press.

Mann, Michael. 1986. *The Sources of Social Power.* Cambridge: Cambridge University Press.

Mansbridge, Jane, ed. 1990. *Beyond Self-Interest.* Chicago and London: University of Chicago Press.

March, J. 1988. *Decisions and Organizations.* Oxford: Blackwell.

Marcus, George E., ed. 1992. *Rereading Cultural Anthropology*. Durham: Duke University Press.

Marcussen, Henrik S., ed. 1993. *Institutional Issues in Natural Resources Management*. Occasional Papers, no. 9. Roskilde, Denmark: International Development Studies, Roskilde University.

Marshall, A. 1920. *Principles of Economics*. London: Macmillan.

Marten, G. 1986. *Traditional Agriculture in Southeast Asia: A Human Ecology Perspective*. Boulder: Westview.

Marx, Emanuel. 1978. The ecology and politics of nomadic pastoralists in the Middle East. In Wolfgang Weissleder, ed., *The Nomadic Alternative: Modes and Models of Interaction in the African-Asian Deserts and Steppes*, 41–74. The Hague: Mouton.

Marx, Karl. [1875] 1972. *Critique of the Gotha Program*. Peking: Foreign Languages Press.

Marx, Karl. [1848] 1948. *The Eighteenth Brumaire of Louis Bonaparte*. Moscow: Foreign Languages Publishing House.

Massey, Garth. 1987. *Subsistence and Change: Lessons of Agropastoralism in Somalia*. Boulder: Westview.

Mauss, Marcel. [1925] 1954. *The Gift: Forms and Functions of Exchange in Archaic Societies*. London: Cohen and West.

McCabe, J. Terrence. 1994. Mobility and land use among African pastoralists: Old conceptual problems and new interpretations. In Elliot Fratkin, Kathleen Galvin, and Eric Roth, eds., *African Pastoralist Systems: An Integrated Approach*, 69–90. Boulder: Lynne Rienner.

McCabe, Terrence. 1985. Livestock management among the Turkana: A social and ecological analysis of herding in an East African pastoral population. Ph.D. diss., State University of New York, Binghampton.

McCay, B., and J. Acheson, eds., 1987. *The Question of the Commons: The Culture and Ecology of Communal Resources*. Tucson: University of Arizona Press.

McCloskey, Donald. 1990. The open fields of England: Rent, risk, and the rate of interest. In David Galenson, ed., *Markets in History: Economic Studies of the Past*, 1–34. Cambridge: Cambridge University Press.

McCloskey, Donald. 1986. *The Rhetoric of Economics*. Cambridge: Cambridge University Press.

McKean, Margaret. 1992. Success on the commons: A comparative examination of institutions for common property resource management. *Journal of Theoretical Politics* 4(3): 247–81.

Mearns, Robin. 1993. Territoriality and land tenure among Mongolian pastoralists: Variation, continuity, and change. *Nomadic Peoples* 33:37–103.

Michaels, Walter Benn. [1992] 1995. Race into culture: A critical genealogy of cultural identity. In K. Anthony Appiah and Henry Louis Gates Jr., eds., *Identities*, 32–62. Chicago: University of Chicago Press.

Migdal, Joel S., Atul Kohli, and Vivienne Shue, eds. 1994. *State Power and Social Forces: Domination and Transformation in the Third World*. Cambridge: Cambridge University Press.

Miller, Daniel, ed. 1995. *Acknowledging Consumption*. London: Routledge.

Mills, C. Wright. 1959. *The Power Elite*. New York: Oxford University Press.

Mirga, Andrzej. 1992. Roma territorial behavior and state policy: The case of the socialist countries of East Europe. In Michael J. Casimir and Aparna Rao, eds., *Mobility and*

Territoriality: Social and Spatial Boundaries among Foragers, Fishers, Pastoralists, and Peripatetics, 259–78. New York: Berg.

Misra, Pramode Kumar. 1977. The Nomadic Gadulia Lohar of Eastern Rajasthan. Calcutta: Anthropological Survey of India, Government of India.

Misra, Pramode Kumar, and Kailash Malhotra, eds. 1982. Nomads in India: Proceedings of the National Seminar. Calcutta: Anthropological Survey of India.

Mitchell, Timothy. 1991. The limits of the state: Beyond statist approaches and their critics. American Political Science Review 85(1): 77–96.

Mitchell, Timothy. 1990. Everyday metaphors of power. Theory and Society 19:545–77.

Mithen S. 1989. Modeling hunter-gatherer decision-making: Complementing optimal foraging theory. Human Ecology 17(1): 59–83.

Mitrany, David. 1961. Marx against the Peasant: A Study in Social Dogmatism. New York: Collier.

Mookherjee, D. 1984. Optimal incentive schemes with many agents. Review of Economic Studies 51:433–56.

Mookherjee, D., and I. Png. 1992. Monitoring vis-à-vis investigation in enforcement of law. American Economic Review 82(3). 556 65.

Moore, Barrington, Jr. 1966. Social Origins of Democracy and Dictatorship: Lord and Peasant in the Making of the Modern World. Boston: Beacon.

Moore, Donald S. 1997. The crucible of cultural politics: Reworking development discourses in Zimbabwe's Eastern Highlands. Institute of International Studies, University of California, Berkeley, Mimeo.

Morris, Brian. 1977. Tappers, trappers, and the hill Pandaram (South India). Anthropos 72:225–41.

Nabli, Mustapha K., and Jeffrey B. Nugent. 1989. The new institutional economics and its applicability to development. World Development 17(9): 1333–47.

Nalebuff, B., and G. Stiglitz. 1983. Prizes and incentives: Towards a general theory of compensation and competition. Bell Journal of Economics 14:21–43.

Ndagala, Deniel Kyaruzi. 1992. Territory, Pastoralists, and Livestock: Resource Control among the Kisongo Maasai. Uppsala and Stockholm: Almqvist & Wiskell.

Ndagala, Deniel Kyaruzi. 1982. Operation Imparnati: The sedentarization of the pastoral Maasai in Tanzania. Nomadic Peoples 10.

Nelson, Cynthia, ed. 1973. The Desert and the Sown. Institute of International Studies Research Series, no. 21. Berkeley: University of California Press.

Nelson, Richard, and Sidney Winter. 1982. An Evolutionary Theory of Economic Change. Cambridge: Harvard University Press.

Netting, Robert M. 1981. Balancing on an Alp. Cambridge: Cambridge University Press.

Niamir, M 1990. Herders' decision making in natural resource management in arid and semi-arid Africa. FAO Forestry Papers. Rome: Food and Agriculture Organization.

Nisbet, Robert. [1953] 1990. The Quest for Community: A Study in the Ethics of Order and Freedom. San Francisco: Institute for Contemporary Studies.

North, Douglass. 1990. Institutions, Institutional Change, and Economic Performance. Cambridge: Cambridge University Press.

North, Douglass. 1981. Structure and Change in Economic History. New York: Norton.

North, Douglass, and Robert Thomas. 1973. The Rise of the Western World: A New Economic History. Cambridge: Cambridge University Press.

NRC (National Research Council). 1986. Proceedings of the Conference on Common Property Resource Management. Washington, DC: National Academy Press.

Nugent, J., and N. Sanchez. 1993. Tribes, chiefs, and transhumance: A comparative institutional analysis. *Economic Development and Cultural Change* 42(1): 87–113.

O'Hanlon, Rosalind. 1992. Issues of widowhood: Gender and resistance in colonial western India. In Douglas Haynes and Gyan Prakash, eds., *Contesting Power: Resistance and Social Relations in South Asia*, 62–108. Delhi: Oxford University Press.

Oldenberg, Veena Talwar. 1992. Lifestyle as resistance: The case of the courtesans of Lucknow. In Douglas Haynes and Gyan Prakash, eds., *Contesting Power: Resistance and Social Relations in South Asia*, 23–61. Delhi: Oxford University Press.

Oldfield, M., and J. Alcorn, eds. 1991. *Biodiversity: Culture, Conservation, and Ecodevelopment*. Boulder: Westview.

Olson, Mancur. 1965. *The Logic of Collective Action*. Cambridge: Harvard University Press.

O'Neill, Barry. 1995. Weak models, nil hypotheses, and decorative statistics: Is there really no hope? *Journal of Conflict Resolution* 39(4): 731–48.

Ophuls, William. 1973. Leviathan or oblivion. In H. E. Daly, ed., *Toward a Steady State Economy*. San Francisco: Freeman.

Ordeshook, P. 1990. Crime and punishment: Are one-shot, two person games enough? *American Political Science Review* 84(2): 573–75.

Ordeshook, P. 1986. *Game Theory and Political Theory*. Cambridge: Cambridge University Press.

Orlove, Benjamin S. 1986. Barter and cash sale on Lake Titicaca: A test of competing approaches. *Current Anthropology* 28(2): 85–106.

Orlove, Benjamin. 1977. *Alpacas, Sheep, and Men: Wool Export Economy and Regional Society in Southern Peru*. New York: Academic.

Ortiz, S. 1967. The structure of decision-making among Indians of Columbia. In R. Firth, ed., *Themes in Economic Anthropology*. London: Tavistock.

Ortiz, S., and S. Lees, eds. 1992. *Understanding Economic Process*. Monographs in Economic Anthropology, no. 10. Lanham: University Press of America.

O'Shea, John. 1989. The role of wild resources in small-scale agricultural systems: Tales from the lakes and the plains. In Paul Halstead and John O'Shea, eds., *Bad Year Economics: Cultural Responses to Risk and Uncertainty*, 57–67. Cambridge: Cambridge University Press.

Ostrom, Elinor. 1992. Community and the endogenous solution of commons problems. *Journal of Theoretical Politics* 4(3): 343–52.

Ostrom, Elinor. 1990. *Governing the Commons: The Evolution of Institutions for Collective Action*. New York: Cambridge University Press.

Ostrom, E., L. Schroeder, and S. Wynne. 1993. *Institutional Incentives and Sustainable Development: Infrastructure Policies in Perspective*. Boulder: Westview.

Parker, H. 1909. *Ancient Ceylon: An Account of the Aborigines and a Part of the Early Civilization*. London: Luzac.

Parry, J. 1989. On the moral perils of exchange. In J. Parry and M. Bloch, eds., *Money and the Morality of Exchange*, 64–93. Cambridge: Cambridge University Press.

Parry, J., and M. Bloch, eds. 1989. *Money and the Morality of Exchange*. Cambridge: Cambridge University Press.

Parsons, Talcott, and Neil Smelser. 1956. *Economy and Society: A Study in the Integration of Economic and Social Theory*. New York: Free Press.

Patwa, Shubhu. 1989. *Paryavaran Ki Sanskriti*. Bikaner, India: Vagdevi Prakashan.

Peters, Pauline. 1994. *Dividing the Commons: Politics, Policy, and Culture in Botswana*. Charlottesville: University of Virginia Press.

Picardi, A., and W. Siefert. 1976. A tragedy of the commons in the Sahel. *Technology Review* 78:42–51.

Pigg, Stacy Leigh. 1992. Constructing social category through place: Social representation and development in Nepal. *Comparative Studies in Society and History* 34(3): 491–513.

Plattner, Stuart, ed. 1985. *Markets and Marketing*. Lanham, MD: University Press of America.

Polanyi, Karl. 1957. *The Great Transformation: The Political and Economic Origins of Our Time*. Boston: Beacon.

Polanyi, Karl, et al. 1944. *Trade and Market in Early Empires*. Glencoe: Free Press.

Pollard, S. 1971. *The Idea of Progress*. Harmondsworth: Penguin.

Popkin, Samuel. 1979. *The Rational Peasant*. Los Angeles and Berkeley: University of California Press.

Poplin, Dennis E. 1972. *Communities: A Survey of Theories and Methods of Research*. New York: Macmillan.

Posey, D., and W. Balee, eds. 1989. *Resource Management in Amazonia: Indigenous and Folk Strategies*. New York: New York Botanical Garden.

Posner, Richard. 1972. *The Economics of Law*. Boston: Little Brown.

Prakash, Gyan, 1994. Subaltern studies as postcolonial criticism. *American Historical Review* 99(5): 1475–90.

Prakash, Gyan. 1992. Can the "subaltern" ride? A reply to O'Hanlon and Washbrook. *Comparative Studies in Society and History* 34(1): 168–84.

Prakash, Gyan. 1991. Becoming a Bhuinya: Oral traditions and contested domination in Eastern India. In Douglas Haynes and Gyan Prakash, eds., *Contesting Power: Resistance and Everyday Social Relations in South Asia*, 145–74. Delhi: Oxford University Press.

Prasad, R. R. 1994. *Pastoral Nomadism in Arid Zones of India: Socio-Demographic and Ecological Aspects*. New Delhi: Discovery.

Pratt, D., and M. Gwynne, eds. 1977. *Rangeland Management and Ecology in East Africa*. London: Hodder and Stoughton.

Preston, Peter. 1992. Models of economic-theoretical engagement. In Roy Dilley, ed., *Contesting Markets: Analyses of Ideology, Discourse, and Practice*, 57–75. Edinburgh: Edinburgh University Press.

Quinn, N. 1975. Decision models of social structure. *American Ethnologist* 2(1): 19–46.

Rabinow, Paul. 1989. *French Modern: Norms and Forms of the Social Environment*. Chicago: University of Chicago Press.

Radhakrishnan, R. 1993. Postcoloniality and the boundaries of identity. *Callaloo* 16(4): 750–71.

Ramos, Alcida R. 1992. Reflecting on the Yanomami: Ethnographic images and the pursuit of the exotic. In George E. Marcus, ed., *Rereading Cultural Anthropology*, 48–68. Durham: Duke University Press.

Randhawa, T. S. 1996. *The Last Wanderers: Nomads and Gypsies of India*. Middletown, NJ: Timeless Books.

Ranger, Terence. 1993. Power, religion and community: The Matobo case. In Partha Chatterjee and Gyanendra Pandey, eds., *Subaltern Studies VII*, 221–46. Delhi: Oxford University Press.

Rao, Aparna, ed. 1987. *The Other Nomads: Peripatetic Minorities in Cross-Cultural Perspective*. Cologne: Bohlau.

Rasmusen, E. 1989. *Games and Information: An Introduction to Game Theory*. Oxford: Blackwell.

Rawls, John. 1971. *A Theory of Justice*. Cambridge: Harvard University Press.

Riefenstahl, L. 1982. *Vanishing Africa*. New York: Harmony.

Rigby, Peter. 1992. *Cattle, Capitalism, and Class: Ilparakuyo Maasai Transformations*. Philadelphia: Temple University Press.

Riley, Denise. 1988. *Am I That Name? Feminism and the Category of "Women" in History*. Minneapolis: University of Minnesota Press.

Robbins, Paul. 1998. Nomadization in western Rajasthan, India: An institutional and economic perspective. *Human Ecology* 26(1): 87–112.

Rogers, Raymond A. 1994. *Nature and the Crisis of Modernity: A Critique of Contemporary Discourse on Managing the Earth*. Montreal: Black Rose.

Root, Hilton. 1987. *Peasant and King in Burgundy: Agrarian Foundations of French Absolutism*. Berkeley: University of California Press.

Rose, Nikolas, and Peter Miller. 1992. Political power beyond the state: Problematics of government. *British Journal of Sociology* 43(2): 173–205.

Ross, S. 1973. The economic theory of agency: The principal's problem. *American Economic Review* 63:134–39.

Rowe, William L. 1968. The New Cauhans: A caste mobility movement in North India. In James Silverberg, ed., *Social Mobility in the Caste System in India*. The Hague: Mouton.

Rudner, O. 1989. Banker's trust and the culture of banking among the Nattukottai chettiars of colonial South India. *Modern Asian Studies* 23(3): 417–58.

Ruhela, Satya Pal. 1968. *The Gaduliya Lohar of Rajasthan: A Study in the Sociology of Nomadism*. New Delhi: Impex India.

Sack, Robert David. 1985. *Human Territoriality: Its Theory and History*. Cambridge: Cambridge University Press.

Sadr, K. 1991. *The Development of Nomadism in Ancient Northeast Africa*. Philadelphia: University of Pennsylvania Press.

Sahlins, Marshall. 1976. *Culture and Practical Reason*. Chicago: University of Chicago Press.

Sahlins, Marshall. 1974. *Stone Age Economics*. London: Tavistock.

Said, Edward. 1986. Foucault and the imagination of power. In David Couzens Hoy, ed., *Foucault: A Critical Reader*, 149–56. Oxford: Blackwell.

Saith, A. 1990. Development strategies and the rural poor. *Journal of Peasant Studies* 17(2): 171–244.

Salzman, Philip Carl. 1987. From nomads to dairymen: Two Gujarati cases. *Nomadic Peoples* 24:44–53.

Salzman, Philip Carl. 1986. Shrinking pasture for Rajasthani pastoralists. *Journal of Sociological Studies* 5(1): 128–38.

Salzman, Philip C. 1972. Multi-resource nomadism in Iranian Baluchistan. In William Irons and Neville Dyson-Hudson, eds., *Perspectives on Nomadism*, 60–68. Leiden: Brill.

Samuelson, Paul. 1947. *Foundations of Economic Analysis*. Cambridge: Harvard University Press.

Sandford, Stephen. 1983. *Management of Pastoral Development in the Third World*. Chichester: Wiley.

Sangari, Kumkum. 1990. The politics of the possible. In Ebdul Jan Mohamed and David Lloyd, eds., *The Nature and Contexts of Minority Discourse*, 216–45. New York: Oxford University Press.

Sangmpam, S. N. 1992. The overpoliticized state and democratization: A theoretical model. *Comparative Politics* 24(2): 401–17.

Sankan, S. S. 1971. *The Maasai*. Nairobi: East African Publishing House.

Sayer, Derek. 1994. Everyday forms of state formation: Some dissident remarks on "hegemony." In Gilbert M. Joseph and Daniel Nugent, eds., *Everyday Forms of State Formation: Revolution and the Negotiation of Rule in Modern Mexico*, 367–77. Durham: Duke University Press.

Schlager, Edella, William Blomquist, and Shui Yan Tang. 1994. Mobile flows, storage, and self-organized institutions for governing common-pool resources. *Land Economics* 700(3): 294–317.

Schlager, Edella, and Elinor Ostrom. 1992. Property rights regimes and natural resources: A conceptual analysis. *Land Economics* 68(3): 249–62.

Schlee, Gunther. 1989. *Identities on the Move: Clanship and Pastoralism in Northern Kenya*. Manchester: Manchester University Press.

Schleifer, A., and R. Vishny. 1993. Corruption. *Quarterly Journal of Economics* 108(3): 599–617.

Schmink, M., and C. Wood, eds. 1984. *Frontier Expansion in Amazonia*. Gainesville: University of Florida Press.

Schneider, Harold. 1990. Development and the pastoralists of East Africa. In Carl Salzman and John Galaty, eds., *Nomads in a Changing World*, 179–210. Naples: Instituto Universitario Orientale.

Schotter, Andrew. 1981. *The Economic Theory of Social Institutions*. Cambridge: Cambridge University Press.

Schumpeter, Joseph. [1942] 1975. *Capitalism, Socialism, and Democracy*. New York: Harper and Row.

Scott, James C. 1990. *Domination and the Arts of Resistance: Hidden Transcripts*. New Haven: Yale University Press.

Scott, James C. 1985. *Weapons of the Weak: Everyday Forms of Peasant Resistance*. New Haven: Yale University Press.

Scott, James C. 1976. *The Moral Economy of the Peasant: Rebellion and Subsistence in Southeast Asia*. New Haven: Yale University Press.

Seed, Patricia. 1991. Colonial and postcolonial discourse. *Latin American Research Review* 26:181–200.

Sen, Amartya. 1994. Markets and the freedom to choose. In Horst Siebert, ed., *The Ethical Foundations of the Market Economy*, 123–38. Tubingen: Mohr.

Sen, Amartya. 1981. *Poverty and Famines: An Essay on Entitlement and Deprivation*. Oxford: Clarendon.

Sharma, G. D. 1977. *Rajput Polity: A Study of Politics and Administration of the State of Marwar, 1638–1749*. New Delhi: Manohar.

Sharma, P. 1972. *Maharaja Man Singh of Jodhpur and His Times, 1803–1843 A.D.* Agra: Shiv Lal Agarwala.

Sharma, Ravindra. 1974. *Village Panchayats in Rajasthan: An Administrative Profile*. Jaipur: Aalekh.

Shepsle, Kenneth A. 1995. Studying institutions: Some lessons from the rational choice approach. In James Farr, John Dryzek, and Stephen T. Leonard, eds., *Political Science in History: Research Program and Political Traditions*, 276–95. Cambridge: Cambridge University Press.

Shepsle, Kenneth A., and Mark Bonchek. 1997. *Analyzing Politics: Rationality, Behavior, and Institutions*. New York: Norton.

Shils, E. 1957. Primordial, personal, sacred, and civil ties. *British Journal of Sociology* 8:130–45.

Shleifer, Andrei, and Robert W. Vishny. 1995. Corruption. *Quarterly Journal of Economics* 108(3): 599–618.

Siebert, Horst. 1994. Introduction to H. Siebert, ed., *The Ethical Foundations of the Market Economy: International Workshop*. Tubingen: Mohr.

Simmel, G. 1978. *The Philosophy of Money*. London: Routledge.

Singleton, Sara, and Michael Taylor. 1992. Common property, collective action, and community. *Journal of Theoretical Politics* 4(3): 309–24.

Sinha, Saurabh. 1996. *The Conditions for Collective Action: Land Tenure and Farmers' Groups in the Rajasthan Canal Project*. Gatekeeper Series, no. 57. London: International Institute for Environment and Development.

Skocpol, Theda. 1985. Bringing the state back in: Strategies of analysis in current research. In Peter Evans, Dietrich Ruschemeyer, and Theda Skocpol, eds., *Bringing the State Back In*, 3–37. Cambridge: Cambridge University Press.

Skocpol, Theda. 1979. *States and Social Revolutions: A Comparative Analysis of France, Russia, and China*. Cambridge: Cambridge University Press.

Smith, Andrew B. 1992. *Pastoralism in Africa: Origins and Development Ecology*. Athens: Ohio University Press.

Smith, Andrew. 1991. Adjusting to drought conditions in an event-driven system: An example from a Namaqualand Reserve. In Jeffrey C. Stone, ed., *Pastoral Economies in Africa and Long-Term Responses to Drought*, 109–13. Aberdeen: Aberdeen University African Studies Group.

Smith, John D. 1991. *The Epic of Pabuji*. Cambridge: Cambridge University Press.

Smith, R. 1981. Resolving the tragedy of the commons by creating private property rights in wildlife. *CATO Journal* 1:439–68.

Smith, Susan E. 1978. The environmental adaptation of nomads in the West African Sahel: A key to understanding prehistoric pastoralists. In Wolfgang Weissleder, ed., *The Nomadic Alternative: Modes and Models of Interaction in the African-Asian Deserts and Steppes*, 75–96. The Hague: Mouton.

Soja, Edward W. 1989. *Postmodern Geographies: The Reassertion of Space in Critical Social Theory*. London: Verso.

Spencer, Paul. 1990. Pastoralists and the ghost of capitalism. In Carl Salzman and John Galaty, eds., *Nomads in a Changing World*, 211–32. Naples: Instituto Universitario Orientale.

Spencer, Paul. 1988. *The Maasai of Matapato*. Bloomington: Indiana University Press.

Spiro, Melford. 1992. Cultural relativism and the future of anthropology. In George E. Marcus, ed., *Rereading Cultural Anthropology*, 124–51. Durham: Duke University Press.

Spivak, Gayatri Chakravarti. 1990. Poststructuralism, marginality, postcoloniality, and value. In Peter Collier and Helga Geyer-Ryan, eds., *Literary Theory Today*, 219–44. Cambridge: Polity Press.

Spivak, Gayatri C. 1988a. Can the subaltern speak? In Cary Nelson and Lawrence Grossberg, eds., *Marxism and the Interpretation of Culture*, 271–313. London: Macmillan.

Spivak, Gayatri C. 1988b. Subaltern studies: Deconstructing historiography. In Ranajit

Guha and Gayatri C. Spivak, eds., *Selected Subaltern Studies*, 3–34. New Delhi: Oxford University Press.

Spooner, Brian. 1973. *The Cultural Ecology of Pastoral Nomads*. Addison-Wesley Modules in Anthropology, no. 45. Reading, MA: Addison-Wesley.

Srivastava, Vinay. 1997. *Religious Renunciation of a Pastoral People*. Delhi: Oxford University Press.

Srivastava, Vinay. 1991. Who are the raikas/rabaris? *Man in India* (special issue) 71(1): 279–304.

Srivastava, Vinay. 1990. In search of harmony between life and environment. *Journal of Human Ecology* 1(3): 291–300.

Stack, Carol B. 1970. *All Our Kin: Strategies for Survival in a Black Community*. New York: Harper and Row.

Stenning, Derrick J. 1959. *Savannah Nomads*. London: Oxford University Press.

Stenning, Derrick J. 1957. Transhumance, migratory drift, migration: Patterns of pastoral Fulani nomadism. *Journal of the Royal Anthropological Institute of Great Britain and Ireland* 87:57–75.

Stewart, Michael. 1992. Gypsies at the horse-fair: A non-market model of trade. In Roy Dilley, ed., *Contested Markets: Analyses of Ideology, Discourse, and Practice*, 97–114. Edinburgh: Edinburgh University Press.

Strathern, Marilyn. 1992. Qualified value: The perspective of gift exchange. In Caroline Humphrey and Stephen Hugh-Jones, eds., *Barter, Exchange, and Value: An Anthropological Approach*, 169–91. Cambridge: Cambridge University Press.

Sugden, Robert. 1986. *The Economics of Rights, Cooperation, and Welfare*. Oxford: Blackwell.

Swallow, Brent. 1994. *The Role of Mobility within the Risk Management Strategies of Pastoralists and Agro-Pastoralists*. Gatekeeper Series, no. 47. London: International Institute for Environment and Development.

Swedberg, Richard. 1987. Economic sociology: Past and present. *Current Sociology* 35(1): 1–221.

Swidler, W. W. 1972. Some demographic factors regulating the formation of flocks and camps among the Brahui of Baluchistan. In William Irons and Neville Dyson-Hudson, eds., *Perspectives on Nomadism*. Leiden: Brill.

Tambiah, Stanley. 1984. *The Buddhist Saints of the Forest and the Cult of Amulets*. Cambridge: Cambridge University Press.

Tawney, R. H. 1966. *Land and Labor in China*. Boston: Beacon.

Taylor, Michael. 1987. *The Possibility of Cooperation*. Cambridge: Cambridge University Press.

Taylor, Michael, 1982. *Community, Anarchy, and Liberty*. Cambridge: Cambridge University Press.

Taylor, Ralph B. 1988. *Human Territorial Functioning: An Empirical, Evolutionary Perspective on Individual and Small Group Territorial Cognitions, Behaviors, and Consequences*. Cambridge: Cambridge University Press.

Thomas, David Hurst. 1981. Complexity among Great Basin Shoshoneans: The world's least affluent hunter-gatherers? *Senri Ethnological Studies* 9:19–52.

Thompson, E. P. 1971. The moral economy of the eighteenth-century English crowd. *Past and Present* 50:76–136.

Thongchai, Winichakul. 1994. *Siam Mapped: A History of the Geo-Body of a Nation.* Honolulu: University of Hawaii Press.

Thornton, Robert J. 1992. The rhetoric of ethnographic holism. In George E. Marcus, ed., *Rereading Cultural Anthropology,* 15–33. Durham: Duke University Press.

Tirole, J. 1986. Hierarchies and bureaucracies: On the role of collusion in organizations. *Journal of Law, Economics, and Organization* 2:181–213.

Tribe, D. E. 1950. Influence of pregnancy and social facilitation on the behavior of grazing sheep. *Nature* 166.

Tribe, K. 1981. *Genealogies of Capitalism.* London: Macmillan.

Trinh T. Minh-ha. 1991. *When the Moon Waxes Red: Representation, Gender, and Cultural Politics.* New York: Routledge.

Tsebelis, G. 1990. Crime and punishment: Are one-shot, two person games enough? *American Political Science Review* 84(2): 576–85.

Tsebelis, George. 1989. The Abuse of Probability in Political Analysis: The Robinson Crusoe Fallacy. *American Political Science Review* 83(1): 77–91.

Tsing, Anna Lowenhaupt. 1993. *In the Realm of the Diamond Queen: Marginality in an Out-of-the-Way Place.* Princeton: Princeton University Press.

Upadhayaya, Nirmala. 1973. *The Administration of Jodhpur State, 1800–1947.* Jodhpur: International.

Useem, Michael. 1979. The social organization of the American business elite and participation of corporation directors in the governance of American institutions. *American Sociological Review* 44:553–72.

Vandergeest, Peter, and Nancy Lee Peluso. 1995. Territorialization and state power in Thailand. *Theory and Society* 24:385–426.

van Ginkel, Rob. 1989. Plunderers into planters: Zeeland oystermen and the enclosure of the marine commons. In J. Borssevain and J. Verrips, eds., *Dutch Dilemmas: Anthropologists Look at the Netherlands,* 89–105. Maastricht, Netherlands: Van Gorcum.

Varshney, Ashutosh. 1995. *Democracy, Development, and the Countryside: Urban-Rural Struggles in India.* Cambridge: Cambridge University Press.

Wade, Robert. 1992. Common property resource management in South Indian villages. In Daniel Bromley, ed., *Making the Commons Work: Theory, Practice, and Policy,* 207–28. San Francisco: Institute for Contemporary Studies.

Wade, Robert. 1988. *Village Republics: Economic Conditions for Collective Action in South India.* Cambridge: Cambridge University Press.

Waller, Richard, and Neal Sobania. 1994. Pastoralism in historical perspective. In Elliot Fratkin, Kathleen Galvin, and Eric Roth, eds., *African Pastoralist Systems: An Integrated Approach,* 45–68. Boulder: Lynne Rienner.

Warren, D. 1991. *Using Indigenous Knowledge in Agricultural Development.* World Bank Discussion Papers, no. 127. Washington, DC: World Bank.

Warren, D., J. Slikkerveer, and D. Brokensha. 1991. *Indigenous Knowledge Systems: The Cultural Dimensions of Development.* London: Kegan Paul.

WCED (World Commission on Environment and Development). 1987. *Our Common Future.* Delhi: Oxford University Press.

Weber, Max. [1922] 1978. *Economy and Society: An Outline of Interpretive Sociology.* Berkeley: University of California Press.

Weiner, Annette. 1976. *Women of Value, Men of Renown: New Perspectives in Trobriand Exchange.* Austin: University of Texas Press.

Weissleder, W., ed. 1978. *The Nomadic Alternative: Modes and Models of Interaction in the African-Asian Deserts and Steppes*. The Hague: Mouton.

Welch, W. 1983. The political feasibility of full-ownership property rights: The case of pollution and fisheries. *Policy Sciences* 16:65–80.

Westoby, M., B. H. Walker, and I. Noy-Meir. 1989. Opportunistic management for rangelands not at equilibrium. *Journal of Range Management* 42:266–74.

Westphal-Hellbusch, S. 1975. Changes in meaning of ethnic names as exemplified by the Jat, Rabari, Bharvad, and Charan in northwestern India. In L. Leshnik and G. Sontheimer, eds., *Pastoralists and Nomads in South Asia*, 117–38. Wiesbaden: Harrasowitz.

White, Hayden. 1973. *Metahistory*. Baltimore: Johns Hopkins University Press.

Wickham, Gary. 1990. The political possibilities of postmodernism. *Economy and Society* 19(1): 121–49.

Wilks, I. 1975. *Asante in the 19th Century: The Structure and Evolution of a Political Order*. Cambridge: Cambridge University Press.

Williams, Donald C. 1996. Reconsidering state and society in Africa: The institutional dimension in land reform policies. *Comparative Politics* 28(2): 207–24.

Williamson, Oliver. 1985. *The Economic Institutions of Capitalism: Firms, Markets, Relational Contracting*. London: Free Press.

Williamson, Oliver. 1981. The economics of organization: The transaction cost approach. *American Journal of Sociology* 87(November): 548–77.

Williamson, Oliver. 1979. Transaction-cost economics: The governance of contractual relations. *Journal of Law and Economics* 22(3): 233–61.

Williamson, Oliver. 1975. *Markets and Hierarchies*. New York: Free Press.

Williamson, Oliver, and William Ouchi. 1981. The markets and hierarchies and visible hand perspectives. In Andrew Van de Ven and William Joyce, eds., *Perspectives on Organizational Design and Behavior*, 347–70. New York: Wiley.

Willis, Paul. 1981. *Learning to Labor: How Working Class Kids Get Working Class Jobs*. New York: Columbia University Press.

Wilmsen, Edwin. 1989. *Land Filled with Flies: A Political Economy of the Kalahari*. Chicago: University of Chicago Press.

Wilmsen, Edwin. 1973. Interaction, spacing behavior, and the organization of hunting bands. *Journal of Anthropological Research* 29(1): 1–31.

Wittgenstein, Ludwig. 1958. *The Blue and the Brown Books*. Oxford: Blackwell.

Wolf, C., Jr. 1990. *Markets or Governments: Choosing between Imperfect Alternatives*. Cambridge: MIT Press.

Wolf, Eric. 1982. *Europe and the People without History*. Berkeley: University of California Press.

Woodburn, J. C. 1972. Ecology, nomadic movement, and the composition of the local group among hunters and gatherers: An East African example and its implications. In P. Ucko, R. Tringham, and G. Dimbleby, eds., *Man, Settlement, and Urbanism*. London: Duckworth.

Young, Iris Marion. 1990. *Justice and the Politics of Difference*. Princeton: Princeton University Press.

Zhao, Ding-Xin, and John A. Hall. 1994. State power and patterns of late development: Resolving the crisis of the sociology of development. *Sociology* 28(1): 211–29.

Index

Forest Department, 53, 55, 57, 87, 106, 173 n.22
forests, 52
Foucault, Michel, 11, 17, 20, 39, 69, 76, 174 n.3, 179 n.32
Fox, Richard, 176 n.5
Fratkin, Elliot, 32, 104, 176 nn.2–3, 184 n.3
free riding, 72, 146
Friedman, M., 131
fuelwood, 35, 55
functionalism, 98, 108
Furubotn, Eirik, 178 n.14

Gaiha, Raghav, 175 n.19
Galaty, John G., 104, 184 n.5
game theory, 129, 149, 151, 180 n.3, 182 n.3; applied to raikas, 157–59
Garber, Judith, 131
Geertz, Clifford, 107, 146, 179 n.31
Gell, Alfred, 179 n.27
Giddens, Anthony, 25
Gladwin, C., 180 n.3
Glover, J., 150
Godelier, Maurice, 175 n.22
Godwara, 28
Goffman, Erving, 3
Goldman, Michael, 174 n.7
Goldschmidt, Walter, 163, 174 n.9
Gooch, Pernille, 176 n.3
government agencies, 9, 73
Gramsci, Antonio, 9, 39, 51
Granovetter, Mark, 119, 177 n.3
Gray, John, 179 n.31
Grayzel, John Aron, 83, 104
grazing days, 56
grazing fees, 63, 87, 174 n.5
Green, Donald, 182 n.2
Guha, Ranajit, 3, 171 n.26
Gujarat, 6, 14, 27–28, 31, 63
Gulliver, P. H., 82
Gupta, Akhil, 11, 178 n.11
Gusfield, Joseph, 180 n.4

habitus, 19
Hahn, Steven, 176 n.2
Hall, Stuart T., 51

Halstead, Paul, 132, 170 n.6, 171 n.14, 176 n.2
Hardin, Garrett, 32, 170 n.9
Harriss, Barbara, 102
Harvey, David, 176 n.29
Haryana, 6, 14, 62–63, 76, 88, 108
Haworth, Alan, 102
Hayami, Yujiro, 176 n.2
Haynes, Douglas, 165
Hebdige, D., 51
Hedlund, H., 175 n.21
hegemony, 39, 51–52, 165; definition of, 51
Herskovits, M., 32
Hewitt de Alcantara, Cynthia, 102
hierarchical exchanges, 107–8
hierarchy, 17, 108, 128, 148, 161, 169 n.11
Hillery, George A. Jr., 180 n.5
Hirschman, A., 182 n.11
Hirschon, Renee B., 181 n.18
history, 23, 29; and teleology, 32, 76
Hogg, Richard, 32
Holling, C. S., 174 n.3
Holmstrom, B., 183 n.17
Homewood, K., 32
Horowitz, Michael M., 181 n.19
Humphrey, Caroline, 116, 179 n.21
hunting and gathering, 32, 170 n.5, 180 n.3
Hurvicz, L., 150, 178 n.14

Ibbetson, D., 171 n.16
identity, 19, 20, 26–30; construction of, 28–29
indigenous peoples, 33, 163, 171 n.25
Indus River, 64
inequality, 17, 38, 44, 172 n.10
information asymmetries, 149, 160, 178 n.14
Ingold, Tim, 82, 170 n.11, 175 n.26
innovations, 32
institutions, 13–14, 41, 47, 59, 72, 93, 99, 169 n.9, 173 n.23; changes in, 40, 59; definition of, 14; and politic, 173 n.24; informal, 132; neoinstitutionalist theories of, 172 n.1; in Patawal, 50, 59; and rural resource management, 35, 38. *See also* common property

Integrated Rural Development Program, 73
irrigation, 14, 62, 64, 106, 109, 112

jagirdars, 48
Jain, H. K., 174 n.12
Jaipur, 27, 109
Jaisalmer, 6, 27, 53, 62
Jalore, 6
James, William, 175 n.25
Jedrej, M. C., 163
Jensen, M., 150
Jodha, Narpat, 46, 49, 173 n.14
Jodhpur, 3, 6, 27, 35, 41, 53, 55, 61, 69,
    109, 169 n.6, 174 n.11
Johnson, Douglas, 134
Johnson, Ronald N., 170 n.7
justice, 9

kamdar, 132
Kavoori, Purnendu, 62, 64, 87, 175 n.17,
    177 n.16
Kellner, Douglas, 179 n.24
Kelly, Robert L., 176 n.3
Kenya, 12
Khalsa, 48
Khazanov, Anatoly, 32, 84, 170 nn.5 and
    11
Kiser, E., 182 n.8
Knight, Jack, 59 n.24
Kohler-Rollefson, I., 27
Koster, Harold A., 86
Krader, L., 170 n.11
Krepps, M., 182 n.6
Kreps, D., 117, 150
Kroeber, A., 131
Kutch, 28

labor, 82, 88
Laffont, J., 150
Lal, Deepak, 98
Lamprey, Hugh, 32
Lancaster, William, 83
landholdings, 109, 172 n.10; of different
    castes, 44
landowners, 36, 43–44, 54–55
Larson, Bruce A., 170 n.7
Latin America, 149

lavas, 86
Leach, J. W., 184 n.1
Leach, Melissa, 169 n.4
Lee, R., 82
Lefebvre, Henri, 20
Lenin, V. I., 61
Levi, Margaret, 173 n.24
Lewis, A., 61
Lewis, I. M., 163
Lewis, T., 150, 183 n.17
Li, S., 182 n.6
Libecap, Gary, 59
Lichbach, Mark, 176 n.4
Little, K., 184 n.5
Lizot, Jacques, 184 n.2
locality, 18, 29, 75, 126, 131, 144
loss, 30–33
lower castes, 42; grazing patterns of, 46;
    unequal landholdings of, 44, 173 n.12
Luce, Duncan, 148
Lupia, A., 160
Lutz, Catherine A., 184 n.5

Madhya Pradesh, 6, 62–63, 88, 108
Mali, 83
Malinowski, B., 184 n.1
Malmberg, Torsten, 176 n.25
Mandelbaum, David, 171 n.18
Mann, Michael, 175 n.23
manure, 81, 84, 86–87, 106, 177 n.17; ex-
    changes for grain, 100–101, 105–8; re-
    turns from, 110–12; statistical data on,
    109–11
March, J., 180 n.3
Marcus, George E., 169 n.1
Marcussen, Henrik S., 170 n.8
marginality, 33; definition of, 5; mobility as
    reflection of, 25–26; protests against, 39
marginal utility, 116
markets: 80, 84, 100–104, 117–18,
    179 n.21; anthropological writings on,
    102; and freedom, 81, 101; political in-
    fluences on, 120–22; and prices, 117–20;
    and property rights, 59; raika decisions
    about, 84–87, 135, 142
Marshall, A., 116
Marwar, 28, 47–48

patels, 8, 43, 49, 54, 58
patron-client relationships, 108
peasants, 71
performativity, 39
Persia, 27
Peters, Pauline, 174 nn.3 and 4
Phalodi, 10
Picardi, A., 32
Pigg, Stacy Leigh, 11
place, 125–27
Polanyi, Karl, 104, 118, 170 n.29
politics, 35–39, 40–41, 149–61; and caste, 49–58; in Patawal, 40–41, 47–51, 54–59
Popkin, Samuel, 102
Poplin, Dennis E., 180 n.4
Posey, D., 180 n.2
postcoloniality, 61, 169 n.2
postmodernity, 20, 171 n.26
poststructuralism, 11
power, 11, 23, 26, 35–39, 74, 76–77, 162; institutions of, 9, 35; marginality as lack of, 5; and mobility, 25, 76
Prakash, Gyan, 171 n.18
Prasad, R. R., 31
Pratt, D., 32
Prezworski, Adam, 20
prices: and politics, 120; of sheep and wool, 155–56; theories of, 118–19, 122
"primitive" economics, 103
principal-agent analysis, 129, 148–50, 160, 183 nn.12 and 17; and cheating, 160; and group size, 161
production, 113–15
profits, 82
property rights, 14, 23, 74, 149, 169 n.10, 170 nn.7 and 8; changes in, 45–46; institutional arrangements, 46; and excludability, 23–25
Punjab, 62, 76

Quinn, N., 180 n.3

Rabinow, Paul, 169 n.5
Radhakrishnan, R., 170 n.2
raikas, 3–4, 6–9, 52, 163–68; associations of, 28; authority of, 17; bargaining

power of, 120–21; caste roles of, 43–44, 52; and collective action, 83; communities of, 125–27; conflicts of, 96–98; and diet, 90; history of, 27–28; identities of, 28–29; origins of, 26–28; participation in markets, 80–81, 104–5, 115, 120–21, 165; political actions of, 28, 30–31, 41, 43–44, 52–58, 70–71, 77; political influence of, 9, 35; social networks of, 28
Rajasthan, 3, 14, 27–28, 31, 35–36, 41–42, 49, 57, 63–64, 76, 87
Rajasthan Tenants Act, 31, 52
rajputs, 3, 42, 54
Randhawa, T. S., 28, 31, 171 n.16
Rasmusen, E., 183 n.23
rational choice, 143, 169 n.9, 181 n.17, 182 n.1
Rawls, John, 9
religion, 90
resistance, 76, 165–66, 169 n.1
Riefenstahl, L., 163
Rigby, Peter, 32
Riley, Denise, 30
Robbins, Paul, 58, 176 n.1
Root, Hilton, 173 n.16
Ross, S., 150
Rowe, William L., 171 n.18
rules: changes in Patawal, 51–52; and institutions, 35, 47–51, 59–60
Rural Landless Employment Guarantee Program, 73

Sachs, Wolfgang, 61
Sack, Robert David, 176 n.24
Sadr, K., 131
sagaras, 44
Sahlins, Marshall, 104
Saith, A., 175 n.19
Salzman, Philip Carl, 31, 82, 172 n.8
Sandford, Stephen, 12, 32, 82, 131, 169 n.7
Sangari, Kumkum, 170 n.2
Sangmpam, S. N., 175 n.28
sarpanch, 50
Sayer, Derek, 174 n.4
Schelling, 148
Schlager, Edella, 170 n.7

Village Councils, 8, 35–36, 47, 50, 67;
and informal panchayats, 55; in Patawal,
50, 53–54, 57, 59; as state in the village,
50

Wade, Robert, 150, 176 nn.2 and 4
Waller, Richard, 184 n.3
Warren, D., 180 n.2
water tanks, 10, 42, 48
Weber, Max, 39, 118–19, 146, 177 n.3,
181 n.12
Weiner, Annette, 184 n.1
Weissleder, W., 180 n.3
Westphal-Hellbusch, S., 27, 169 n.2
Wickham, Gary, 171 n.26

Wilks, I., 102
Williams, Donald C., 175 n.28
Williamson, Oliver, 107, 182 nn.4 and 8
Willis, Paul, 174 n.3
Wilmsen, Edwin, 175 n.25, 176 n.5
Woodburn, J. C., 82
wool, 12, 80, 86, 141, 181 n.15; sale of,
155
Wool Marketing Federation, 31
World Bank, 10, 65

Young, Iris Marion, 131

Zhao, Ding-Xin, 175 n.28
Zimbabwe, 12

Arun Agrawal is Assistant Professor of Political Science,
Yale University, and the author of *The Grass is Greener on
the Other Side: A Study of Raikas, Migrant Pastoralists of
Rajasthan* (1992).

Library of Congress Cataloging-in-Publication Data
Agrawal, Arun.
   Greener pastures : politics, markets, and community
among a migrant pastoral people / Arun Agrawal.
   Includes bibliographical references and index.
   ISBN 0-8223-2233-1 (cloth: alk. paper).
ISBN 0-8223-2122-X (pbk. : alk. paper).
   1. Rabaris.   2. Shepherds — India — Rajasthan.
3. Nomads — India — Rajasthan.   4. Pastoral systems —
India — Rajasthan.   5. Political anthropology.   I. Title.
DS432.R13A37 1999 305.9'0691 — dc21 98-21274 CIP